Words and Worlds: New Directions in the Philosophy of Language

ROYAL INSTITUTE OF PHILOSOPHY SUPPLEMENT: 95

EDITED BY

Julian Baggini

PUBLISHED BY THE PRESS SYNDICATE OF THE UNIVERSITY OF CAMBRIDGE
The Pitt Building, Trumpington Street, Cambridge, CB2 1RP,
United Kingdom

CAMBRIDGE UNIVERSITY PRESS
Shaftesbury Road, Cambridge CB2 8EA, United Kingdom
32 Avenue of the Americas, New York, NY 10013–2473, USA
477 Williamstown Road, Port Melbourne, VIC 3207, Australia
C/Orense, 4, planta 13, 28020 Madrid, Spain
Lower Ground Floor, Nautica Building, The Water Club, Beach Road,
Granger Bay, 8005 Cape Town, South Africa

© The Royal Institute of Philosophy and the contributors 2024

Printed and bound by CPI Group (UK) Ltd, Croydon, CR0 4YY
Typeset by Techset Composition Ltd, Salisbury, UK

A catalogue record for this book is available from the British Library

ISBN 9781009544320
ISSN 1358-2461

Contents

Notes on the Contributors	v
Introduction JULIAN BAGGINI	1
Racial Realities LUVELL ANDERSON	15
Misunderstanding and Meaning Change ANDREW HINES	33
Politics, Words, and Concepts: On the Impossibility and Undesirability of 'Amelioration' LOUISE ANTONY	47
Inflammatory Language ERNIE LEPORE	63
Games, Norms, and Utterances MIHAELA POPA-WYATT AND JEREMY L. WYATT	73
Prejudicial Speech: What's a Liberal to Do? MARI MIKKOLA	87
What Is It to Be Responsible for What You Say? EMMA BORG	107
On Discussing What We Should Do JANE HEAL	127
How To Get *About* DAVID SOSA	143
Stories and Selves: A Twisted Love Story about the Meaning of Life ELISABETH CAMP	157
A New Look at the Classical Chinese *Dào* of the Relation between Word and World CHAD HANSEN	181
Index of Names	199

Notes on the Contributors

Luvell Anderson (lander04@syr.edu) is Associate Professor of Philosophy and Affiliate Faculty in African American Studies and Women's and Gender Studies at Syracuse University. He primarily works in the Philosophy of Language, Philosophy of Humor, and Philosophy of Race. Professor Anderson is co-editor of the *Routledge Companion to the Philosophy of Race* and the forthcoming *Oxford Handbook on Applied Philosophy of Language*. He is also the author of *The Ethics of Racial Humor*, to appear with Oxford University Press.

Andrew Hines (drandrewhines@gmail.com) is the Programme Manager of the Westminster Abbey Institute and Philosopher in Residence at King's High School Warwick. From 2020 to 2023 he was Lecturer in World Philosophies at SOAS University of London and the Thyssen Research Fellow at the Centre for Anglo-German Cultural Relations. His research takes an interdisciplinary approach to philosophy that draws from comparative literature, intellectual history, and post-Kantian philosophy. In 2020, his first book, *Metaphor in European Philosophy after Nietzsche*, was published by Legenda and his second book, *Communication Breakdown: Misunderstanding in the Public Use of Reason* will be published by Bloomsbury in 2024. Beyond his work as a writer, Dr Hines is a keen chorister and open water swimmer.

Louise Antony (lantony@philos.umass.edu) is Professor of Philosophy Emerita at the University of Massachusetts and Regular Visiting Professor at Rutgers University. She has published many articles on topics in philosophy of mind, philosophy of language, feminist philosophy, epistemology, and philosophy of religion, and lectured on these topics throughout the United States and many other countries. She is the author of *Only Natural: Gender, Knowledge, and Human Kind*, and the editor of *Philosophers Without Gods: Meditations on Atheism and the Secular Life*. Committed to bringing philosophical ideas to non-academic audiences, she has published opinion pieces in *The New York Times* and in blogs and online journals, and regularly engages in public debates, most recently with Alex Byrne on the relation between sex and gender (presented by the Houston Institute: https://houstoninstitute.org/media).

Notes on the Contributors

Ernie Lepore (lepore.ruccs.rutgers.edu@gmail.com) is a Board of Governors professor of philosophy. He is the author of numerous books and papers in the philosophy of language, philosophical logic, metaphysics and philosophy of mind, including with Matthew Stone, *Imagination and Convention* (Oxford University Press, 2015), *Meaning, Mind and Matter: Philosophical Essays* with Barry Loewer (Oxford University Press, 2011), *Liberating Content* (2016) and *Language Turned on Itself* (2007, Oxford University Press), *Insensitive Semantics* (2004, Basil Blackwell) all with Herman Cappelen, *Donald Davidson: Meaning, Truth, Language and Reality* (Oxford University Press, 2005) and *Donald Davidson's Truth-Theoretic Semantics* (Oxford University Press, 2007) both with Kirk Ludwig, *Meaning and Argument*, and co-authored, with Jerry Fodor, *Holism: A Shopper's Guide* (Blackwell, 1991) and *The Compositionality Papers* (Oxford University Press, 2002); and with Sarah-Jane Leslie *What Every Student Should* Know (Rutgers Press, 2002). He has edited several books, including *Handbook in Philosophy of Language* (with B. Smith, Oxford University Press, 2006), *Truth and Interpretation* (Blackwell, 1989), and is co-editor with Zenon Pylyshyn of *What is Cognitive Science?* (Blackwell, 1999). He is also general editor of the Blackwell series *Philosophers and Their Critics*.

Mihaela Popa-Wyatt (mihaela.popa-wyatt@manchester.ac.uk) is a lecturer in philosophy at the University of Manchester. She received her PhD from the university of Geneva. Her main research interests are in Philosophy of Language and Linguistics, Meta-ethics, Social and Political Philosophy, Social Epistemology, and Philosophy of Race and Gender. Her recent work focuses on how slurs and oppressive speech shift social norms and re-entrench social hierarchies. She combines philosophical analysis with tools from game theory and sociology to make testable predictions.

Jeremy L. Wyatt (jeremy.l.wyatt@gmail.com) has published in artificial intelligence, decision theory, and philosophy of language. He has a BA (Bristol), MS (Sussex) and PhD (Edinburgh).

Mari Mikkola (m.mikkola@uva.nl) is a Professor of Philosophy and Chair of Metaphysics at the University of Amsterdam. Her areas of expertise are in feminist philosophy (particularly feminist metaphysics), social ontology, and pornography debates in philosophy. She has published widely on these topics being the sole author of two books (*The Wrong of Injustice: Dehumanization and Its Role in*

Notes on the Contributors

Feminist Philosophy and *Pornography: A Philosophical Introduction*, both with Oxford University Press) and of several articles. In addition to working on various conceptions of prejudicial speech, Mikkola's current work deals with philosophical methodology. Prior to coming to Amsterdam, she has worked at the University of Oxford / Somerville College, Humboldt-Universität zu Berlin, Lancaster University, and University of Stirling.

Emma Borg (emma.borg@sas.ac.uk) is Professor at the Institute of Philosophy in the School of Advanced Study, University of London. Emma's main research interests lie in philosophy of language (where she defends a position known as 'minimal semantics'), philosophy of mind (where she is interested in rational decision-making and what philosophers call 'mindreading'), and business ethics (asking what private sector organisations owe to society). She has published widely in these areas, including two monographs with Oxford University Press, with a third (*Acting for Reasons*) forthcoming. She is also the author (with Sarah Fisher) of *A Very Short Introduction to Meaning* (forthcoming, Oxford University Press).

Jane Heal (jane.heal@phil.cam.ac.uk) studied History and Philosophy at Cambridge where she also took her Ph.D. After a Research Fellowship at Newnham, she travelled to the US with a Harkness Fellowship, visiting Princeton and Berkeley. In 1976 she became a lecturer at the University of Newcastle upon Tyne and in 1986 returned to Cambridge where she is now an Emeritus Professor. She has written on meaning, self-knowledge, indexicality, and rationality. She is particularly known for work exploring the importance of co-operative action and cognition as underpinnings for our grasp of the psychological. The importance of the first person plural is a recent focus. She is a Fellow of St John's College, where she was President from 1999 to 2003. She has also served as President of the Aristotelian Society and the Mind Association. She was elected a Fellow of the British Academy in 1997.

David Sosa (david_sosa@austin.utexas.edu) is Temple Centennial Professor in the Humanities, and Professor and Chair in Philosophy, at the University of Texas at Austin, where he's been since 1997. Sosa works across the discipline, with publications including 'Consequences of Consequentialism', *Mind* 1993, 'The Import of the Puzzle About Belief', *Philosophical Review* 1996, 'Rigidity in the Scope of Russell's Theory', *Noûs* 2001, 'Standard Bearers', *Episteme* 2017, and 'Truth within Reason', *Midwest*

Notes on the Contributors

Studies in Philosophy 2023. He is editor of the journal *Analytic Philosophy*, and co-editor (with A.P. Martinich) of *Philosophy of Language* (Oxford, 6th edition), and of *Analytic Philosophy: An Anthology* (Wiley, 2nd edition) and *A Companion to Analytic Philosophy* (Wiley).

Elisabeth Camp (emc233@philosophy.rutgers.edu) is a Professor of Philosophy at Rutgers University, New Brunswick, specializing in language, mind, and aesthetics. Her research focuses on thoughts and utterances that don't fit a standard propositional model of minds and languages, including metaphor and sarcasm, slurs and insinuation, and maps and animal cognition. She is the author of over forty articles and chapters, and recently edited *The Poetry of Emily Dickinson: Philosophical Perspectives* (Oxford University Press, 2021).

Chad Hansen (chadzi@gmail.com) is Chair Professor of Chinese Philosophy, Emeritus at the University of Hong Kong, where he has taught for over 30 years. He previously held positions at the University of Pittsburgh (1972–77) and the University of Vermont (1978–1991). He has held visiting positions at universities around the world, including the University of Michigan, Stanford, University of Hawaii, UCLA, University of Auckland, Smith College, Hong Kong University of Science and Technology, and National University of Singapore. He took his BA at the University of Utah and PhD at the University of Michigan. He was named University Scholar at the University of Vermont for his second book, *A Daoist Theory of Chinese Thought,* before returning to Hong Kong to finish his career as Chair Professor.

Introduction

JULIAN BAGGINI

Around a century ago, philosophy in the English-speaking world took a 'linguistic turn', as it was retrospectively baptised by Richard Rorty in an edited volume of the same name in 1967 (Rorty, 1967). As Simon Blackburn later wrote, philosophy has always been interested in the relationship between language, mind, and world, but at different periods in history the emphasis has been on different corners of the triangle (Blackburn, 1984).

The linguistic turn led philosophers to focus on issues such as the meaning of 'meaning', the relationship between words and world, and the logical structure of propositions. A stock set of key problems in the philosophy of language emerged and most scholars stuck to ploughing these increasingly familiar and deeply-dug furrows.

In the last decade or so, however, the philosophy of language has been somewhat reinvigorated. The old problems have not been left behind but new issues have come to the fore, many of them concerning the political, ethical, and social aspects of language. Philosophers are increasingly interested in how language shapes social reality, and how it might be used to reshape it for the better.

Consider, for example, Wittgenstein's now well-worn adage that *the limits of my language* mean the limits of my world' (Wittgenstein, 2023, §5.6). As with so many of his aphorisms, many people agree with it but few agree on what exactly it means. One of the least contentious ways to make the claim true is that our experience of the world is shaped by our concepts, and so language literally determines what we can and cannot experience. For example, without a concept of 'sexual harassment', a woman working in an office in 1950s America could not understand the way her male colleagues treated her in the way that women today readily can.

Luvell Anderson calls this the '*different worlds* thesis'. It entails that 'people come to radically different understandings of the world because they inhabit incompatible conceptual realities'. These different worlds are often inhabited by people with different ethnic origins, but Anderson argues that people do not inhabit 'different worlds' purely as a result of racial differences. Rather, borrowing a concept from Penelope Eckert and Sally McConnell-Ginet (Eckert and

Julian Baggini

McConnell-Ginet, 1992), he argues that different worlds are rooted in 'communities of practice', defined as 'an aggregate of people who come together around mutual engagement in an endeavor'. This results not only in different concepts, but also 'ways of talking, beliefs, values, power relations – in short, practices'.

If this is true, however, then misunderstandings between people who inhabit different communities of practice are inevitable. To go back to our office example, a 50s female secretary would be baffled by a claim that she was subject to sexual harassment, while a twenty-first century professional woman would be equally perplexed that her 50s counterpart did not interpret the way she was being treated as prejudicial.

However, Anderson cautions against reaching too extreme a conclusion from this. Yes, the distance of 'different worlds' makes mutual comprehension more difficult. But it does not make it impossible. That is why over time female workers did come to see their treatment by many male colleagues as unacceptable, and why it does not take too much effort for a woman today to understand why her predecessors complained so little. Humans have 'imaginative capacities' that enable us to understand worlds other than our own. 'The different worlds thesis encourages us to contemplate the differences between human beings,' writes Anderson, 'but we should not neglect those aspects that also tie us together.'

At the same time, we should not make the old Western mistake of universalisation, by which we understand our shared humanity by reducing our myriad worlds to a singular, universal one. Following the Martinican scholar Édouard Glissant, he argues that 'the true way to unity is the recognition of opacities, which he says can coexist and converge.' As Glissant wrote, 'There would be something great and noble about initiating such a movement, referring not to Humanity but to the exultant divergence of humanities' (Glissant, 1997, p. 190).

Misunderstanding is also the subject of Andrew Hines's contribution. His starting point is the phenomenon of meaning change, in particular in politics. Many people who have for decades thought that they believed in conservatism, socialism, or democracy have found the current referents of those terms unrecognisable. Somehow, the meanings of each have changed. This leads to misunderstandings between people who use the terms in the old or new senses.

Hines argues that this sheds light on the nature of misunderstanding. This, he argues, has been an under-analysed concept. It has been assumed that *misunderstanding* can be understood simply as a *failure of understanding*. This simple 'failure' model is sometimes adequate,

Introduction

but all too often it is not. Rather, misunderstanding very often occurs 'when human understanding is caught between two different meanings'. This is especially likely to happen when meanings change.

One reason why this is important is that misunderstanding often results in 'communication breakdown', when neither side can even comprehend the other. The failure model, argues Hines, encourages this, since it attributes misunderstanding to a failure of one party to understand what is perfectly intelligible to others. If, rather, we see misunderstanding as the product of meaning change, misunderstanding becomes both understandable and capable of being overcome. It is not that those who understand a meaning one way and those that understand it another are in entirely different semantic worlds. Nor must we embrace a relativism in which neither party is right or wrong but simply uses different meanings. Rather, we have the scope to make the different meanings clear to both sides and so allow them to overcome communication breakdown and understand each other better, even if that does not lead to agreement.

If language limits our world, do we sometimes have to change it in order to overcome certain restrictions it places on us? This question has become socially and politically hot due to the issue of transgender rights. While there are still many who stand opposed to equal rights for trans men and women, among those who support equality, there is a disagreement about whether the terms 'man' and 'woman' apply equally and without qualification to those born biologically male and female and those whose gender identity does not match their biological sex. (Even this characterisation of the debate will be seen by some as inaccurate, since some deny the legitimacy of the category of 'biological sex' and talk instead of 'gender assigned a birth'.)

Among those who argue that 'trans women are women, trans men are men, period', there are many who argue that accepting this requires us to engage in some 'conceptual engineering' since the concept of 'woman' that we have inherited is not fit for a trans-inclusive world. Sally Haslanger is one such philosopher, arguing that we have to ask what *purpose* a concept is meant to serve, and give up those that serve no good purpose or revise them so that they do.

In her contribution to his volume, Louise Antony argues that this strategy is mistaken. In a sense, she believes that the mistake is simple: 'WOMAN is a social concept, not a biological concept, meaning that our concept WOMAN picks out or is connected to individuals who are assigned or who come to play a certain social role, one that is generally and for the most part attached to the biological property of being female.' Whether this is the case or not is a matter of fact, determined by how language is actually used. What we believe or want to be the case is irrelevant.

As Antony argues:

> If WOMAN is in fact a social concept, and not a biological concept, that means that those who think the thought TRANSWOMEN ARE NOT WOMEN *are wrong, as a matter of fact*, and *in virtue of the reference of their own concept WOMAN*. Those of us who realize that this thought is false must then work to persuade those who think this that they are wrong.

Of course, many will disagree that 'woman' is a social concept, but that is a debate for another time. One interesting feature of Antony's argument is that she argues that while 'the reference of concepts is not under our control, but the reference of *words* is'. In other words, the concept 'woman' either does or does not refer to a trans woman as much as it does to any other kind of woman. But in law and social practice, people may not use the word 'woman' to refer in the same way. Antony sees the political goal to make sure that people use words so that they match the reference of their associated concepts.

Although Antony and Haslanger disagree, both their views assume that the power of language can be immense, for good and for ill. Slur words, for example, can get people fired, cancelled, or even killed. Why are such words taboo? The obvious answer is that their meaning is offensive. But Ernie Lepore argues that this cannot explain why they cannot be uttered. Using the fiction slur term 'muggleborns' from the Harry Potter universe as an example, it would be offensive to use the word even if one is denying any negative associations it may have. Saying 'Hermione is a mudblood, but I don't think muggleborn wizards are despicable on account of being muggleborn' does not nullify the offensiveness of the term. Replace the term with a genuine slur term and you'll get the point.

Another explanation Lepore calls 'prohibitionism'. On this view, slur terms are taboo words and so it is never acceptable to use them, even in ostensibly non-offensive contexts. The problem with this view is that many taboo words just aren't slur terms, such as names for God in Judaism. Taboos function differently from slur words so one cannot explain the prohibition of slur words in the same terms as one explains the prohibition of taboo words.

Lepore's conclusion is that there is no need to appeal to meaning 'in order to account for an offensive sting'. Merely articulating a slur word is enough to trigger its offensive, negative associations. That

Introduction

cannot be explained by the meaning of the word itself, since words with identical or very similar meanings just don't have the same power to offend. Also, slur words can lose their power and become acceptable, even though their meaning may not change at all. A final piece of evidence for Lepore's view is that non-standard articulations of a slur word can be acceptable, even though they are in effect the same word with the same meaning. In a context like this volume for example, it would be acceptable to refer the N-word or even to write n***er, whereas to use the word itself would not be.

Lepore sums up his surprising conclusion as 'it is not slur terms, but their standard articulations that carry offensive potential. This means that, however this potential is determined, it has little to do with semantics or pragmatics, or indeed even with language at all'. Think about it: the power of some language to offend cannot be explained by any explanation of what language standardly does.

A background assumption to the debates both Lepore and Antony engage with is that social norms can be changed by what people say. Mihaela Popa-Wyatt and Jeremy L. Wyatt set out to explain how this is possible. One conceptual tool they use is J.L. Austin's idea of a speech act. Austin argued that some utterances can actually change the world merely by their being said. Such 'performative' speech acts include proclaiming a couple husband and wife or banning a book. By declaring something to be forbidden or permitted, such speech acts can change social norms directly.

Popa-Wyatt and Wyatt also make use of David Lewis's concept of a 'conversational game'. Conversations are considered analogous with games, with each new contribution adding something to the 'score', changing what it acceptable or unacceptable to say later. For example, saying 'I drove to London last week' gives you the information that I can drive, a fact that is added to the conversational score. This means that later in the conversation, you are able to assume I can drive and it would be inappropriate to ask if I can.

Combine these two ideas, as Mary Kate McGowan (2004) did, and you have a kind of speech act she called a 'conversational exercitive', which Popa-Wyatt and Wyatt define as 'a particular utterance which updates the conversational score so that new norms apply'. To give an example: 'When addressing a target with a slur, the speaker's purpose is to grab power by changing the social norms governing the conversation.' The slur undermines the person slurred, in turn raising the status of the slurrer.

Popa-Wyatt and Wyatt take this further, using both game theory and Bayesian probability theory. At the risk of oversimplifying a rich argument, the key idea here is that our interactions with others

Julian Baggini

depend upon us having certain expectations of how they will act and react; and that these expectations are constantly being revised in light of new information that comes to light. Concerning norms, these expectations can be both empirical – which norms we expect others to adhere to – and normative – which norms we think they *should* adhere to.

Popa-Wyatt and Wyatt's model is both philosophically rigorous and true to the dynamic, open-ended character of actual speech. It is a terrific example of how good theorising does not take us further away from the messy reality of the world, but helps us to makes sense of it better.

Although people may disagree about which slur words are worst and how far they should be removed from public discourse, there is general agreement on which are and are not acceptable. The same is not true of many forms of prejudicial speech. Terms and phrases that some judge to be beyond the pale others think of as little more than bawdy fun. Mari Mikkola begins her exploration of the problems of prejudicial speech by insisting that we cannot generalise about it. We have to consider it in its different forms. Mikkola notes the tendency to use the term 'hate speech' to cover all kinds of prejudicial discourse. She argues that if we need an umbrella term, 'prejudicial speech' serves the purpose better. And if we want to understand how this kind of speech works and how to deal with it, we are better off considering it in its different forms in turn, such as hate, discriminatory, and toxic speech. Note that 'this division isn't about the seriousness or harmfulness of speech, with hate speech being the most serious kind'.

Start with hate speech. This can be harmful when 'it limits its recipients' participation in deliberative exchanges and prevents recipients from getting a fair hearing when they try to participate'. In other words, hate speech can delegitimise certain groups, making it more difficult for their voices to be heard in public discourse. Importantly, this means that the harm is not primarily any offence a person may feel. It is rather the effect one has on their capacities to participate in civic and public life. A person may not even hear the hate speech in question, and so not be offended by it, yet be disadvantaged by it.

The same can be true of discriminatory speech, which also perpetuates negative stereotypes without actively vilifying the groups concerned, as is the case with hate speech. For example, speech which suggests women are not suited to professions may be couched in ways that praise so-called 'womanly virtues' but their effect is to limit female participation in work and political life. Mikkola also

Introduction

argues that it undermines self-trust: those to whom discriminatory speech refer may themselves question their competencies.

Toxic speech is even more insidious. It works by undermining trust, spreading suspicion, and kindling fear, all on the basis of false claims, such as that an election was stolen or that something bad happening in the world is a result of a plot by an (often racial) elite. This corrodes the very fabric of a democratic society, undermining our capacity to engage in sincere debate in which we take the views of others as genuine.

Given all this, classic liberal defences of free speech are insufficient as objections to measures to prevent or at least limit the uses of prejudicial speech. Allowing such unfettered speech is not to allow free competition in the marketplace of ideas, but to give the users of such speech the power to undermine the credibility and democratic agency of others. Speech of this kind is not just an expression of opinions: it has damaging, material effects.

Generally speaking, we hold people to account for prejudicial speech. This is an example of 'linguistic liability'. For instance, if you lie to me, you have 'linguistic liability' for any consequences that might follow from that. That much seems obvious. But as Emma Borg points out, once you start to ask just how absolute or limited this liability is, things quickly become difficult. If I tell you in a casual conversation what I think the weather will be and you set off up a mountain, it's not my fault if you get caught in a storm. If, however, a teacher misinforms their students and they answer an examination question incorrectly as a result, the teacher is blameworthy.

One way into solving the issue of linguistic liability is to think about precisely what is required in order for an utterance to be understood. Borg highlights three broad approaches. 'Semantic minimalism' is the view that a well-formed sentence can be understood and judged true or false in the absence of most, if not all, context. 'Contextualism', as the name implies, denies this, while a third approach, associated with Paul Grice, claims that we need to know 'what a speaker conversationally implies by what they say', as Borg puts it.

There seems to be some truth in all three approaches. Borg gives the example of a person being asked 'Do you want to have lunch?' and replying 'I've eaten.' Semantic minimalism highlights the fact that, irrespective of context, the sentence 'I have eaten' tells us something that can be understood and is true or false: that the speaker has eaten. Contextualism, however, highlights the fact that to understand properly what this means, you have to understand that the person has eaten *recently*, which in context would be clear. The Gricean would add that even this doesn't fully explicate the utterance, as in this situation it implies that the person is turning down the invitation.

What has this to do with linguistic liability? For a start, to attribute liability fairly we have to be sensitive to the different ways in which utterances can have meaning in themselves, in context, and in their implications. People are generally good at this: 'Ordinary speakers are adept at making different kinds of liability judgments, where these judgements are sensitive to different kinds of content.' Sometimes, we need to hold people liable for the non-literal content of their utterances. For example, one can make a promise without saying 'I promise' or similar. If it is clear from the context that a promise was made, a person is responsible for keeping it, even if the literal sentence they uttered (perhaps just 'ok') did not take the form of a promise.

However, Borg argues that sometimes, 'strict linguistic liability' is appropriate, by which we hold a speaker liable for the literal content of the sentences they utter. 'Semantic minimalism' may seem to be an overly literal and limited way to understand sentences, but, Borg argues, 'Some judgements of linguistic liability are strict and strict judgements require a grasp of minimal content.' Her example is Donald Trump saying that the crowd for his inauguration stretched 'all the way back to the Washington Monument'. So, although 'in the cut and thrust of communication it is often non-minimal content which is to the fore,' we cannot do away with the notion of minimal semantic content if we are to hold people liable for their utterances.

The contributions to this volume discussed so far all concern the political, social, and ethical dimensions of language. However, the philosophy of language has plenty of other questions to grapple with and many old problems have been taken in new directions. For example, Jane Heal uses considerations of language as a springboard into an inquiry into a somewhat puzzling phenomenon: 'plural intentionality'. Singular intentionality concerns the intentions and desires of individuals. For example, the question 'What should I do?' is one that concerns singular intentionality. Plural intentionality concerns the intentions or desires of more than one person, as raised by the question 'What should *we* do?' Until quite recently, plural intentionality was thought of as simply the sum of singular intentionalities, 'convenient (perhaps in practice unavoidable) shorthand for talking about what would be more accurately (if far more lengthily) reported as assemblages of instances of singular intentionality'.

Introduction

This assumption is a manifestation of a wider 'analytic' strategy of 'trying to understand some complex and interesting thing by looking for its separable parts'. Heal does not think that this strategy is always wrong, but it 'may get us into trouble if used inappropriately.'

Heal acknowledges that plural intentionality 'is apt to strike analytic philosophers as strange and paradoxical, as requiring telepathy or as needing the co-subjects to become somehow identical with each other'. But, she argues, it is 'not mysterious at all.' Human beings are social animals and 'making common knowledge usable is one key role of language'. Linguistic communication is a social, co-operative practice, and so we should not be surprised that we can use language to form and express collective intentions, as well as individual ones.

Intentionality has another philosophical meaning, which confusingly has nothing to do with intentions. Intentionality in this second sense concerns the 'aboutness' of mental states or language. It seems to be a key feature of language that it is about things, events, or states of affairs. But this is curious: how can anything in the natural world be *about* something else? Atoms, rocks, plants, animals, minerals and so on are not about anything, they just are. So how do things like words and thoughts get to be about other things?

David Sosa returns to this age-old problem in his inquiry into the aboutness of language. He conjectures that the reason why the problem has remained intractable is that it has been assumed that an explanation for the aboutness of language will also work as an explanation for the aboutness of thoughts, and vice-versa. 'The story of aboutness will be *uniform*, simplex, or so the presupposition has it.' A related assumption is what Sosa calls 'monosemanticism', that the meaningfulness of thoughts and linguistic expressions 'are fundamentally akin and correlated phenomena'. But what if we reject these assumptions?

Sosa's proposal takes as its starting point another old puzzle from Frege. Hesperus (the evening star) and Phosphorus (the morning star) are the same celestial body: Venus. So there is a sense in which 'Hesperus is the evening star' means that 'Hesperus is Phosphorus' as 'the evening star' is the same things as 'the morning star'. But someone may not know this. There is information they lack even though there is nothing lacking in the meaning of the words they use. Frege concluded from this that there is a difference between a word's *sense* and its *reference*, so sometimes we can fail to know that a word has a certain reference because we only understand one sense of it (Frege, 1952). Sosa takes a different approach. He

Julian Baggini

argues that sentences can have the same meaning yet cause different beliefs. Simply knowing 'Hesperus is the evening star' does not cause you to believe that it is also the morning star, even though that is what it means.

Sosa advocates for 'polysemanticism', the idea that the content of a mental state and the semantic value of a sentence are 'fundamentally different – indeed independent – phenomena'. Our minds can be about one thing and our sentences about something else, in part because the 'aboutness' in each case is of a different kind. Take someone who thinks 'Gödel must have been a really smart guy', knowing him only as the man who discovered the incompleteness theorem. But what if we found out that he didn't discover the theorem after all, and that a woman called Schmidt did? 'Gödel' still refers to Gödel, but it turns out the person we thought was really smart was actually Schmidt. Hence 'our mind is about Schmidt and our sentence is about Gödel. Aboutness bifurcates'.

It follows from this that the truth of such sentences does not determine the contents of our minds. For example, we can truthfully say, in an important sense, that 'If Lois believes that Superman can fly then she believes that Clark Kent can fly' because Superman is Clark Kent. But Lois doesn't know this and so the truth of 'Superman can fly' does not determine the content of Lois's beliefs about Kent. It further follows that when we express our thoughts in ordinary sentences, such utterances may not make the contents of our thoughts explicit.

Sosa's paper is a good illustration of the traditional tendency of philosophers to use language precisely and formally. Words are the building blocks of propositions, used to construct arguments and truth claims. But for the rest of humanity one of language's main uses is very different: to tell stories. The question of why we tell each other so many tales has fascinated psychologists, anthropologists, and many other scholars for millennia. Elizabeth Camp, like many others, sees narratives as important tools for making sense of ourselves and the world. There are many ways in which stories can do this. One, suggested by Jerome Bruner, is that stories are 'part of our armamentarium for dealing with surprise' (2002, p. 29). They help prepare us for what might go wrong or for what we might not otherwise have foreseen, as well as reassuring us that surprise is to be expected and no matter how much we may be thrown by life, we can react. For Louis Mink, in contrast, narratives bring coherence to what would otherwise be a sequence of actions and events lacking in overall significance. Camp sums this up as the view that 'stories are a technology for making events tractable by knitting

Introduction

them together into coherent patterns'. These two views can be combined into the idea that 'We use stories to achieve a comprehensive understanding of a sequence of events, often partly in order to guide action'.

One aim such story-telling serves is the construction of a unified self. As biological animals we are born, live, and ultimately die. But what happens along the way does not necessarily add up to a coherent autobiography, unless we take on the role of author and help create that coherence ourselves. Something like this view has become very popular in philosophy and psychology, and although Camp is broadly supportive of it, she points our various ways in which this project of self-construction can be distorted by the norms of story-telling. For example, biographical narratives tend to be constructed as 'a lifelong quest in pursuit of an overarching goal'. Think of how many heroic stories and fables centre on the protagonist realising and then fulfilling their destiny. The problem is that many of us do not have any such ultimate goal. If we imagine that we must, we either end up telling a false story of our actual life trajectory or imposing some kind of inappropriate end goal on what perhaps should be a more rambling journey through life. Also, making the final destination the entire point of life 'holds the meaning and value of those selves hostage to the ends of their lives, in a way that leaves radically underdetermined not just who we might eventually become, but who we are right *now*'. The conviction of a singular, predetermined destiny highlights 'a particular path forward only by imposing blinders that conceal alternative paths'.

This is not the only way in which narratives can impose what Camp calls 'frames' on our lives, frames that may distort the true picture. For example, if we see our lives in the 'parenthood' framing we may neglect those aspects of ourselves that are not related to parenting. We may also prime ourselves to react as parents, rather than as the more rounded human beings we could be. Other identity labels can also lead to overly narrow self-understandings.

Camp does not dispute that narrative is a tool to be used in the art of self-making. But it is not the only one, and the risk is that when we focus too much on narratives, we occlude other important non-narrative resources. Self-making is an art which draws on more than narrative. For example, one way to grow is to be open, following our curiosities whether they fit neatly into existing narratives or not. We should not make the mistake of identifying selves with the lives that they live. We all contain more possibilities than can be told in any single, neat story.

Julian Baggini

The papers in the volume all deliver on the promise of its subtitle: new directions in the philosophy of language. But this also invites the question: new for whom? Chinese philosophy of language is not just old, it's ancient. But for many anglophone philosophers, it is unknown territory. Chad Hansen's contribution is a useful and challenging reminder that many of the things some thinkers take most for granted are utterly alien to others, and *vice versa*.

Generalisations about Western and Chinese are always potentially problematic, if they are taken to indicate neat binaries and uniformity on both sides. However, some generalisations are both helpful and true: there are general currents in both traditions of thought that have tended to dominate and are contrastive. One difference identified by the philosophers David Hall and Roger Ames is that Western philosophy has traditionally been primarily 'truth-seeking' while Chinese philosophy has been 'way-seeking'. In other words, the ultimate goal of Western philosophy is to achieve a full and objective understanding of ultimate reality as it really is. In Chinese philosophy, the aim has generally been to find the best way to live and organise society. Living rightly has required following the 'way', or *dao*, which means following the path of nature. But the point is that Chinese thinkers are not concerned about whether we represent nature fully as it is, as long as we live in accordance with it.

The relationship of this to language is clear. Western philosophers have sought that their words and concepts map on to reality as accurately as possible. As Hansen puts it, this means ensuring that each individual mind stands in the correct relationship with the world. Chinese philosophers, in contrast, are less interested in the mind-world relation. 'The implicit goal of "knowledge" was not of picturing a material reality, but of competence, mastery, and know-how in behaving in real contexts,' says Hansen. Their concern is for 'a natural world in which humans cooperated via historically evolved social-political structures'.

Hansen has plenty of other things to say about how differences is the ways in which language is conceived affects philosophical theorising. One of the most intriguing is that the common-sense ontology (theory of being) in Western philosophy distinguishes between substance and attribute: substance being the 'stuff' the universe is made of and attribute being the properties of that stuff. But this is not at all common sense for Chinese, for linguistic reasons: 'Chinese grammar does not require a subject so can't require that there be an underlying substance with properties for something to exist.'

It is often says that philosophy questions everything. Anglophone philosophers of language should familiarise themselves with their

Introduction

Chinese counterparts, if only to enable them to question their own assumptions more robustly.

References

Simon Blackburn, *Spreading the Word* (Oxford: Clarendon Press, 1984).

Jerome Bruner, *Making Stories: Law, Literature, Life* (Cambridge, MA: Harvard University Press, 2002).

Penelope Eckert and Sally McConnell-Ginet, 'Communities of Practice: Where Language, Gender, and Power All Live', in *Locating Power: Proceedings of the Second Berkeley Women and Language Conference, April 4 and 5, 1992* (Berkeley, CA: Berkeley Women and Language Group, University of California, 1992), 89–99.

Gottlob Frege, 'On Sense and Reference', in P. Geach and M. Black (eds), *Translations from the Philosophical Writings of Gottlob Frege* (Oxford: Blackwell, 1952).

Édouard Glissant, *Poetics of Relation*, Betsy Wing (trans.), (Ann Arbor: University of Michigan Press, 1997).

David Hall and Roger Ames, *Thinking from the Han* (Albany: State University of New York Press, 1998).

M.K. McGowan, 'Conversational Exercitives: Something Else We Do with Our Words', *Linguistics and Philosophy*, 27 (2004), 93–111.

Richard Rorty (ed.), *The Linguistic Turn: Recent Essays in Philosophical Method* (Chicago: The University of Chicago Press, 1967).

Ludwig Wittgenstein, *Tractatus Logico-Philosophicus*, Alexander Booth (trans.), (London: Penguin, 2023).

Racial Realities

LUVELL ANDERSON

Abstract

How should we conceive of conflicts that seem intractable? Is there any hope of a resolution? We observe impasses between various groups concerning the Israeli and Palestinian conflict, the Movement for Black Lives and racial conservatives, and Indigenous voices versus settler colonial states. Some aspects of these impasses can surely be explained by an unwillingness by one or more parties to the conflict to yield any ground. Might there also be room for misunderstanding generated by radically different ways of conceiving the world? According to the different worlds thesis, people come to radically different understandings of the world because they inhabit incompatible conceptual realities. In this article, I endeavor to explore possible ways of understanding the thesis and its potential impact on certain normative practices we tend to take for granted.

1. Racial Memory and Racial History

Fights over the right conception of racial history are often passionate and marked by deeply entrenched impasses. Many in the US remember the 1960s as a turbulent period, especially with respect to racial conflict. This was, after all, the decade in which Medgar Evers, Martin Luther King Jr., and Malcolm X were assassinated, and major riots in Harlem, Watts, Newark, and Detroit were set off by violence perpetrated by white police officers against Black people. (The Brixton riots in 1981 were similarly sparked by police violence against Black people.)

Perhaps the event that took place at the Cambridge Union in 1965 between James Baldwin and William F. Buckley Jr. crystallizes this turbulence in verbal form. The two debated the motion 'The American Dream is at the expense of the American Negro', with Baldwin representing the affirmative and Buckley the opposition. Nicholas Buccola recounts the debate and the events that led up to it in his wonderful book *The Fire is Upon Us* (2020). He describes the two debaters in the following way:

> Baldwin was the grandson of slaves and had risen from the Harlem ghetto to become one of the world's most famous writers [...]. Baldwin believed that the soul of the country was desperately in need of redemption, and he had devoted his voice and pen to hasten the nation's deliverance.

Luvell Anderson

> Buckley may as well have been from another planet [...]. At the heart of [his] message was the belief that American society was basically good, and that it was the sacred duty of conservatives to defend it from any ideas, personalities, or movements that were deemed threats to it. (Buccola, 2020, p. 2)

Baldwin and Buckley represented the stark impasse that existed between many Black and white Americans. How could such radically different worldviews even begin to figure out how to fix what is broken, especially when one of those voices thinks the world is basically fine?

How should we conceive of conflicts that seem intractable? Is there any hope of a resolution? We observe impasses between various groups concerning the Israeli and Palestinian conflict, the Movement for Black Lives and racial conservatives, and Indigenous voices versus settler colonial states. Some aspects of these impasses can surely be explained by an unwillingness by one or more parties to the conflict to yield any ground. Might there also be room for misunderstanding generated by radically different ways of conceiving the world?

Some people deny or downplay the role race plays in explaining social ills. Disparities in wealth, employment, or incarceration are better explained by personal or cultural failings than by racism. In the UK, for instance, the Commission on Race and Ethnic Disparities released a report that stated the British system was no longer deliberately rigged against ethnic minorities; rather, geography, family influence, socio-economic background, culture, and religion play a more significant role in one's life chances.[1] The report's conclusion contradicts Nahella Ashraf's sentiment – a sentiment I presume is widely shared by many of the UK's Black residents – that systemic racism is inherent in Britain's police force and British society in general (Thomas and Kahn, 2022). We see here yet again an apparent clash of worlds.

The impasses I have been highlighting so far are sometimes explained by the *different worlds* thesis. According to the thesis, people come to radically different understandings of the world because they inhabit incompatible conceptual realities. This could perhaps explain the chasm between, for example, Baldwin and Buckley. The thesis is also applied to the perception of broader group-based chasms. In this article, I endeavor to

---

[1] *Inclusive Britain: Government Response to the Commission on Race and Ethnic Disparities* (2022).

explore possible ways of understanding the thesis and its potential impact on certain normative practices we tend to take for granted.

2. Some Preliminary Issues

Before examining proposals for the different worlds thesis, it would be useful to discuss two broad ideas: the presumed connection between race and language and the nature of these worlds. Key theorists observed a connection between language and race, sometimes stating that language is the characteristic feature of race. For example, early philologists like Ernest Renan proposed the existence of linguistic races, decipherable on the basis of language (Omoniyi, 2016). W.E.B. Du Bois included shared language among the features in his definition of race (Du Bois, 2014). Bill Ashcroft remarks that language 'has always "inscribed" rather than "described" human difference' by using 'chromatic signifiers' and that 'the reality of racial experience centres […] in language' (Ashcroft, 2001, pp. 314–15). Ashcroft also cites English historian Edward Freeman as representative of late nineteenth-century thought on the link between race and language:

> If races and nations, though largely formed by the workings of an artificial law, are still real and living things, groups in which the idea of kindred is the idea around which everything has grown, how are we to define our races and nations? How are we to mark them off from one another? […] I say unhesitatingly that for practical purposes there is one test, and one only, and that that test is language. (Ashcroft, 2001, p. 316)

Thus, a presumed link between race and language is longstanding.

Ashcroft highlights philologist and historian Ernest Renan's work on the connection between race and language. Renan claims 'race' refers to two things: physical race and culture. Language plays a central role in his understanding of race, which is characterized in the following statement:

> Language is thus almost completely substituted for race in the division of humanity into groups, or rather the word 'race' changes meaning. Language, religion, laws, mores brought the race into being much more than blood did. (Ashcroft, 2001, p. 320)

The Aryan and Semitic races are two prime examples of linguistic races for Renan. According to Renan, there are five factors that determine a race: 'a separate language, a literature with identifiable characteristics, a religion, a history, and a civilisation' (Ashcroft, 2001, p. 320).

We should take care to resist views like Renan's because they entail troublesome ideas that ought to be rejected. First, Ashcroft claims Renan's notion of linguistic races fails to disentangle itself from biological race. Even though Renan explicitly rejected biological race, his characterizations of linguistic races appeared to rely on what Ashcroft calls the 'racialist priority of color' (Ashcroft, 2001, p. 321). In short, distinguishing linguistic races from one another presupposed biological race. Second, though Renan posits a determinative link between language and culture, he cannot say which comes first in order of explanation. Ashcroft quotes Renan: 'The spirit of each people and its language are very closely connected: the spirit creates the language, and the language in turn serves as formula and limit for the spirit' (Ashcroft, 2001, p. 321). Ashcroft's main point is that there is a vicious circularity here that undermines Renan's claim.

Though the story about language, race, and identity told by people like Renan ultimately falters, that there is a connection is surely right. As I have already noted, we can observe differences in interpretation that trend along racial lines. The question before us is why that is so. I resist stories that suggest interpretive differences can be reduced to racial identity. But this need not put us off completely from explanations that draw on race in some way.

Turning to the second issue, what is it we are discussing when speaking of 'different worlds'? The proposed distance between relevant groups can be described as epistemic, hermeneutic, metaphysical, or some combination of these. According to the first, divergent worlds are epistemically distinct. This may mean explaining the divide by way of standpoint theory. Appeals to hermeneutics could mean characterizing divergent worlds in terms of different meanings. Lastly, if the basis of the divide is metaphysical, we are encouraged to think these worlds are ontologically distinct. For now, I will leave it to each candidate view to say how it approaches the nature of worlds question.

Now that we've considered these preliminary issues, we can start to view proposals for the *different worlds thesis*.

3. The Different Worlds Thesis

What does it mean to say that various groups inhabit different worlds? This question sets our agenda. The thesis is an intriguing proposal for explaining the existence of deep impasses between various groups. It is fairly easy to think of someone who seemingly observes the same things but perceives the world puzzlingly differently from you as living in a different world. There are even occasions when reading or listening to someone speak gives this impression as well. Sometimes this is a hasty judgment whose function is to protect your own views and biases. But at other times, it can feel like a real explanation. What we should figure out is whether the phrase has anything more than metaphorical value to offer. Let us examine it closer to judge its viability.

Perhaps Thomas Kuhn's reflections on scientific revolutions provide the strongest form of the different worlds thesis. Kuhn describes scientific revolutions as 'those non-cumulative developmental episodes in which an older paradigm is replaced in whole or in part by an incompatible new one' (Kuhn, 1962). According to Thomas Nickels, Kuhn describes a radical change between two paradigms in which they 'cannot be compared against the same goals and methodological standards and values' and that 'scientists on different sides of a paradigm debate "live in different worlds"' (Nickles, 2017). These paradigm changes typically involve changes in meanings, goals, practices, and world perception. Changes in meaning correspond to a radical change in the perceived ontology of the world.

For Kuhn, revolutionary changes produce discontinuities between paradigms. These discontinuities make two paradigms *incommensurable*. There is plenty of debate about the concept's meaning, but I will draw on Daian Florez's characterization of it (Florez, 2024). According to Florez, the semantic version says:

Incommensurability
Theories T1 and T2 are incommensurable if and only if the terms in the language of T1 are not semantically equivalent to terms in the language of T2.

According to this definition, it is enough for translation failure to go in one direction. T2 can lack semantically equivalent terms for expressions in T1, while T1 can contain semantically equivalent terms for expressions in T2. What is left unclear is how much translation failure is required before we conclude the languages are incommensurable. Perhaps there is a threshold where the lack of semantically equivalent terms undermines communication, making it virtually impossible to reconstruct truths in that language. Alternatively, we could imagine a language organized much like a Quinean web of belief, with some concepts more central to the network and others more peripheral. On this conception, two languages are incommensurable if there is a lack of semantically equivalent terms for central concepts. Rather than get bogged down in the details, let's assume we all have a good idea of when incommensurability has been met.

Before we can apply Kuhn's account, we need to characterize the relata. Consider the conflicting views represented by Baldwin and Buckley. Let us suppose both act as representatives for black and white English speakers. Clearly, neither represents 100% of each respective group. We are not dealing with organisms linked by a hive mind as in some science fiction narrative. Human beings have differing opinions and perceptions. Falling under a particular racial classification does not alter that reality. Thus, we need a more fine-grained characterization.

I believe the concept *community of practice* serves our purposes. Penelope Eckert and Sally McConnell-Ginet define a community of practice as:

> an aggregate of people who come together around mutual engagement in an endeavor. Ways of doing things, ways of talking, beliefs, values, power relations—in short, practices—emerge in the course of this mutual endeavor. (Eckert and McConnell-Ginet, 1992, p. 97)

Eckert and McConnell-Ginet list as examples people working in a factory, a neighborhood play group, a family, and the Supreme Court. The examples highlight smaller units, but communities of practice can also be large, intensive, or diffuse and can survive significant changes in group membership. Essentially, the nature of the community's practices distinguishes one group from another. The virtue of the concept, according to Eckert and McConnell-Ginet, is that it 'takes us away from the community defined by a location or by a population. Instead, it focuses on a community defined by social engagement' (Eckert and McConnell-Ginet, 1992, p. 96).

Eckert and McConnell-Ginet's insights share affinities with an idea James Baldwin expresses about the relationship between language and experience. He eloquently wrote that people 'evolve a language in order to describe and thus control their circumstances, or in order not to be submerged by a reality that they cannot articulate' (Baldwin, 1979). This is consistent with the community of practice concept insofar as we restrict our focus to groups whose members share the relevant kind of social interaction. Baldwin emphasizes a shared endeavor around which linguistic practices emerge. Given these insights, the relevant relata are discursive communities of practice. This characterization allows us to apply the incommensurability thesis – two racialized discursive communities RD_1 and RD_2 are incommensurable if and only if the terms in the language of RD_1 are not semantically equivalent to the terms in the language of RD_2.

Donald Davidson raises powerful objections to views like Kuhn's that we should now consider. The first thing he notes is that the metaphor of different viewpoints only makes sense 'if there is a common co-ordinate system on which to plot them' (Davidson, 1984, p. 184). However, if we admit to a common system, then these points of view cannot be radically incomparable.

Secondly, Davidson argues it is not clear the change in meaning from an old paradigm to a new one that Kuhn suggests amounts to radical conceptual change. To illustrate the point, Davidson supposes he is a Minister of Scientific Language who oversees a new policy – a prohibition on using words that refer to emotions, feelings, thoughts, and intentions and instead refer to physiological states and happenings. Davidson wonders: 'How do I tell whether my advice has been heeded if the new man speaks a new language? For all I know, the shiny new phrases, though stolen from the old language in which they refer to physiological stirrings, may in his mouth play the role of the messy old mental concepts' (Davidson, 1984, p. 189). His point is that the vocabulary provides no basis for determining whether the new scheme is the same as or different from the old one. We can also apply this to different racial conceptual schemes.

Additionally, I doubt Kuhn's account can explain some of our normative practices. For one, if worlds are really incommensurable in the Kuhnian way, then how can we make sense of the normative demands we often place on one another? It is reasonable to assume that demands of justice require correctly identifying the instances of injustice that must be addressed. But if the two conflicting discursive communities significantly lack semantically equivalent terms, it makes the project of identification fraught. Presumably, the source of this difficulty is the relativism the view appears to entail. If the divergences in meaning really do signal radical differences in ontology – social ontology included – then there would be no basis for shared normative demands.

Another concern that emerges from the previous one is that the absence of a shared basis for normative demand and descriptive adequacy makes disagreement impossible. As has been pointed out countless times, the possibility of disagreement requires a shared basis of understanding at some level. Relativizing reality to a discursive community's conceptual scheme would undermine this basis.

Globalization and multiculturality also threaten the different worlds thesis. Distinct worldviews are tied to the distinctiveness of the groups with whom the language is associated. But in an ever-increasing multilingual and multicultural world, the viability of such distinctiveness becomes more difficult. You may think establishing a distinct discursive world depends on relatively isolated conditions in which they can be reproduced. We can draw an analogy with the racial naturalist's view about races. According to racial naturalism, races result from relative reproductive isolation – members located in a specific geographic region produce offspring with one another. It is reasonable to assume language production also occurs in these relatively isolated contexts, a process that includes the mutual construction of concepts and discursive norms that order one's perception of the world.

We find a less contentious version of the different worlds thesis in Kenyan writer and thinker Ngugi Wa Thiong'o's book *Decolonising the Mind* (1986). Thiong'o believes language serves a dual purpose: it is a means of communication as well as a carrier of culture. Thiong'o points to English as used in Britain, Sweden, and Denmark and Swahili in East and Central Africa as illustrations of his claim. English for the British, he says, 'is [...] inseparably from its use as a tool of communication, a carrier of [British] culture and history', whereas it is only a means of communication for Swedes and Danes (Thiong'o, 1986, p. 13). Likewise, Swahili is a carrier of culture for parts of Kenya and Tanzania, particularly in Zanzibar, but only a means of communication for others.

Thiong'o says communication is the basis and process of evolving culture: 'In doing similar kinds of things and actions over and over again under similar circumstances, similar even in their mutability, certain patterns, moves, rhythms, habits, attitudes, experiences and knowledge emerge' (Thiong'o, 1986, p. 14). These experiences are handed over to subsequent generations as inherited bases for interactions with nature and each other. Thiong'o goes on to say these established patterns give rise to:

> a gradual accumulation of values which in time become almost self-evident truths governing their conception of what is right and wrong, good and bad, beautiful and ugly, courageous and cowardly, generous and mean in their internal and external relations. Over a time this becomes a way of life distinguishable from other ways of life. (Thiong'o, 1986, p. 14)

The repetition of speech in certain circumstances brings about a shared way of life. These values become second nature for members of this speech community, guiding judgments and perceptions of the world.

Racial Realities

Thiong'o also identifies three aspects of language as culture. First, culture is a product of and reflects history – 'Culture [...] is a product and a reflection of human beings communicating with one another in the very struggle to create wealth and to control it' (Thiong'o, 1986, p. 15). Culture reflects history by forming images or pictures of the world of nature and nurture. Second, culture is an 'image-forming agent in the mind of a child' (Thiong'o, 1986, p. 15). We base our conception of ourselves as individuals and collectives on these images, which needn't necessarily correspond to the reality of the struggles that gave rise to them. The quality of those images impacts our capacity to creatively confront the world because they either clarify or distort 'the reality of our struggles' (Thiong'o, 1986, p. 15). Third, culture transmits or imparts these images through a specific language. Thiong'o writes, 'a specific culture is not transmitted through language in its universality but in its particularity as the language of a specific community with a specific history' (Thiong'o, 1986, p. 15). He says literature and orature are the main means of transmission. Thiong'o then characterizes the connection between language and culture in this way:

> Language carries culture, and culture carries, particularly through orature and literature, the entire body of values by which we come to perceive ourselves and our place in the world. How people perceive themselves affects how they look at their culture, at their politics and at the social production of wealth, at their entire relationship to nature and to other beings. Language is thus inseparable from ourselves as a community of human beings with a specific form and character, a specific history, a specific relationship to the world. (Thiong'o, 1986, p. 16)

In Thiong'o, I believe we find a more realistic basis for the different worlds thesis. Although he does not strictly offer a race-based conception, Thiong'o is talking about the impact colonizing language has on the colonized, a subject not unrelated to race. In Thiong'o's view, we can see how different languages can come to diverge in conceptualization given the environments in which they are developed. Further, Thiong'o's distinction between *language as communication* and *language as culture* provides a way for us to make sense of cross-racial convergences in language while also maintaining the idea of important divergences between racialized discourses. If language carries culture and impacts the speaker's imagination the way he suggests, then there is a very real sense in which divergent collective interpretations of historical events can be attributed to different worlds.

However, Bill Ashcroft sees in Thiong'o a danger of conflating race with culture. Contrary to Thiong'o's idea that language carries culture, Ashcroft retorts, 'use of language is a signifier of culture, language does not contain that culture' (Ashcroft, 2001, p. 324). Ashcroft sees the potential in appropriating language for resistant ends, contrary to what he thinks is suggested in views like Thiong'o's. In fact, he sees Thiong'o's own English writing as an instance of resistance. Ashcroft appears to interpret Thiong'o as saying languages determine one's imaginative outlook irrevocably.

Additionally, Ashcroft denies a connection between 'race' and language. He understands 'race' to mean those biological groupings primarily characterized by physical attributes – especially color – and lines of descent. If we use race as a purported means of understanding particular speech, we err in appealing to something that is disconnected from reality. Further, we risk imprisoning resistance in an 'inward looking world'. Ashcroft insists post-colonial intellectuals must realize language has no race because the consequence of linking the two is the undermining of linguistic resistance: 'The ultimate consequence of the belief that language embodies race is the deafening silence of a rage that cannot be heard' (Ashcroft, 2001, p. 326).

I am not entirely convinced Ashcroft's objections are damning since it is not necessary to understand race as biological race. Social constructionist and anti-realist views might avoid the consequences Ashcroft anticipates. However, I do think we should heed his warnings about the effects of drawing too tight a connection between language and culture might provoke. If one is too insistent on this point, it leaves open the idea that addressing social injustice is futile. Albert Hirschman, for instance, details ways reactionaries have appealed to this strategy to resist calls for reform.[2]

Maybe the different worlds we are after can best be described as either an *epistemic bubble* or an *echo chamber*. As C. Thi Nguyen (2020) defines them, epistemic bubbles are social epistemic structures in which some relevant voices are excluded through omission, and echo chambers are social epistemic structures in which other relevant voices are actively discredited. Let us examine each in turn.

Nguyen claims epistemic bubbles form when certain information or voices are excluded from one's epistemic social network. For instance, we sometimes selectively expose ourselves only to like-

---

[2] For more, see Hirschman (1991).

minded people or information. There are also instances in which the information we receive is filtered by authority figures or algorithmic processes. People who only watch Fox News or MSNBC, for example, are receiving a heavily curated news presentation and not comprehensive coverage. Nguyen thinks inadequate coverage is a central feature of epistemic bubbles; it is the result of omissive exclusions.

Should we understand racialized discourses in terms of epistemic bubbles? One advantage of doing so would be that it separates the presumed tight connection between race and language we saw reason to worry about earlier. Equating worlds with epistemic bubbles would allow us to capture observations about relative cohesiveness in thought without presupposing the existence of biological races. It would also avoid claiming a certain group of speakers are monolithic because they share a race. The network aspect of bubble communities localizes the group's membership in important ways.

That being said, the fact of epistemic bubbles' relative fragility makes me think this isn't the right explanation. The examples we observed in the introduction feel more deeply entrenched than what's on offer here. They don't seem like the sorts of things one could be extracted from simply by being introduced to a more comprehensive set of sources. What is left unaccounted for is the mode of interpretation people bring to the things they encounter. Essentially, our linguistic socialization leaves a heavy imprint on how our perceptual capacities work. Merely encountering a more comprehensive set of views will not necessarily alter our interpretations in positive ways.

Understanding racialized worlds in terms of echo chambers could offer a better option. Keeping with the theme of community, Nguyen clarifies the notion: 'I use the term "echo chamber" to mean an epistemic community which creates a significant disparity in trust between members and non-members' (Nguyen, 2020, p. 146). Non-members are excluded through epistemic discrediting while members' epistemic credentials are simultaneously boosted. Also, gaining membership in the group requires general agreement with the group's core set of beliefs, including beliefs that support the disparity in trust.

Admittedly, there is something to this. People who strongly identify with a particular group may indeed find themselves crediting members more highly while discrediting and distrusting non-members more. However, I do not believe racialized discourses are echo chambers. There are many who engage views from different groups in good faith and who do their best to understand a counterview. This approach goes against the proclivities of someone caught up in an echo chamber. Though the disparity in trust and credit represented by this concept is a real phenomenon, it does not work as a general explanation for conflicting racialized discourses.

I speculate a proposal that views the nature of difference as metaphysical could draw inspiration from Afro-pessimist discussions of ontology. Roughly, the idea is that if you conceive of beings with different ontological statuses, you could say these beings inhabit different worlds because the dominant discourse's use of 'universal humanism' is specious; it surreptitiously claims certain humanoid beings are not human. In so far as this discourse is used, it obscures the relevant realities for these various groups. I'm not entirely sure this follows, but I raise it as a possible path to explore. I leave it to others to work out.

Although we've seen some compelling reasons to be skeptical of the different worlds thesis, I am inclined to defend it, nonetheless. But instead of centering epistemological, hermeneutical, or metaphysical considerations, I turn instead to *normative* ones. In short, racial realities amount to a network of normative relations that make different things permissible or impermissible. The idea I am going for here is about the kinds of things you can do and say to a person based on the role their perceived social identity plays in a system of power relations. These are group-level attributions that come to affect their members in various ways.

By and large, societies are racially stratified social orders. In part, racial identities heavily influence the distribution of benefits and burdens. Race is one dimension used to divide people in order to regulate access. Race is also informed by and helps inform the shape of other dimensions like gender, sexuality, class, and ability. Stratification refers to 'the unequal distribution of people across social categories that are characterized by differential access to scarce resources' (Massey, 2007, p. 1). Sociologist Douglas Massey notes that resources can be material, symbolic, or emotional.

I submit that one effect of this stratification is the production of significantly different 'worlds', zones of ethical concern that vary in scope. These zones do not strictly follow racial lines, but race can often play a significant explanatory role in a person's response to some event. Note that by *race*, I am not using it in the classificatory sense, but something like race as culture. The race/culture nexus both influences and is influenced by the kinds of practices localized communities devise in pursuit of a shared endeavor.

This is not to deny that epistemological, hermeneutical, or metaphysical considerations play a role; it is just that they do not take center stage as the main explanatory element. In my view, those elements are things that emerge with the development of a practice. I draw once again on Eckert and McConnell-Ginet's use of a community of practice to help conceptualize how these things come together.

Eckert and McConnell-Ginet aver that the community of practice 'is where observable action and interaction do the work of producing, reproducing, and resisting the organization of power in society, and societal discourses of gender, age, race, etc.' (Eckert and McConnell-Ginet, 1992, p. 98). The affirmation or denial of racial realities hinges largely on differences in power and one's relation to it. The privileges a group has, or the detriments, are part of the environment it must address. A group's predicament understandably conditions linguistic patterns that, as Baldwin attests, attempt to control or articulate one's experience. Groups with widely divergent predicaments develop discourses that can feel worlds apart.

4. Understanding

The relationship between the 'worlds' question and understanding is motivated by the former's impact on the latter. If people inhabit different worlds with different perceptual, semantic, and ethical norms, we rightly expect divergences in understanding. For example, this idea seemingly explains how two people can observe the 'same' data and come to conflicting conclusions.

Depending on how these worlds are characterized, different worlds talk could also require bold revisions of basic concepts we take for granted. For instance, what would be the basis for justice claims if these worlds are understood as incommensurable, even partially? Surely, the hope of converging on an overlapping concept between different worlds would be unlikely, if not impossible.

We've spent the last several pages attempting to clarify the notion of different worlds. Perhaps we should now take a moment to clarify how we should understand *understanding*. Scholars have offered various characterizations. Jonathan Kvanvig (2003), for instance, distinguishes between two senses: *propositional* and *objectual* understanding. Propositional understanding takes the form 'I understand that P' while objectual understanding takes the grammatical form 'I understand P.' Neil Cooper (1994) refers to *cognitive understanding* – 'the understanding of things, phenomena, events, truths, situations, states of affairs and so on' (Cooper, 1994, p. 1).

There are differences in understanding at the *discursive* level. You will readily recognize some of these immediately. If you are not an avid poetry reader, you will likely find it hard to understand what is happening in a poem. You may need to learn the various writing styles and conventions poets use in their work before you can understand their poetry. Kvanvig's two senses of understanding may work well at this level. You can fail to understand Lucille Clifton's poem *Brothers* in the objectual sense. This would be failing to understand why, for example, she makes some of the choices she does. You could also experience failure in propositional understanding, not knowing that the poem is a dialogue between Lucifer and God.

Presumably, there can be both objectual and propositional failures of understanding at work in the racial conflicts we observed earlier. We also allow for a multiplicity of different understandings on certain occasions. In aesthetic contexts, for example, open-ended interpretation is often welcome and appreciated. Such open-endedness is more restricted in political contexts. I suspect this is because there is an assumption of universality or commonness driving good-faith discussion.

Until now, we've been operating on the assumption that inhabiting different worlds potentially impacts one's understanding. Perhaps some of us have also assumed being associated with one world (or related set of worlds) restricts our ability to understand a different one. It is not entirely clear to me that this is true. The different worlds thesis encourages us to contemplate the differences between human beings, but we should not neglect those aspects that also tie us together.

Differences in imagination can serve as the source of an impasse. For example, former US Secretary of Commerce Wilbur Ross could not imagine why federal workers would need to line up at food banks after not receiving paychecks due to a government shutdown (Mallin, 2019). There is a palpable sense in which Ross' inability to imagine and hence understand the plight of federal workers is explained by his living in a different world. Yet, humans, in general, have imaginative capacities that are, in principle, refinable.

Ian York and I (Anderson and York, 2024) illustrate this point by discussing the story of Derek Black, a former white nationalist whose experience as a student at the New College of Florida transformed his imaginative capacities. Black's interactions with Jewish student Matthew Stevenson and with courses on race and medieval Islamic culture helped to dislodge imaginative blocks that prevented him from empathic understanding of others. There is, of course, no guarantee that encounters like these will yield transformations of the sort Black experienced, but they are possible.

However, Martinican scholar Édouard Glissant interestingly challenges the underlying assumption of universality. He says Western perspectives on *understanding* require transparency that ultimately demands that one 'reduce' (Glissant, 1997, p. 190). Essentially, this version of understanding assumes an implicit scale that allows for comparisons and judgments to measure others by. Glissant observes,

> Accepting differences does, of course, upset the hierarchy of this scale. I understand your difference, or in other words, without creating a hierarchy, I relate it to my norm. I admit you to existence, within my system. I create you afresh.—But perhaps we need to bring an end to the very notion of a scale. Displace all reduction. (Glissant, 1997, p. 190)

Glissant argues that the search for a unifying story about what makes us all the same inevitably results in disunity because of the impulse to assimilate an Other into one's own system. The true way to unity is the recognition of *opacities*, which he says can coexist and converge: 'There would be something great and noble about initiating such a movement, referring not to Humanity but to the exultant divergence of humanities' (Glissant, 1997, p. 190).

If Glissant is right, pursuing a universal form of understanding actually undermines social justice projects. Instead, we need to reconcile ourselves to unbridgeable chasms, come to peace with not understanding everything about a perceived Other, but not let these differences motivate power grabs that maintain relationships of dominance. Observe that admitting this would be to admit a more robust version of the different worlds thesis.

5. Conclusion

The consequences of embracing conceptual relativity would be harsh and disruptive. One consequence would be a loss of perceived connection to discursive expressions of the past. If truth is relative to a particular conceptual scheme, we need to identify past cultures' schemes to make sense of their ideas and concepts.

I think we all acknowledge that bare racial identities in the classificatory sense do not cause divergent discursive worlds. It is difficult to contemplate any naturally occurring feature that would separate human understanding according to race. This also means we should not expect to find totally distinct racial worlds. But as was stated previously, this does not mean race plays no part in an explanation of why certain impasses exist.

I have offered what I hope is a fruitful discussion about a tempting idea that needs further clarity. The challenge raised by Glissant leaves

Luvell Anderson

us without a clear resolution, but it does force us to examine the often-unacknowledged assumption of universality many social justice projects tend to adopt.

References

Luvell Anderson and Ian York, 'Online Propaganda and the Manipulation of Imaginative Possibilities', in Patrick Connolly, Sanford Goldberg, and Jennifer Saul (eds), *Conversations Online* (Oxford: Oxford University Press, 2024).

Bill Ashcroft, 'Language and Race', *Social Identities: Journal for the Study of Race, Nation and Culture*, 7:3 (2001), 311–28.

James Baldwin, 'If Black English Isn't a Language, Then Tell Me, What Is?', *New York Times*, July 29, 1979.

Nicholas Buccola, *The Fire Is upon Us: James Baldwin, William F. Buckley Jr., and the Debate over Race in America* (Princeton: Princeton University Press, 2020).

Neil Cooper, 'Understanding', *Proceedings of the Aristotelian Society, Supplementary Volumes*, 68 (1994), 1–26.

Donald Davidson, *Inquiries Into Truth And Interpretation* (Oxford: Oxford University Press, 1984).

W.E.B. Du Bois, 'The Conservation of Races', (1897), in N.D. Chandler (ed.), *The Problem of the Color Line at the Turn of the Twentieth Century* (New York: Fordham University Press, 2014), 51–66.

Penelope Eckert and Sally McConnell-Ginet, 'Communities of Practice: Where Language, Gender, and Power All Live', in Kira Hall, Mary Bucholtz, and Birch Moonwomon (eds), *Locating Power: Proceedings of the Second Berkeley Women and Language Conference* (Berkely, California: Berkeley Women and Language Group, 1992), 89–99.

Daian Florez, 'Semantic Change in the Language of Technology', in Luvell Anderson and Ernest Lepore (eds), *The Oxford Handbook of Applied Philosophy of Language* (Oxford: Oxford University Press, 2024).

Édouard Glissant, *Poetics of Relation*, Betsy Wing (trans.), (Ann Arbor: University of Michigan, 1997).

Albert O. Hirschman, *The Rhetoric of Reaction: Perversity, Futility, Jeopardy* (Cambridge, MA: Belknap Press, 1991).

'Inclusive Britain: Government Response to the Commission on Race and Ethnic Disparities', (2022). Accessed August 19, 2023, https://www.gov.uk/government/publications/inclusive-britain-action-plan-government-response-to-the-commission-on-race-and-ethnic-disparities.

Thomas Kuhn, *The Structure of Scientific Revolutions* (Chicago: University of Chicago Press, 1962).

Jonathan L. Kvanvig, *The Value of Knowledge and the Pursuit of Understanding* (Cambridge University Press, 2003).

Alexander Mallin, 'Trump Commerce Secretary Wilbur Ross Says He Doesn't "Understand" Why Federal Workers Lining up at Food Banks', *ABC News*, 24 January 2019, https://abcnews.go.com/Politics/trump-commerce-secretary-wilbur-ross-understand-federal-workers/story?id=60595988.

Douglas Massey, *Categorically Unequal: The American Stratification System* (Russell Sage Foundation, 2007).

C. Thi Nguyen, 'ECHO CHAMBERS AND EPISTEMIC BUBBLES', *Episteme*, 17:2 (2020), 141–61.

Thomas Nickles, 'Scientific Revolutions', in Edward N. Zalta (ed.), *The Stanford Encyclopedia of Philosophy* (Winter 2017), https://plato.stanford.edu/archives/win2017/entries/scientific-revolutions/.

Tope Omoniyi, 'Language, Race and Identity', in Sian Preece (ed.), *The Routledge Handbook of Language and Identity* (Abingdon: Routledge, 2016), 146–62.

Ngugi Wa Thiong'o, *Decolonising the Mind: The Politics of Language in African Literature* (London: James Currey Ltd / Heinemann, 1986).

Tobi Thomas and Aina J. Khan, 'Protests across UK over Killing of Unarmed Black Man Chris Kaba', *The Observer*, 17 September 2022, https://www.theguardian.com/uk-news/2022/sep/17/protest-uk-met-police-killing-black-chris-kaba.

Misunderstanding and Meaning Change

ANDREW HINES

Abstract

Today, the tone of discussion in the public sphere is dominated by misunderstanding. A common assumption is that misunderstanding comes from a failure of understanding. This article argues that misunderstanding is in fact a type of meaning change. To fully understand the contrast between misunderstanding as a failure of understanding and misunderstanding as a type of meaning change, the article uses Ludwig Wittgenstein and Hans-Georg Gadamer as a starting point to tease out an unthought assumption. Both thinkers challenge traditional preconceptions of how language shapes understanding and they make prominent use of the concept of misunderstanding to do so. Yet both rely on a de facto model of misunderstanding as a failure of understanding. To consider an alternative notion of misunderstanding, the article looks at examples from thinkers influenced by Wittgenstein's and Gadamer's philosophy. Finally, the article concludes by positing a new definition of misunderstanding.

1. Introduction

Seven years ago, Gina Miller took a case to the UK high court to argue that the government couldn't go ahead with Brexit without first consulting parliament. Some labelled her a 'traitor to democracy' for her actions and the judges who ruled in her favour 'enemies of the people'. Miller expressed confusion about this. In her perspective, the pro-Brexit activists who called her a 'traitor to democracy' had incorrectly judged how democracy works in the UK, highlighting how the UK is a representative rather than a direct democracy (Hines, 2016). Whether through a lack of experience, of education, or even laziness, when Miller suggests that the activist misunderstands the nature of democracy, she is suggesting that their judgement is committed to something that is incorrect and that further reflection would show is fundamentally improbable. Despite the fact that the EU referendum is nearly ten years old and that the UK has since left the EU, the example of the clash of meaning over a key term like 'democracy' still haunts us today. While Brexit may not be as close to the headlines today as Ukraine or Gaza, the tone of the discussion in the public sphere is still dominated by that of misunderstanding and communication breakdown.

One phenomenon in particular is clearly observed in such examples: while often assumed to come from ignorance or a failure of understanding, the communication breakdown in public discourse of the last ten years is fundamentally linked to a change in meaning. The meaning of words, such as 'democracy' in the Miller example, which are central to providing stability for a community's identity and daily life, has undergone a rapid shift. While one may argue, rightly in some instances, that these meaning changes are not actual changes at all but rather ignorance of the terms involved or a failure to understand them, there is also something else at work. The meaning changes we see today are cross-cutting. The shift in such terms affects all classes, all levels of education, all political alliances. Due to the nature of how we experience information today through social media, the internet and video, these meaning shifts have not simply been observed by academics, but rather have taken place with the whole world watching. The global public of Western democracies have all experienced moments in the last ten years where they found themselves thinking, 'I thought I supported Labour, but not that meaning of Labour', or 'I thought I was a Conservative, but not that type of Conservative', or 'I thought I believed in democracy, but not that meaning of democracy'. These meaning changes that the majority of us have found ourselves within go deeper than a simple ignorance or failure of understanding. And it is these changes in meaning that, at least in part, have caused such publicly visible misunderstandings. Because of this, they leave public consciousness with a gap: we think to ourselves, 'what I see in front of me is misunderstanding'. And yet, try as we might to reduce it to failure, we see our own communities collapsing and fragmenting around us as the meanings of central ideas shift.

This essay will make the case that these meaning changes are not simply an associated phenomenon, brought about by ignorance, failure or error, but rather a part of the very nature of misunderstanding itself. Far from being an assertion of relativism, investigating the relationship between meaning change and misunderstanding does not seek to revert to a post-war critique of metaphysics or to challenge our assumptions about the nature of truth or the nature of fact. Rather, such an investigation seeks to challenge our assumptions about the nature of misunderstanding itself. That is because our contemporary moment suggests that our use of the term is no longer fit for purpose.

Misunderstanding and Meaning Change

2. An Unthought Assumption in the History of Philosophy

What do we actually know of misunderstanding? It could be said to be the word of our age, yet we know so little about it. As an example, one only need to look to a philosophical dictionary. *The Dictionary of Untranslatables: A Philosophical Lexicon* and the *Historisches Wörterbuch der Philosophie* represent distinct currents for those studying the history of concepts in the humanities. However, one thing they share is the absence of an entry on 'misunderstanding'. Both simply say: 'see understanding'. This conceptual dependency implies an assumption about the nature of misunderstanding. If misunderstanding is simply a word we use to describe the absence or lack of a fully formed concept with a distinct canonical history, then the concept of misunderstanding itself is a lacking or even absent concept. This essay maintains that, given this absence, the concept of misunderstanding is taken de facto on a model of 'failure of understanding'. But far from addressing the phenomenon of meaning change seen in our contemporary moment, the de facto model points us towards an assumption of failure. While sometimes useful, the failure model is severely limited, particularly in a moment like ours when a new type of misunderstanding is emerging.

Such a de facto model is largely reflected in both the everyday definition and the history of the term's usage in European philosophy. In both the verb and noun form in the English language, dating from at least 1225 and 1443 respectively, misunderstanding is defined as a 'failure to understand something rightly'.[1] This is reflected in its very construction: the root of the term is 'understanding' and the 'mis' doesn't tell us new information about the lack of understanding occurring but only acts a prefix to denote understanding's opposite. This dictionary definition, that reflects popular usage, is also often reflected in the philosophical usage of the term and its associated satellites. These uses, in a history we do not have room to go into here, largely do not reflect on misunderstanding in its own right.[2]

---

[1] 'Misunderstanding, N. (1)', and 'Misunderstand, V.', in the *Oxford English Dictionary* (2023).

[2] The author is aware there is a long history of various investigations about how misunderstanding occurs. However, these instances on the whole tend to assume the de facto 'failure' model. The author's argument is not that the history of philosophy does not involve important investigations of misunderstanding, but rather, that it is often the case that such investigations assume the de facto failure model. Because of this they tend to shed more light on human cognition, understanding, language *etc.* than on misunderstanding itself.

Andrew Hines

When they do, they often reinforce the de facto, 'misunderstanding is a failure of understanding' model. Such is the case in Locke's *An Essay Concerning Human Understanding* from 1689 where he argues that our understanding is in error when we have failed to match up probability, evidence, and truth correctly (Locke, 2008, p. 454).

We can see the de facto 'failure of understanding' model reinforced even when the nature of understanding itself is subject to critical reflection. We can illustrate this with two examples from the twentieth century's most influential thinkers on language: Ludwig Wittgenstein and Hans-Georg Gadamer. Both contributed profoundly to the development of Western thinking on language, meaning, and understanding in the twentieth century. Perhaps it is fitting, then, to see the failure model in contrast alongside two thinkers who transformed our conception of meaning and understanding. It is also fitting to look at 'historic' as opposed to current thinkers that have impacted later movements as we can see how rooted later developments are in these descriptions. Finally, what is even more fitting is that Wittgenstein and Gadamer appear to have fundamentally different projects relating to understanding, and yet, when they use the term misunderstanding, they both seem to invoke the de facto failure model in their use of the term.

2.1 Wittgenstein and Gadamer

At first glance, Gadamer utilises the concept of misunderstanding in a very different way for his philosophical programme from Wittgenstein. Gadamer follows along with the larger tradition of German hermeneutics in asserting that misunderstanding happens as a matter of course in the process of interpretation. The father of hermeneutics, Friedrich Schleiermacher, asserts that hermeneutics is the art of overcoming the misunderstandings inherent in language and tradition. These misunderstandings, Schleiermacher argues, happen as a matter of course because of how the parts of speech work.

In *The General Theory and Art of Interpretation*, Schleiermacher is suggesting that the traditional notion of interpretation and translation is incorrect. In the traditional view, if one were to pick up a copy of Cicero and read the Latin word *narratio* and misunderstand it for something other than the English word 'narrative', the reason for misunderstanding would be to do with the translator, the education of the reader, *etc*. As Schleiermacher states, 'the assumption [behind interpretation] is that understanding occurs as a matter of course' (Schleiermacher, 1986, p. 82). However, Schleiermacher's genius lies in the fact that he was able to discern that it is language itself, its historicity, and the parts of speech that can lead to misunderstandings, and this is the starting point of interpretation. The art of hermeneutics is a way of overcoming misunderstandings and achieving understanding.

Building on this tradition in German scholarship, in *Truth and Method* Gadamer famously ontologises Schleiermacher's insight drawing on the philosophy of Martin Heidegger to do so. Gadamer makes the basic hermeneutic principle of misunderstanding not simply a technical matter of importance to textual exegesis, but a basic function of how our consciousness interprets our own existence and the existence of the world around us. Speaking about the 'reflective' nature of language, one of the things that Gadamer's philosophy asserts is that language impacts our understanding and reflects the local, colloquial situation we find ourselves in (Gadamer, 2019, pp. 401–23). Because of this, in a philosophical outlook like Gadamer's, misunderstanding appears to be inherent within language, tradition, and experience of the world.

As is well known, Wittgenstein, in stark contrast to Gadamer, was not drawing on a lengthy tradition, but rather responding, at least in part, to aspects of Bertrand Russell's attempt to distil the problems of both philosophy and mathematics with a highly precise approach (see Ray, 2005, pp. 11–19). About this approach, and indeed seemingly all the problems of philosophy, Wittgenstein sums them up as a misunderstanding. At the beginning of the *Tractatus*, it is not that misunderstanding is inherently *within* language, as is the case with Gadamer, but rather that *we* misunderstand the logic of our language. To paraphrase his famous pronouncement, it is our misunderstanding of language which creates the problems of philosophy (Wittgenstein, 1974, p. 3). A cursory, and arguably superficial reading of this, suggests that *we* as thinking human beings are the ones doing the misunderstanding. The *Philosophical Investigations* expands and deepens this initial idea. In §90, Wittgenstein suggests the investigation he's carrying out clears a misunderstanding away over the use of words and analogies (Wittgenstein, 1989, pp. 42–43). In §111, he clarifies that 'these misunderstandings are deep, their roots are as deep in us as the forms of language' (*ibid.*, p. 47). One could argue that this type of misunderstanding then is closer to Gadamer's use of the term, because Wittgenstein seems to suggest it is not just *we* who misunderstand but that there is misunderstanding *within* the roots of the form of language itself.

However, whatever view one takes about the location of misunderstanding (within us or within language), there is a fundamental overlap in both Gadamer and Wittgenstein's use of the term that is

Andrew Hines

not connected to their respective philosophical programmes. Gadamer's and Wittgenstein's use of the term simply tells us something distinct about the *location* at which a misunderstanding occurs as human beings, think, experience, and use language. One may even argue that they disagree on the location of misunderstanding. But both thinkers' use of the term ultimately connotes the same thing: that a failure of understanding has taken place.

Gadamer and Wittgenstein both produced two of the most influential theories of language to emerge from Europe in the last hundred years. Yet, despite the highly nuanced and pioneering theories both thinkers bring to the theme of how meaning is created or produced, both thinkers, perhaps unthinkingly, invoke the de facto 'failure' model of misunderstanding. Such a model relies primarily on a static view of meaning, as it assumes a basic tripartite correspondence between meaning, word, and truth. The irony, of course, is that, in their own way, the philosophy of both thinkers involves an explicit critique of the traditional correspondence model of meaning. Wittgenstein even goes so far as explicitly stating this in sections 1–5 of his *Philosophical Investigations* and Gadamer's reliance on Heidegger also assumes such a critique.

Because of this, what we have in both thinkers are progressive, paradigm-shifting models of how the creation of meaning relates to human understanding. Yet both models rely on a very traditional, centuries-old model of misunderstanding. Furthermore, in many ways the misunderstanding model they rely on represents the very thing they are critiquing. In some instances, this centuries-old model is very useful. Its description of misunderstanding is quite apt to describe some instances. But 'some instances' is not at all the same as 'in every case' and the fact that this centuries-old de facto model relies on a static view of meaning, makes it increasingly hard to defend, especially when our contemporary lived experience suggests a much deeper relationship between meaning change and misunderstanding. Close examination of these experiences reveals that misunderstanding is rooted not simply within a failure of understanding, but more broadly within a type of meaning change of which failure of understanding is only one sub-variety.

There is one point of clarification needed before we proceed to an explication of the relationship between misunderstanding and meaning change. And that is to do with why I have avoided attempting to establish a normative foundation for the concept of misunderstanding. One might suggest that, to clear up our confusion about misunderstanding, could we not begin by establishing a normative foundation for when a misunderstanding has occurred? This paper will maintain that we can't simply create normative foundations for judging misunderstanding because, as I've attempted to demonstrate above, we don't know what misunderstanding is beyond the de facto model. Because of this, we can't reap the functional benefits of any potential normative foundation. Such a normative foundation would assume that we know what a misunderstanding is and who it is happening to, and that this assumption is suitable 'in every case'.

So, if we can't assume the de facto model of failure of understanding, where does that leave us? We can perhaps best illustrate a different route into the concept of misunderstanding by looking at two further examples in the philosophical literature. While by no means exhaustive, both examples show the mechanics of meaning change as it relates to misunderstanding. Mainly that, a misunderstanding takes place when human language, thought, and experience are caught between two different meanings. Both, incidentally, also take place in the aftereffects of both Wittgenstein's and Gadamer's philosophy.

3. Two Examples: Kwasi Wiredu and Jürgen Habermas

3.1 Wiredu

One of the most influential African philosophers of his generation, Kwasi Wiredu provides us with an example of how misunderstanding is produced when a speaker of a given language is caught between two grammatical realities. He begins with the assumption that grammar produces meaning, but that such meaning is 'tongue dependent'. In his brief but powerful and deeply influential essay, 'The Concept of Truth in the Akan Language', Wiredu reminds the reader of the correlative nature of meaning and that there are different types of correlation. He makes the distinction between moral and cognitive correlation in pointing out the difference between a moral and a cognitive concept of truth. To flesh out this distinction, he uses an example from his native Akan language (Wiredu, 1998, pp. 239–43).

Wiredu points out that the differences between the moral and cognitive correlations of the meaning of a concept, in this case truth, causes a discrepancy in our understanding of meaning production. For Wiredu, an example of such a discrepancy appears when attempting to explain to a native Akan speaker, who hasn't made a specialist study of the subject, a traditionally expressed theory of truth (such as the correspondence theory) (*ibid.*, p. 240). Wiredu's conclusion isn't that the correspondence theory is wrong, but rather that meaning and correlation are 'tongue dependent'. Specifically, this means that philosophical claims are dependent on the grammatical structure of a given language (in this case Akan) (*ibid.*, pp. 240–42).

'Tongue dependency' of course became one of Wiredu's foundational contributions to the African philosophical movement of the twentieth century. While Wiredu is broadly highlighting the relative nature of meaning, he is doing it through largely empirical means (referencing the evidence of his own language) rather than through a critique of metaphysics as we may find in another thinker such as Nietzsche. Thus, Wiredu's critique is not of the nature of truth (as we find in Nietzsche), but rather of the nature of meaning and with it the constructive assertion that the nature of meaning and its tendency to have a correlative capacity is always 'tongue dependent'. This, Wiredu argues, has special significance for the African philosophical movement. For our purposes, if we take a step back, we can see a concept of misunderstanding and a concept of meaning change take a distinctive shape.

Wiredu opens the piece by explaining the Akan words for truth, falsity, and lies. He uses this to tease out the ambiguous and vague nature of the everyday use of the English word 'truth'. It tends to suggest truthfulness (i.e., the moral concept), not truth *an sich* (the cognitive concept) (*ibid.*, pp. 239–40). So if the average Akan were to encounter the correspondence theory and were asked to translate it, they would encounter a difficulty. The difficulty, Wiredu argues, is quite a good reason, and related not to education or culture (as we might expect if misunderstanding were simply ignorance or failure), but to grammar. This inescapable grammatical reality causes a small misunderstanding in the attempt to translate a theory like the correspondence theory of truth. Wiredu writes,

> Consider the correspondence theory of truth. This is supposed to assert something like this: 'p is true' means 'p corresponds to a fact'. What does this come to in Akan? Simply that 'p *te saa*' which in truth, is nothing more than saying that 'p *te saa*' means 'p *te saa*'. In other words, the correspondence definition amounts to a tautology in Akan [...]. If we now assert that the statement form [in English] 'p if and only if q' is equivalent to '(if p then q) and (if q then p)' we are obviously asserting a logical truth in English, but no such logical truth exists in Akan. There is nothing necessary about the form 'p if and only if q', so that it might be thought obligatory that the Akan should have a phrase literally corresponding to it. (Wiredu, 1998, pp. 240, 242)

Misunderstanding and Meaning Change

Wiredu's point of course is not that the Akan speaker can't understand the correspondence theory of truth if they made a special study of it, but rather that the way the correspondence theory of truth is expressed in English is partially due to the structure (or peculiarity, as Wiredu puts it) of English grammar. The grammar of the Akan language, as Wiredu points out, prioritises a moral, rather than cognitive concept of truth. This is where he derives his famous concept of 'tongue dependency' from.

What are we to make of this? The meaning change between grammatical structures causes a misunderstanding. Wiredu highlights an important truth for our purposes. It is not that the Akan speaker has simply *failed to understand*, nor is it even strictly a cultural paradigm clash. Rather, it is a change of meaning between grammatical structures that causes the misunderstanding. Therefore, the 'home' of meaning in this case, is the grammatical structure and its correlates. Misunderstanding, then, occurs when a meaning change is attempted but fails to land within the 'home' grammar of the language (English in this case) which produces this specialist usage.

As we will see in the next example, misunderstanding does not rest solely (or even primarily) within the individual, but rather as meaning is caught in the 'in-between' state created by meaning change. There are so many impossible transformations of meaning attempted between Akan and English, and yet, these transformations are not fully realised, because the subject experiences a meaning change, even if one party perceives it as a failure.

3.2 Habermas

For our next example, let us look at the definition of ideological misunderstanding Jürgen Habermas provides in his critique of philosophical hermeneutics. This exchange of essays between friends (often characterised as a debate) has come to stand in for an intellectual conflict that runs not only through the length of the critical theory tradition, but through a basic tendency of Western thought: it is simply the question, do we conserve or critique tradition? This binary, often a false one, is a basic habit of Western thought. Do we conserve or do we critique? And what is the capacity of human cognition in this regard?

This question, and the way that Habermas poses it, also has significance for the problem of meaning change. Commentators about this exchange often skip over the attention, care, and respect that Habermas pays to the hermeneutic tradition. In fact, if we simply take a moment to read the first half of the essay, his critique is born of both admiration and a deep recognition that one cannot have critique without cognition.[3] What was it about philosophical hermeneutics that Habermas so admired in its description of cognition? It was the fact that meaning is always produced colloquially or through 'colloquial communication' as he calls it (Habermas, 1986, p. 296). For Habermas, colloquial communication is an indispensable aspect of assessing communication. Because of this he makes clear that an approach like Chomsky's Universal Grammar cannot adequately address the full scale of the socio-political questions Habermas is concerned with in his reflections on communication (*ibid.*, p. 296). Because of this, Habermas feels there is something essential in hermeneutics, namely its recognition of the colloquial dimension of the production of meaning.

For our purposes, we must also pay attention to colloquial communication to understand the relationship between misunderstanding and meaning change. It is important to note that examining the role of colloquial communication in misunderstanding is fundamentally different from a call to revitalise philosophical hermeneutics in its canonical form. So much philosophy, so much life, has transpired in the fifty years since the publication of Habermas' critique. Because of this, there are many cases where philosophical hermeneutics as an answer to cultural questions is either severely limited or no longer valid. The developments in cognitive science alone, or fundamental changes to the practice of dialogue (due to technological developments and irreversible geopolitical moments), are a few of the several candidates that rupture many of the foundational assumptions of the tradition. This is of course even before we engage with the 'Heidegger question'.

But Habermas' desire to preserve something about colloquial communication in his analysis of the production of meaning is in the spirit, if not the letter, of what we must return to today. So how does he articulate this problem? And how does it relate to misunderstanding and meaning change? Habermas agrees with the hermeneutic tradition that colloquial communication is essential to understanding language as a socio-cultural phenomenon. However, he argues that there is a problem central to the role of colloquial communication in the production of meaning. Colloquial communication both feeds and reflects tradition, and while it is central to our understanding both as individuals and communities, colloquial communication also produces

---

[3] A point which critical theorists of today would be well served to remember.

Misunderstanding and Meaning Change

misunderstanding. While colloquial communication can build consensus, Habermas also points out that it can build 'false consensus', being the vehicle not simply for understanding but for oppression (Habermas, 1986, pp. 303, 314).

These few lines present us with a distinct definition of misunderstanding and how it relates to meaning change, particularly from the perspective of ideology. It provides the perfect case study for our purposes. What does Habermas suggest is occurring? The key philosophical insight we need to take from this is that, while colloquial communication creates meaning through the process of the hermeneutic circle and its relationship to tradition (both informing and being informed by tradition), the same relationship can also change meaning. Habermas writes that it even has the potential to do so in a systematic fashion through a centralised authority. This meaning change, Habermas writes, produces misunderstanding. Therefore, Habermas suggests, the very hermeneutic process he values because of the importance it places on colloquial communication also has the potential to systematically produce misunderstandings in our collective consciousness. If we think for example about Boris Johnson's use of the metaphor of Britain as a roaring lion to argue for a distinctive post-Brexit economic policy, we can see Habermas' meaning. The 'roaring lion' of British mythology is a broad figurative truth with several meanings. But in the case of a particular economic policy argument such as Johnson's, it is reduced to one particular meaning (Hines, 2017).

Because of this reality of political rhetoric, what follows for Habermas is not a total rejection of hermeneutics, but rather a critical dialogue about how a theory of language with colloquial meaning in the centre can also recognise the ideological danger of misunderstanding. In particular, Habermas wants to keep front and centre the fact that the danger of misunderstanding comes from the very tradition that produces colloquial meaning itself.

This is what is so essential to grasp. Habermas initially affirms hermeneutics because it reminds us of the truth that we are not outside tradition and colloquial meaning. Yet both tradition and colloquial meaning have the capacity to oppress or to generate ideological misunderstandings. In this critical distinction, we see Habermas create a fundamental link between misunderstanding and meaning change. For Habermas, the idiomatic quality of our colloquial communication produces meaning. This meaning is stabilised, not by some metaphysical or 'natural' truth, and not solely (though definitely partially) by grammar, but by the continual use of language by a community of speakers. This process of stabilisation informs and is informed by tradition.

Here is where the ideological misunderstanding comes, according to Habermas. That which is common suddenly is changed and destabilised. The interesting and key thing is the fact that the community of speakers doesn't necessarily immediately notice the meaning has changed. What exactly is changing here? It is the consensus of meaning that has changed. How? Let us use the example of an individual in a community of speakers that hears or uses a term that has been systematically produced by a structure of power or centralised authority. Because the structure of power uses colloquial communication, the phrases are familiar to the listener and automatically register as a part of the common consensus that has held together meaning, such as the roaring lion as a metaphor for Britain.

However, the consensus of meaning has also been nudged in the direction of a certain interpretation of that larger metaphor, such as the post-Brexit economic policy. While the particular word or metaphor, in this case the roaring lion, is traditionally associated with a fairly general idea, the ideological meaning has nudged it into a more concrete literal meaning. The broader, more figurative meaning has shifted to a specific and more literal use of language for a particular aim.[4] In our reading, we can see Habermas suggesting that the individual consciousness will eventually recognise this change, even if subtly, but that their understanding is caught between the two different consensuses: the polyphony of the figurative, broad colloquial meaning, and the more literal, specific meaning of ideology. Here again, as we saw with Wiredu, an individual's understanding is caught between two different meanings. This is thus ultimately what happens when a misunderstanding occurs.

4. A New Definition of Misunderstanding?

From both of these examples, we can suggest a new definition of misunderstanding that moves beyond the de facto 'failure of understanding' model. Misunderstanding is not simply a failure of understanding but rather a type of meaning change of which failures of understanding are subvarieties. In its broadest sense, misunderstanding is when human understanding is caught between two different meanings. It

---

[4] This principle is similar to the concept of 'prefiguration' that Hans Blumenberg develops in his posthumously published text *Präfiguration: Arbeit am politischen Mythos* (2014).

Misunderstanding and Meaning Change

is when understanding rests in the space between meanings. Both failures of understanding and intentional misunderstandings (ideological *etc.*) can happen within this phenomenon but are never reducible to it. Finally, one of the socio-political conclusions of this article is that we will not be able to adequately confront the problems of our age if we reduce public sphere misunderstandings simply to ideological misunderstandings, failures of understanding *etc*. This article maintains that our 'communication breakdown' is in fact partially created by such a reduction. In defining misunderstanding in this new way, there are three things that become clear. First, we have seen that while the 'failure of understanding' model is a useful model in some instances, it is ultimately an insufficient model. This article's assertion is that even in a failure of understanding, meaning change is present. That is to say, failure of understanding is simply a subvariety of the understanding's being caught in between meanings. Secondly, it poses questions about who is misunderstanding or experiencing misunderstanding. Finally, it asks us to reflect more on the location of misunderstanding. Is it a social phenomenon? A grammatical one? A cognitive one?

One of the great problems we are left with, then, is how do we affirm the 'in between meanings' state of misunderstanding, while simultaneously affirming the need for some form of shared understanding for communities. Alongside this, how do we affirm the 'in between meanings' state and also affirm that there are indeed failures of understanding and failures that are poisonous to the health of communities? These are the questions that we must turn our attention to if we hope to comprehend the communication breakdown in the public sphere. A starting point is recognising the absence of a philosophical exploration of misunderstanding beyond the de facto 'failure' model and the need for more reflection on the relationship between misunderstanding and meaning change. This article has maintained that misunderstanding is in fact a type of meaning change, a state of being 'in between' meanings. Far from being a throwback to a post-war relativism, considering misunderstanding as a type of meaning change can potentially open the door for a more constructive reflection on the different types of misunderstanding seen in the public sphere, and how acknowledging these can be a constructive tool in building a new type of dialogue in our communities.

Andrew Hines

References

Hans Blumenberg, *Präfiguration: Arbeit am politischen Mythos*, Angus Nicholls and Felix Heidenreich (eds), (Berlin: Suhrkamp Verlag, 2014).

Hans-Georg Gadamer, *Truth and Method*, Joel Weinsheimer and Donald G. Marshall (trans.), (London: Bloomsbury, 2019).

Jürgen Habermas, 'On Hermeneutics' Claim to Universality', in Kurt Mueller-Vollmer (ed.), *The Hermeneutics Reader* (Oxford: Basil Blackwell, 1986), 294–319.

Andrew Hines, 'After Brexit, What does Democracy Mean?', *The Converstation* (2016), https://theconversation.com/after-brexit-what-does-democracy-mean-69251. Accessed 20 December 2023.

Andrew Hines, 'The Roaring Lion and the Dutiful Public Servant', *The Huffington Post* (2017), https://www.huffingtonpost.co.uk/andrew-hines/boris-johnson-theresa-may_b_18184272.html. Accessed 20 December 2023.

John Locke, *An Essay Concerning Human Understanding* (Oxford: Oxford University Press, 2008).

Ray Monk, *How to Read Wittgenstein* (London: Granta Books, 2005).

Friedrich D.E. Schleiermacher, 'The General Theory and Art of Interpretation', in Kurt Mueller-Vollmer (ed.), *The Hermeneutics Reader* (Oxford: Basil Blackwell, 1986), 72–97.

Kwasi Wiredu, 'The Concept of Truth in the Akan Language', in P.H. Coetzee (ed.), *The African Philosophy Reader* (Milton Park: Taylor & Francis, 1998), 239–43.

Ludwig Wittgenstein, *Philosophical Investigations*, G.E.M. Anscombe (trans.), (Oxford: Basil Blackwell, 1989).

Ludwig Wittgenstein, *Tractatus Logico-Philosophicus*, D.F. Pears and B.F. McGuinness (trans.), (London: Routledge, 1974).

Politics, Words, and Concepts: On the Impossibility and Undesirability of 'Amelioration'

LOUISE ANTONY

Abstract

Recently, several philosophers have argued that there is a political necessity to alter certain important concepts, such as WOMAN, in order to give us better tools to understand and change oppressive conditions. I argue that conceptual change of this sort is impossible. But I also argue that it is politically unnecessary – we can effect progressive change using the same old concepts we've always had.

1. Introduction

I came of political age in the early 1970s in the US, a period of intense activism around ending the Vietnam war, establishing the civil rights of Black people, and pressing for equal rights and opportunities for women, for gays and lesbians, and for persons with disabilities. At the time, we activists thought that a large part of our job – though certainly not *all* of it – was to correct many mistaken *beliefs* that were widely held by members of the American public: that the war in Vietnam was being fought to preserve democracy against Communist aggression; that Black people were inferior to white people and needed to be kept separate from them; that women were, by their natures, fit only for domestic and subservient roles in society; that heterosexuality was the only morally acceptable form of sexuality; and that disabled persons simply couldn't do certain things and needed to accept that. This is not to ignore the fact that powerful people had vested *interests* in maintaining US imperialism, racism, sexism, homophobia, and ableism, but insofar as we were interested in producing accurate and useful *theories* of the problems that beset our society, it was the *propositions* that were advanced in defense of these and other forms of injustice that needed to be articulated and refuted.

Those battles were, of course, never decisively won by progressives – all these social malignancies are, unfortunately, still with us. New generations of activists have joined us old-timers in battling these too-familiar cancers as well as more recently identified ills, such as

Louise Antony

transphobia. Among these new activists is a group of philosophers who are arguing that what is needed at this point is a revision not of *propositions believed* but of the *concepts* that compose these propositions. Here is philosopher Sally Haslanger:

> On my view, to say that I am a white woman is to situate me in complicated and interconnected systems of privilege and subordination that are triggered by interpretations of my physical capacities and appearance. *Justice requires that we undermine these systems, and in order to do so, we need conceptual categories that enable us to describe them and their effects* [...].
>
> Much recent debate over race, in particular, seems to have become bogged down in the question whether this or that account of race can claim to be an analysis of *our* concept of race [...]. I've maintained that my goal is *not* to capture the ordinary meanings of 'race' or 'man' or 'woman', nor is it to capture our ordinary race and gender concepts. I've cast my inquiry as an analytical—or what I here call an *ameliorative*—*project that seeks to identify what legitimate purposes we might have (if any) in categorizing people on the basis of race or gender, and to develop concepts that would help us achieve these ends.* (Haslanger, 2005, p. 11)

Haslanger is saying several things here. Let's look at the first paragraph:

1. That gender is a hierarchical social system, and that being a woman involves standing in the lower rung of this system.
2. That gender justice requires dismantling this system.
3. That our current concept of WOMAN does not enable us to describe this system or its unjust effects.

Now I completely agree with the first two points. Haslanger and I are both materialist feminists – 'materialist' in the sense that we believe that oppression is not *just* a matter of what people believe, but also a matter of the objective physical and social factors that structure our options and choices. However, I disagree with Haslanger on the third point. I don't see why our concept WOMAN is any less adequate for activist purposes now than it was back in the twentieth century, when many of us were working with the same social analysis and pursuing the same political goals that Haslanger and I are both committed to today.

In fact, I actually believe that it makes no sense to call for the revision of our *concept* of WOMAN. That's one of the points I'll be arguing for below.

Politics, Words, and Concepts

But to get everything out onto the table, let's look at the second paragraph. Here Haslanger is calling for a different kind of adjustment to our conceptual repertoire. She is claiming that:

1. Too much time is being spent (by activist philosophers) in trying to figure out what our *ordinary* concept of RACE, or WOMAN, is.
2. We should instead question whether it serves any good purpose to *have* such concepts.
3. If the answer to question 2 is 'yes' – that is, that there is an important purpose to our having such concepts – then we ought to try to either revise or produce concepts that better serve those purposes. This is the *ameliorative* project.

Here Haslanger is, first of all, criticizing a type of philosophical project, called 'conceptual analysis' that aims to elucidate the concepts that we (and I use the term 'we' advisedly[1]) use in ordinary life. The procedure was to propose a definition of a concept – e.g., KNOWLEDGE – and then test it against speakers' intuitions, making revisions, if necessary, until the revised definition pretty much accorded with speakers' judgements about what was and was not knowledge. Haslanger is suggesting that we give up on projects like that, and instead ask what *purpose* a concept is meant to serve, with the idea that we might either give up concepts that serve no good purpose (like, perhaps, RACE) or else revise existing concepts to enable them to serve their purposes better.

Although I agree with Haslanger's criticism of conceptual analysis as it has been pursued in philosophy, I must again disagree with Haslanger on a couple of counts, regarding two presumptions that lie behind her ameliorative project. First, I think, once we *have* a concept, we are stuck with it. That is, once we have the conceptual resources to represent a category, we have them, and cannot get rid of them without something like brain surgery. Second, I think that the only 'purpose' a concept has is simply to enable us to refer to, or pick out, objects and properties in the world. And referring to or

---

[1] Philosophers have been rightly criticized for presuming that their own individual intuitions – about language use as well as about substantive issues such as freedom and justice – are shared by *everyone*, or, if not everyone, by members of some kind of intellectual or social elite whose opinions about such things are authoritative, regardless of the linguistic practices or opinions of *hoi polloi*. It's a toss-up which presumption is more offensive. Haslanger, I know, means to be talking about *general* usage when she speaks of what 'we' mean by a concept.

Louise Antony

picking out an object, set of objects, or property is neutral with respect to whatever it is we want to *assert* about the objects or *attribute* the property to. I think that Haslanger, and other proponents of 'amelioration' or 'conceptual engineering' are failing to distinguish the essentially *referential* function of concepts with the *assertoric* function of propositions.

I'll try to make these abstract points more concrete by working through the cases of the concepts RACE and WOMAN, but first, some general philosophical background.

2. Background

Let's start with the distinction between concepts and words.[2] Words, or terms, are the primitive elements of *language*. Put together in accordance with the syntactic rules of a language, words strung together form sentences, which can be used to assert things, to ask questions, to issue commands, and do all the other things we use language to do.[3] Although the general *structure* of naturally occurring human languages is governed by innate rules, the *semantics* of language – the determination of what particular words refer to – is up to us. That the sound 'dog' refers, in English, to the particular animals it does is a matter of *convention*. It's the fact that speakers of English all use the same word to refer to the same animals that enables us to communicate with each other. We know that this regularity – using 'dog' to refer to <dogs> is a *convention*, as opposed to a natural law, because different societies have *different* conventions to do the same job – the French use the word 'chien' and the Germans use the word 'Hund' – just as the English regularize automobile traffic by requiring drivers to keep to the left, while Americans do it by requiring drivers to keep to the right.

Conventions are thus, in an important sense, our creatures – we made them, we can change them. No one individual can do this

---

[2] A note on orthography: when I am talking about a word, I will enclose the word in quotation marks – e.g., the word 'word' has four letters in it. When I'm talking about a concept, I will designate the concept with all capital letters – e.g., the concept WOMAN is typically expressed by the word 'woman'. I will use italics only for emphasis. When I want to refer to the things to which a predicate refers, I'll use angle brackets, e.g., the word 'dog' picks out <dogs>.

[3] Actually, we don't need syntactically correct strings of words in order to communicate. But there is system to the ungrammaticality that we can tolerate.

Politics, Words, and Concepts

unilaterally – conventions *essentially* involve social cooperation – but enough individuals can, with enough time, manage to do it. We have seen plenty of cases where a word changes its reference: 'awful' used to pick out a quality that (Americans, at least) now express with the word 'awesome'; the word 'hopefully' used to be an adverb of *manner*, so that one could say 'She walked hopefully toward the train'. Nowadays, the word functions as a sentence operator, meaning, roughly, 'It is to be hoped that ...', rendering the previous sentence virtually uninterpretable for many speakers (e.g., students in my undergraduate classes). In science, too, there can be what's called 'semantic drift' – the word 'atom' originally (in the Greek, or so I'm told) referred to the ultimate constituents of reality, whatever they were. As modern science developed, however, it became clear that the things regarded as atoms were in fact composed of even smaller things. Did the discovery of atomic structure mean that 'atom' changed its reference? Or did it mean that we discovered that (cleaving to the original reference) the things we had called 'atoms' were *not* atoms? This is an unanswerable question – the relation between words and their references is not definite enough for there to be a clear yes or no.

One arena where there can be a clear yes or no, however, is the law. In order to prevent vagueness in enforcement, certain terms are explicitly defined: 'citizen', 'contract', 'homicide', etc. These legal contexts are also ones in which we can intentionally and abruptly change the reference of a word. In the US, this can be done through a constitutional amendment, such as the ones that made formerly enslaved Black men citizens, and made women of all races eligible voters. In Canada, it took legislation to redefine 'marriage' so as to make marriage legal between members of the same gender. Such changes can also be accomplished legislatively in the US, as happened with the gradual elimination, in state law, of the abhorrent 'marital exclusion' in rape law. It used to be, in every state in the US, that 'rape' was defined or understood in such a way as to make it legally impossible for a husband to rape his wife – the law took it that a wife, in marrying, gave her husband blanket consent to sexual intercourse, making rape a legal impossibility (see Ryan, 1995).

But all this is about *words*. What about concepts?

Just as words are the primitive components of sentences, concepts are primitive components of *thoughts*. Concepts are prior to words. We know this for several reasons: (1) concepts are required in order for language to be acquired;[4] (2) fascinating research on infants

---
[4] See Pinker (1994, Chs. 2 and 5).

makes clear that from the earliest testable ages, human babies possess and employ a rich stock of concepts representing the general properties of physical objects and animals, as well as social and even moral properties of persons, all antecedent to the sort and quantity of experience that would have been necessary for them to pick them up from observation,[5] and (3) there's strong empirical evidence that non-linguistic creatures – quite a large number of them – are capable of thought.[6] According to the developmental psychologists and ethologists whose work I follow (or try to), many non-human animals are capable of quite sophisticated reasoning. All of our closest primate cousins – chimpanzees, gorillas, bonobos, orangutans and many species of monkey – engage in *mind-reading*, that is, they seem to possess, natively, an understanding that others of their species have mental states, and an appreciation of the structure of those mental states. Many other species – horses, dogs, cats, elephants – also appear to have such capacities. (Interestingly, dogs seem to be better interpreters of human minds than are our closest relatives, the chimpanzees.[7]) Since these creatures do not have overt languages as human beings do, the comprehension and reasoning displayed by these non-human creatures requires an *internal*, language-like system of representation.

The philosopher Jerry Fodor made this theoretical postulate explicit and argued that humans and many other creatures possess a *language of thought* – 'Mentalese', if you will. On this view, concepts are essentially the words in a native system of mental representation.[8] I'll speak of our *conceptual repertoire* as the postulated set of Mentalese words that form the basis of the thoughts we can think.

Evidence that we have such an internal representational system, one that is independent of whatever public language we acquire, comes from many sources: everyday experience as well as carefully designed and controlled psychological experiments. Here are some samples.[9] First, from everyday life:

---

[5] For a comprehensive review of research supporting this claim, see Elizabeth Spelke, *What Babies Know: Core Knowledge and Composition*, Vol. 1 (2023), esp. 'Prologue' and Ch. 5, 'Core Knowledge'.

[6] For a review of empirical and philosophical literature on animal cognition, see Andrews and Monsó (2021).

[7] Yale Psychologist Laurie Santos heads labs studying both non-human primate and canine cognition, see https://caplab.yale.edu/research.

[8] The *locus classicus* is Fodor, *The Language of Thought* (1975), but for an accessible explanation of the hypothesis and the philosophical controversy surrounding it, see Michael Rescorla (2023).

[9] And see the sections of *The Language Instinct* referred to above.

Politics, Words, and Concepts

1) 'tip-of-the-tongue' phenomena

You probably have had the experience of knowing that there is a word that expresses the idea you have, but being unable to produce it. This suggests that you are tokening the *concept*, and just cannot locate in memory the *word* that expresses it. I might be able to induce the experience in you right now. See if you can come up with the name for the object that fits the following description:

> an archway in a garden or park consisting of a framework covered with trained climbing or trailing plants.

Do you feel that you know what this is, and just cannot think of the thing's name? (The answer is 'pergola'.)

2) detection of ambiguity

Consider the following sentence: 'Visiting relatives can be tedious.' Did you, right away, appreciate that there were two different things that this sentence can mean? Now, once you recognize that the sentence is ambiguous, you can probably formulate each of the two readings in natural language ('It can be tedious to visit relatives' vs. 'Relatives who are visiting can be tedious'). But I'll bet that you recognized that there *were* two different readings before you actually formulated them in your head.

3) planning

When you set out to do something, you often make a plan, but you don't often explicitly formulate the plan in language, even to yourself. Think of cooking a familiar dish. You often go about collecting the ingredients, preparing them, cooking them in a certain sequence, without formulating the sequence explicitly. The plan is in place, though, as you can tell from what happens if there is a glitch. 'Oh no,' you think, 'I forgot to get eggs!' *This* is a thought you might articulate explicitly, but what about the *intention* to get eggs from the fridge?

The point that plans and intentions needn't be explicitly formulated in a natural language is also borne out by the fact that non-human animals can and do produce novel plans. Crows (actually, rooks) confronted with a novel situation – a tube of water with a tasty grub floating on the surface, and a pile of small stones beside it – were able to figure out to drop stones into the tube to raise the

Louise Antony

water level high enough for the crow to pluck the grub out of the water (see Jelbert *et al.*, 2014). (There's also my dear departed dog, Freya, who spent one entire morning working out how to get hold of a donut someone had tossed onto the sidewalk in front of our house: 'Gotta get outside. How do I get outside? Get Louise. Why do I want to get outside again? Oh yeah, the *donut!*')

The fact that intentions must be formulated *in thought*, using *concepts*, is a point that I'll make much of in my criticism of the project of amelioration, to which I now turn.

3. Against Amelioration

Amelioration, if it is possible, must grapple with the following: what is the connection between Mentalese words – concepts – and words in human public (or what is confusingly called *natural*) languages? This is a vast and unsettled question, not just for advocates of amelioration, but for everyone. One view that has been popular in philosophy, and in some branches of linguistics, is that concepts are actually determined by words in natural language – that language determines the expressive potential of thought – this is a view championed by Benjamin Whorf (1956), and defended in a limited way by psychologists such as Lera Boroditsky (2003). But the thesis that (public) language determines thought founders on the evidence for structured thought in pre-linguistic humans and non-linguistic animals that I alluded to above.

What about the other way around? Does our native conceptual repertoire determine what thoughts we can think, or can language extend the boundaries of thought? Here we need to separate two questions: 1) Can we acquire *new concepts*? 2) If we can, do we acquire them *through language*? I think the answer to the first question is 'yes', but that the answer to the second question is 'no'. That is, I think that we certainly do *acquire* new concepts – that we can and do enrich our conceptual repertoire – but that we don't do it *by means of language*. When we coin new words – as we certainly do – we can only give sense to these words by recombining concepts (words in the language of thought) that we already possess. Usually new words are essentially *abbreviations* of complex expressions in the language of thought. Insofar as new *words* can be defined in terms of combinations of old words – that is, essentially, *definitions* – there is no reason to think that there's any expansion of our conceptual repertoire involved. This is important to keep in mind with respect to the project of amelioration – there are certainly new *words* that come into use as the result of expanding knowledge of the world or cultural changes. But the addition of new words does not necessarily involve the generation of new concepts.

Fodor made an important distinction between the *acquisition* of a new concept – which he thought was not only possible, but something that happened all the time – and the *learning* of a new concept, which he thought was impossible. 'Learning', as he used the term, requires there to be a *rational* connection between the external circumstances that give rise to a concept (or to a thought) and the concept that results. If we could *learn* concepts, the process would have to proceed this way: we would have to first generate a hypothesis about what the reference of the concept was, and then test to see if that hypothesis was correct. So if we were *learning* the concept WOMAN, we would have to first think, say, 'I bet that to be a WOMAN is to be an adult human female' and then try to figure out whether our hypothesis was correct – maybe by saying of various individuals we judged to be adult human females 'So-and-so is a woman' (using the word as a proxy for the concept) and seeing if the others in our linguistic community accepted such sayings, or corrected us. Acceptance or rejection of such sayings would be rational evidence about whether our hypothesis as to the reference of the new word was correct.

But the thing to notice is that, if we are to ever successfully carry out this process of forming and confirming hypotheses about what the 'new' concept referred to, we *already have to possess* concepts which, combined in the right way, refer to exactly the same things as the *new* concept we are *learning*. Therefore, *if* there is some process by which we can make genuinely new additions to our conceptual repertoire, it *cannot* be by first postulating what the new concept stands for, and then getting evidence whether our postulate is correct or not. The postulate has to already contain the conceptual resources for picking out what the *new* concept picks out. I'll later explain the pertinence of this point to the debate about amelioration.

Here's another essential point about concepts, also pertinent to the amelioration debate: concepts are simply used in thought to pick out the *subjects* of thought; tokening a concept is not to *say anything about* those subjects. To think to yourself 'Women bear children' is to, first of all, *refer to* women (whoever those individuals might be), and *then* to attribute to women (those individuals the concept picks out) the property of bearing children. Now this *thought* can be true or false – it is true if the subjects of the thought, women, possess the property that is attributed to them in the thought, namely the property of bearing children. Some of you might judge that this thought is

55

not true, because of the fact that not all women do bear children. Some of you, though, might think it *is* true, so to speak, 'in general' the way it's true 'in general' that dogs have four legs or bark, or that birds fly. These claims all have exceptions, but are usually accepted as true by speakers of English. The case of the *sentence* 'women bear children' is one of those cases, by the way, where the linguistic representation of thought can be ambiguous – the same sentence in English can express any of these more specific thoughts: 'All women bear children' (false); 'Bearing children is a distinctive property of women' (true);[10] or 'Most women bear children' (true).

The point I am focusing on right now, however, is that the function of the concept WOMEN in thought is *just to pick out the class of women*. But now you probably want to know – how does this concept do this work? What about the concept WOMAN *connects it to* women? And also – who are these individuals, women, to whom this concept is connected?

I cannot answer the first question, although I and many other philosophers have tried to provide theories of how concepts might be connected to their references. (There are problems with all of the theories that I know of.[11]) But we *can* say something about the question of what the references of our concepts *are*. That is, with respect to the question 'who are these individuals that the concept WOMAN picks out?' we have an idea how to provide an answer. The general program is, basically, to *gather up* the individuals who a large number of thinkers will judge to be women, and then see what these individuals have in common. That's the program, but it can be – and is in this case – difficult to carry out.

There is, first of all, the fact that thinkers sometimes *make mistakes* – they might see someone who is dressed in a way that is atypical for women in their culture, and mistakenly judge that individual to be a man (i.e., not a woman). This is a perceptual mistake. But there's another kind of mistake an individual might make. They might have a *mistaken belief* about what properties an individual has to have in order to *be* a woman. Such a person might *believe*, for example, that in order to be a woman, an individual must be *capable* of bearing children. This person would then judge an infertile female, or a post-menopausal female, or a transwoman to be *not a woman*.

---

[10] Or perhaps not: if 'distinctive' means '*exclusively* true of' then the claim would be false, since some transmen have this characteristic as well.

[11] See Jacob (2023).

Politics, Words, and Concepts

Another inherent difficulty in trying to characterize what it is to be a woman – that is, what it is to fall under the concept WOMAN – is that women (whatever they are, exactly) will have *many* properties in common. In fact, most women have a great deal in common *biologically* – they have the same chromosomal properties (two X chromosomes), they have the same general endocrinology (hormonal properties), and the same morphology (body shape and structure).

But not all women share these properties. Many of you will be aware of the existence of intersex individuals – individuals who do not have the set of biological properties typical for either females or males – yet many intersex individuals are women. And apart from women who are biologically intersex, there is the fact that many girls and women lose one or more of these biological properties either permanently or temporarily through illness or accident. These considerations prompt many theorists – including myself – to argue that the commonalities that actually unite individuals into the category <women> are a matter of the social role women play in human societies.[12] On this view, women are united as a class by a system that assigns distinctive social roles, governed by distinctive norms, about dress, behavior, and occupations to individuals, usually at birth, on the basis of what is, or is perceived to be their biological properties. Feminists who believe this will often say that WOMAN is a *social* concept, not a *biological* concept, meaning that our concept WOMAN picks out or is connected to individuals who are assigned or who come to play a certain social role, one that is generally and for the most part attached to the biological property of being female.

Now this disagreement about whether our concept WOMAN picks out biological females or individuals who occupy a certain social role, is, in my view, a question of fact about what our concept actually picks out. It may be – it is – a very difficult question to answer, but there is a fact of the matter, and it is *independent* of what we might believe or want to be the case. What our concept *does* pick out is pre-

---

[12] I am not denying how rare intersex births are – the vast majority of human beings – 97% or higher – do fall unambiguously into one of these two biological categories. Thus, unlike some philosophers working on gender, I think the biological distinction between human males and human females is objective and robust. It is also worth noting that intersex conditions occur in non-human animals as well, but that the existence of these conditions does not seem to anyone to problematize biological categorizations for cattle, dogs, or other non-human species.

determined; and what it picks out determines whether our thoughts involving the concept are true or false.

This may sound very bad to progressive ears. What I'm saying is that *if* our concept WOMAN picks out individuals who have certain biological features, then this will have the consequence that the thought 'transwomen are women' will be false. And that is – I absolutely agree – a difficult conclusion to accept. And this is where amelioration might look attractive. Suppose, you might think, our *current* concept has the reference <female human beings> – can't we just *change* it? Can't we revise – or *re-engineer* or *ameliorate* – that concept so that it has a reference that *includes* transwomen? The answer, I'm afraid, is 'no'. In order to make such a change we would have to use the *old* concept in framing our intention to change *its own* reference – it would amount to thinking 'WOMAN (old) should mean WOMAN (new)' but such a thought would be incoherent. The first occurrence of the concept WOMAN in that thought would have to retain the old reference, which would put it into conflict with the intended reference of the new concept. We cannot alter the reference of a concept we already have by wishing into existence a different concept. We can *add* to our conceptual repertoire a new complex concept: WOMAN-OR-OCCUPANT-OF-THE-SOCIAL-ROLE-GENERALLY-OCCUPIED-BY-WOMEN, but that won't change the reference of the component concept WOMAN. But this all seems politically inadequate, offensive to transwomen (even if their own concept WOMAN has, unbeknownst to them, that content) and even morally repulsive.

I think this sort of consequence is one of the things that advocates of amelioration have in mind when they call for revision of our concepts. But if amelioration is impossible, what can we do? Quite a bit. In the first place, what the impossibility of amelioration shows is simply that *if* the reference of WOMAN is determined by biological properties, then it cannot be changed to be determined by social properties. But the *if*-part of that conditional might be *false*. Indeed, the very strong intuitions that many of us have that transwomen *are* women is in itself *evidence* that the reference of our concept WOMAN is *not* determined biologically after all. If WOMAN is in fact a social concept, and not a biological concept, that means that those who think the thought TRANSWOMEN ARE NOT WOMEN are *wrong*, as *a matter of fact*, and *in virtue of the reference of their own concept WOMAN*. Those of us who realize that this thought is false must then work to persuade those who think this that they are wrong. This would be analogous to persuading someone in the eighteenth century who thought WHALES ARE

FISH that they were wrong, because whales are in fact mammals. The mistake such a person would be making is the same as the mistake made by someone who thinks TRANSWOMEN ARE NOT WOMEN – they'd be *incorrect* about the properties that actually make an individual an individual of the type in question. If this turns out to be the problem, it would be a very welcome result, politically speaking.

There's another issue about the properties that determine whether an individual falls within the reference of a concept or not. Haslanger, in the quote above, says that to say that she is a woman is 'to situate her in complicated and interconnected systems of privilege and subordination', and then goes on to recommend that we 'ameliorate' our concept of women to reflect this fact. Now I agree with Haslanger that the gender role, being a woman, is part of a hierarchical system of privilege, and that it has been a regularity in human societies that the women in those societies – that is the individuals who are assigned the woman-role – are subordinated, often severely so, relative to the men. It may even be that the description Haslanger gives expresses a property that in fact coincides perfectly with the set of individuals that our (current) concept WOMAN picks out. If it is, then there is *no need* to revise or 'ameliorate' our concept. If it is not, then it is *impossible* to revise our concept, if my arguments above are correct.

The crucial point to realize here is that whatever the properties are that determine what the concept WOMAN refers to, *possessing the concept does* NOT *mean knowing what properties connect the concept to its reference*. So even if Haslanger is right, that being subordinated is one of the properties in virtue of which WOMAN refers to women, no one has to *know* that in order to use the concept. Compare: WATER refers to substances with the chemical structure H_2O – that chemical structure is necessary to being water. But for most of human history, and probably even today, most people who have the concept WATER don't know this.

But suppose we did introduce a new, abbreviatory concept WOMAN(sub) that is defined to mean INDIVIDUALS-WHO-ARE-IN-A-SUBORDINATED POSITION RELATIVE TO MEN. Then the thought WOMEN(sub) ARE SUBORDINATED would not be an interesting, substantive thought. It would be akin to thinking BACHELORS ARE UNMARRIED. It would express a *conceptual*, rather than an *empirical, discoverable* fact. And it would be a fact of no *political* significance. That is an unwanted consequence. So amelioration is not something that is politically desirable, even if it is possible.

Louise Antony

There are two more things I want to say to mitigate what may appear to be morally or politically discouraging consequences of the view of concepts I've been defending.

First, concepts, as I pointed out earlier, are not *propositions* – they are elements of propositions. That means that having a concept with the reference <biological females> does not condemn a person to being transphobic. Nor does having an inclusive concept ensure that one is trans-friendly. One can construct the proposition TRANSWOMEN SHOULD BE ALLOWED TO USE 'LADIES' ROOMS' with either concept, and one can deny it using either concept. The content of a proposition is not determined by the subject concept – it's determined by that concept, *plus* the other concepts, *plus* the structure in which they are put together.

Second – and here I want to return to what I regard as the most fundamental matter in this debate. The political work that urgently needs to be done neither requires nor would obviously be served by conceptual change. Where does that leave us? Well, the reference of concepts is not under our control, but the reference of *words* is. And that is hardly a trivial matter. We have the power, and politically the duty, to ensure that our laws, institutions, and *ways of speaking* respect each other's identities, and realize our ideals of justice. Redefining 'marriage' so that the laws recognized loving unions between members of the same gender as equivalent to those involving members of different genders; redefining 'rape' by removing clauses in the law that permitted husbands to sexually assault their wives with impunity; explicitly adding the category 'non-binary' to permissible options for legal identity documents – all these measures have had real, salutary and even transformative consequences for many people. Explicitly stipulating in law that the categories 'woman' and 'man' are to include transwomen and transmen would do the same. Language, as I've been saying, is our creature, and language has power.

Of course such changes will not, in themselves, change anyone's *opinions* about sex, gender, and justice. To the extent that a just social order depends upon what people believe, we must still do the taxing and uncertain work of trying to *change* what people believe. But to the extent that people are motivated to obey the law, legal reforms can change what people *do*. And that is absolutely not nothing.

References

Kristin Andrews and Susana Monsó, 'Animal Cognition', in Edward N. Zalta (ed.), *The Stanford Encyclopedia of Philosophy* (Spring

2021), accessed October 2023 at https://plato.stanford.edu/archives/spr2021/entries/cognition-animal.

Lera Boroditsky, 'Linguistic Relativity', in L. Nadel (ed.), *Encyclopedia of Cognitive Science* (London: Macmillan Publishers, 2003), 917–22.

Jerry Fodor, *The Language of Thought* (New York: Thomas Y. Crowell, 1975).

Sally Haslanger, 'What are We Talking About? The Semantics and Politics of Social Kinds', *Hypatia*, 20:4 (2005), 10–26.

Pierre Jacob, 'Intentionality', in Edward N. Zalta and Uri Nodelman (eds), *The Stanford Encyclopedia of Philosophy* (Spring 2023), accessed January 2024 at https://plato.stanford.edu/archives/spr2023/entries/intentionality.

Sarah A. Jelbert, Alex H. Taylor, Lucy G. Cheke, Nicola S. Clayton, and Russell D. Gray, 'Using the Aesop's Fable Paradigm to Investigate Causal Understanding of Water Displacement by New Caledonian Crows', *PLOS ONE* (2014), np.

Steven Pinker, *The Language Instinct* (New York, NY: William Morrow Publishers, 1994).

Michael Rescorla, 'The Language of Thought Hypothesis', in Edward N. Zalta & Uri Nodelman (eds), *The Stanford Encyclopedia of Philosophy* (Winter 2023), accessed October 2023 at https://plato.stanford.edu/archives/win2023/entries/language-thought.

Rebecca M. Ryan, 'The Sex Right: A Legal History of the Marital Rape Exemption', *Law & Social Inquiry*, 20:4 (1995), 941–1001.

Elizabeth Spelke, *What Babies Know: Core Knowledge and Composition, Volume 1* (New York, NY: Oxford University Press, 2023).

Benjamin Lee Whorf, *Language, Thought, and Reality. Selected Writings of Benjamin Lee Whorf* (Cambridge, MA: MIT Press, 1956).

Inflammatory Language

ERNIE LEPORE

Abstract

This is a paper is about a particular subclass of pejoratives, namely, slurs. These are epithets that denigrate a group on the basis of membership alone, e.g., on the basis of race, ethnicity, origin, religion, gender, or ideology. They carrry a characteristic sting, prone to cause outrage and even injury. As to the source of their characteristic sting, the predominant position invokes some aspect of meaning. Some of the few who reject this assumption locate the source of the sting in the taboo status of pejoratives. Others think slurs can sting because of negative associations they carry across time. We challenge both approaches and defend an alternative, for which negative associations are triggered *not* by every token of a pejorative, but rather by certain of its *articulations*.

This paper is sort of a precis of my forthcoming book with Una Stojnic, *On Inflammatory Language: The Linguistics and Philosophy of Pejoratives* (OUP, 2024).[1] Various versions of this paper have been presented in various places, each in the service of either introducing novel data about the distribution of slur terms or trying to account for what makes their usage offensive. The key question guiding these discussions has always been: why are slur terms offensive? The obvious answer is that it is because of a combination of what they mean (or convey). And how this information is encoded (or calculated).

The simplest such proposal is that slur terms are offensive because of what they predicate of their target group (Hom, 2008, 2012; Hom and May, 2013, 2018; Neufeld, 2019). In order for an assertion of (1) to be true, whatever its predicate means should be true of Hermione; in this case, having the property of being a muggle-born wizard.

1. Hermione is a muggle-born wizard.

One problem with this kind of meaning proposal is that it doesn't permit a slur term's meaning to project. The negation of a predicative sentence is true just in case the predicate does not apply to its subject.

---

[1] The book by Stojnic and myself is more formal and thorough than this paper could be. This paper is intended to introduce various proposals of what makes slur terms so offensive. Any mistakes or other infelicities are due to me; everything else is based on our joint effort.

Ernie Lepore

So, on the current account, whatever is expressed by the predicate in (1)'s negation (2) does not apply to Hermione.

2. Hermione is not a muggle-born wizard.

But, in this regard, the offense that slurs carry does not behave like a predicative content. Instead, whichever offense (3) carries is carried by (4) as well:

3. Hermione is a mudblood.[2]
4. Hermione is not a mudblood.

In lingo, it is said that the offense potential of a slur term takes wide scope over negation.

At this critical juncture, some theorists conclude that, regardless of whatever the specific meaning of a slur term is, it behaves more like a presupposition than a predicate (Schlenker, 2007; Cepollaro et al., 2019; Cepollaro and Stojanovic, 2016). So, for example, both (5) and (6) presuppose (7); neither can be true if (7) is not true.

5. John quit smoking.
6. John has not quit smoking.
7. John used to smoke.

Although a presupposition account better explains projectability than predicative accounts do, it does not go far enough. This is because there are environments that take a wider scope than presuppositional content. For example, placing (5) in the consequent of conditional (8) can block presuppositional content (7) from taking wider scope than the conditional. Ditto for (9); placing (5) inside an indirect speech report can block presuppositional content (7) from taking a wider scope. Put somewhat differently, the conditional in (8) takes a wider scope than presupposition (7); and the indirect report 'said that' takes wider scope than (7) in (9). This explains why (8) and (9) can be true even if (7) is false,

8. If John used to smoke, then he quit smoking.
9. Mary said that John quit smoking, but he never smoked.

In short, if slur terms have meaning, it is not encoded presuppositionally; (10) and (11) behave like (8) and (9): placing a meaning of

---

[2] I assume sufficient familiarity with slur terms and their effects that these effects can be evoked even without my mentioning them. Instead, I will present relevant data using the fictional slur term 'mudblood', targeting wizards born to non-wizard parents – in the fictional world of Harry Potter, as a placeholder for actual slur terms.

a slur term in the antecedent of a conditional or inside an indirect speech or attitudinal report does not block its offense potential.

10. If muggleborns are inferior on account of being muggleborns, then Hermione is a mudblood.
11. Draco said that Hermione is a mudblood, but I don't think muggleborn wizards are despicable on account of being muggleborn.[3]

In short, the slur term in (10) and (11) is offensive. Any appeal to meaning to account for this offense potential of a slur term requires an encoding broader in scope than what is needed to account for presupposition distribution. One popular emendation is to appeal to Conventional Implicature items, since they are alleged always to take widest scope (Williamson, 2009; Potts, 2005; McCready, 2010).

The main idea is that, though sentences (12) and (13) agree in truth conditions, the meaning of (13) requires a contrast between height and speed, and so, (14) is incoherent as a matter of meaning since its second clause denies what 'but' means. It's like saying that John is a bachelor who is married.

12. John is tall and fast.
13. John is tall but fast.
14. #John is tall but fast, and there's no specific contrast between height and speed.[4]

In defense of the wide scope claim on behalf of Conventional Implicature items perhaps a better datum is provided by a denial of the first conjunct in (15):

15. #Joe, who is a spy, is in hiding; and he's not a spy.

No matter where we embed this appositive, e.g., inside a negation, conditional, indirect speech report, modal or any well-formed combination of these, the speaker remains committed to the appositive, namely, that Joe is a spy. So, we ask whether slur terms are, or

---

[3] Notice that in both (10) and (11) I posit distinct meanings for 'mudblood': in (10), I posit the proposition that muggleborns are inferior on account of being muggleborns as its meaning, and in (11), I posit the proposition that muggleborn wizards are despicable on account of being muggleborn as its meaning. Not only do I not defend either of these proposals, I believe both are false. This raises the sticky question as to whether it is ever possible to articulate its meaning. We will return to specificity below.

[4] '#' indicates something is off with the sentence grammatically or semantically.

behave like, Conventional Implicature items with respect to taking the widest possible scope.

One problem with this suggestion is that sentences with slur terms do not feel oddly off when their alleged definition is violated. So, although (14)–(16) are all off (i.e., the meanings of their components are incompatible), (17)–(19) remain perfectly acceptable.

16. #[angrily] That goddamned dog is barking again! [cheerily] I'm pleased with the dog.
17. Hermione is a mudblood, but muggleborns are not inferior on account of being muggleborn; they have nothing but my respect!
18. I love mudbloods!
19. (A recovering bigot:) Our entire way of thinking about mudbloods is wrong!

(17)–(19) are all acceptable and each is offensive. It seems obvious that we need to find an account that underwrites a very robust projection of offense; but how? Once, again, we confront the Problem of Specifying Content: it is hard to see what meaning could be the linguistically encoded content of the slur term. Clearly, given the acceptability of sentences (17)–(19), it's hard to imagine what content candidates for 'mudblood' have not been ruled out; indeed, it's hard to rule in any reprehensible state of mind as supplying the specific meaning of a slur term.

The projectability constraint we need is actually much harder to respect than any we have been exploring. Consider sentences (20)–(23).

20. '"John is French" means John is French' does not predicate anything of John.
21. '"John is tall but handsome" means John is tall but handsome' draws no contrast between height and handsomeness.
22. '"Joe stopped smoking" means Joe stopped smoking' doesn't presuppose Joe smoked.
23. '"ouch" means ouch' does not express a state of mind (e.g., pain).

Each of these sentences mentions a true meaning attribution; and although in each attribution the expression to which meaning is being attributed is mentioned, it is also used on the right-hand side in this sense: consider a sentence where the term in question is replaced by a synonym. If the term were only being mentioned the truth value might change, but it doesn't. For example, consider '"bachelor" has eight letters' vs '"unmarried male" has eight letters' – assuming 'bachelor' and 'unmarried male' are synonyms. But now compare (20)–(23) with (24)–(26)

24. 'mudblood' means mudblood.
25. 'mudblood' has 8 letters.
26. 'mudblood' is a slur term.

Each of these is potentially offensive, and so, were meaning theorists correct, it would follow that the meaning of a slur term projects out of even quotation – a sort of Hyper-projectivity. Indeed, the Opinion letters section in the *New York Times* explicitly discussed the editorial decision to publish a Sunday Review essay 'How the N Word Became Unsayable' by J. McWhorter that spells out the N-word; the essay was prefaced with an editorial disclaimer stating, 'This article contains obscenities and racial slurs, fully spelled out. Ezekiel Kweku, the Opinion politics editor, and Kathleen Kingsbury, the Opinion editor, wrote about how and why we came to the decision to publish these words in Friday's edition of the Opinion Today.'[5]

It is sort of a reductio of the meaning thesis that using slur terms in quotations (or meaning attributions) remain offensive; quotations are universally taken to render the meaning of the quoted item semantically inert. And yet it is undeniable that (24)–(26) can be offensive. But if not meaning, then what's left to account for the offense that audiences can suffer through tokens of slur terms?

The Problem of Specificity together with the Hyper-projectivity Constraint drive some contributors to wonder whether confrontations with slur terms aren't offensive simply because slur terms are taboo words; their tokenings are always prohibited – wherever they might occur – even in quotational and meaning attribution contexts. It is the violation of their prohibition that offends witnesses to their tokenings.

Let's call this non-meaning account of the offensiveness of slur terms Prohibitionism. One obvious problem with Prohibitionism is simply that many taboos fail to generate the same pattern of offense as tokenings of slur terms. No one would deem that Tetragrammaton is a slur term for God. The name is prohibited because of the sacredness of what it names. Other religious taboos illustrate a similar point. Also, historically there was a taboo against tokening of the name of the devil for fear of summoning him. But the devil's name didn't thereby become a slur term; its tokening

[5] https://www.nytimes.com/2021/05/09/opinion/letters/n-word.html.

was associated with fear of misfortune, not with offense of the sort that a slur term can produce. Other examples illustrate the same point. In the 19th century, Ukrainian, Polish, Lithuanian, and Belarusian were banned in the Russian Empire. These prohibitions didn't engender feelings of offense in anyone when violated. Nor did expressions of these languages become slur terms among Russians or anyone else.

Another serious problem with Prohibitionism is that it looks to get the worry backwards. Intuitively, a slur term is taboo because it is offensive, not the other way around. After all, violations of many taboos don't cause offense (Anderson and Lepore, 2013a,b). Since Prohibitionism states it's the violation of a prohibition that generates the offensive potential, it would seem to lack resources to explain the differences between slur terms and other taboo terms, violations of which have rather distinctive effects.

But there is an even more serious problem with Prohibitionism, namely, what I call the Problem of Inheritance. The pejorative potential of a slur term is 'infectious', carrying over to expressions incidentally matching slur terms in articulation. For example, there is the controversy over the incident of tokening an English adverb that orthographically and phonetically resembles, but is etymologically and semantically entirely unrelated to, the N-word; its inherited offensiveness, which has persisted despite the recognized etymological and semantic independence, has been well documented (Kennedy, 2002, pp. 94–95).

Illustration

As O'Hehir writes: 'We pretty much have dumped that word, because it is so easily misunderstood and other words will do, and also because it carries a permanent taint: The only person who would conceivably use it now would be a snickering, anti-p.c. asshole trying to make an obnoxious point. Do we miss it? I submit that we don't' (O'Hehir, 2020).

Or take a more recent case involving a tokening of a Mandarin demonstrative term ('那个'), which acoustically resembles the N-word. The word was tokened in a language class setting, in describing the correlate of the English demonstrative 'that' in Mandarin. The speaker announced which word of which language is about to be tokened.[6]

---

[6] See also the discussion on https://languagelog.ldc.upenn.edu/nll/?p=23691 for other incidents involving the same Mandarin expression.

Inflammatory Language

Where does this leave us? I am not claiming that the speaker who tokens a slur term is blameworthy (or not), that any offense taken is warranted (or not). Nor am I claiming that the tokening was apt or inapt, necessary or gratuitous in achieving a particular point (whether it be rhetorical, pedagogical, artistic, *etc.*). These questions are downstream from the presence or absence of any offense effect. That is, first comes the offensive speech and then its moral assessment. No one should deny that typical tokenings of slur terms can give rise to negative associations rooted in socio-historical, cultural, and psychological factors; these are open-ended, and so, not content-like. However, what I am claiming is that the trigger of these negative associations is *not* the word itself, but rather standard articulations of the word.

Note that on this proposal it becomes quite easy to account for the Hyper-projectivity Constraint. You cannot token a slur term without articulating it. But if I am right that it is standard articulations of slur terms which cause the offensive sting, then regardless of where that articulation occurs so does the potential to offend, even inside quotes or meaning attributions or even homonyms. And as far as meaning goes, as was illustrated above, we are able to deny any particular negative content without fear of linguistic incoherence because we are not appealing to meaning in order to account for an offensive sting. Indeed, for our purposes, slur terms may turn out be synonymous with their neutral counterparts.

The Inheritance Constraint now being endorsed is akin to what we find with offensive gestures, symbols, and imagery. A gesture or a symbol that accidentally shares a shape with an offensive one is prone to trigger the same offensive effect. So, for instance, consider the Nazi *Hakenkreuz* and corresponding ancient Swastika symbols that carry positive connotations in various Eurasian religions, including Hinduism, Jainism, and Buddhism. The Hakenkreuz's violent and offensive symbolism does not only give rise to taboo and prohibitions – often legally codified – against its displays, but its offensive potential easily transfers to closely resembling symbols. This is exactly the same phenomenon we find with the inheritance of the offensive potential of slurs. This is why the unfortunately sounding adverb remains tainted even once all confusion has been cleared.

I need to emphasize that the effect triggered by an articulation of a slur term can be triggered even if no slur (or word) is tokened; and conversely, a slur term can lose its potent sting when its articulation is sufficiently far off from a standard articulation; or even when the articulation itself becomes less and less used. That is, the status of a slur term can change over time, without a change in meaning. And, of course, the presence and severity of the offensive potential can vary itself with articulations. Further, I must caution not to confuse tokenings of articulations with tokenings of words (Stojnic, 2022).

I want to end this discussion with some more data in support of the articulation account. I begin with the vivid example of the phenomenon of graphic slurs in logographic languages like Mandarin, where it is possible that only certain written, but not spoken, articulations of a particular term can be offensive. For example, the Mandarin exonym 'Yáo', the pronunciation of which triggers no offensive effect, when written, can receive either an offensive or a non-offensive rendition, depending on the choice of alternative (phonetically indistinguishable) phono-semantic compounds (either featuring the person-radical or the beast-radical). That can be interpreted as a slur term when written with one, but not another, phonetically indistinguishable choice of a character, depending on the semantic component of the phono-semantic compound (see Matisoff, 1986).

It is thus only one of several possible standard articulations, a particular spelling, that triggers the offensive potential. If the offensive potential were tied to either the word or its meaning, this would be rather puzzling – a word retains its identity regardless of the choice of whatever acceptable spelling it is rendered in; and it retains whatever meaning it has regardless of how it is articulated. Our account, by contrast, readily explains this: it is a particular articulation, not the word itself, that harbors the offensive potential.

Then there is the so-called censoring asterisk. Consider (27)–(28):

27. 'You mudbl**d,' Draco yelled.
28. #'You the M-word,' Draco yelled.

You might think they are equivalent, but they are not. (28) consists of the subject 'you' concatenated with a canonical description for a slur term. But (27) seems to be saying Draco called you something. So, what did he call you? If you are of the opinion that replacing the two 'o'-s with two asterisks derives a new word, then (27) is false. Its only reasonable reading that allows it to be true is to permit 'mudbl**d' to be a non-standard articulation of a slur term that has as its standard articulation 'mudblood'. These kinds of data show how non-standard articulations of bad words need not be offensive.

Conclusion

There is obviously much more to discuss, including the prospects of success of other sorts of meaning theories for slur terms (expressivism

(Potts, 2007; Jeshion, 2013), perspectivalism (Camp, 2013, 2018), and even pragmatic accounts of content (Nunberg, 2018; Jorgensen Bolinger, 2020)). Another key topic without enough space to discuss is *reclamation* of slur terms. The forthcoming book mentioned in the first footnote by me and Una Stojnic takes on these central topics and much more.

The major focus of this discussion has been that it is not slur terms, but their standard articulations that carry offensive potential. This means that, however this potential is determined, it has little to do with semantics or pragmatics, or indeed even with language at all.

References

Luvell Anderson and Ernie Lepore, 'Slurring Words', *Noûs*, 47:3 (2013a), 25–48.
Luvell Anderson and Ernie Lepore, 'What Did You Call Me: Slurs as Prohibited Words', *Analytic Philosophy*, 54 (2013b), 350–63.
Elisabeth Camp, 'Slurring Perspectives', *Analytic Philosophy*, 54:3 (2013), 330–49.
Elisabeth Camp, 'A Dual Act Analysis of Slurs', in David Sosa (ed.), *Bad Words: Philosophical Perspectives on Slurs* (Oxford: Oxford University Press, 2018), 29–59.
Bianca Cepollaro and Isidora Stojanovic, 'Hybrid Evaluatives', *Grazer Philosophische Studien*, 93 (2016), 458–88.
Bianca Cepollaro, Simone Sulpizio, and Claudia Bianchi, 'How Bad Is It to Report a Slur? An Empirical Investigation', *Journal of Pragmatics*, 146 (2019), 32–42.
Christopher Hom, 'The Semantics of Racial Epithets', *The Journal of Philosophy*, 105:8 (2008), 416–40.
Christopher Hom, 'A Puzzle About Pejoratives', *Philosophical Studies*, 159 (2012), 383–405.
Christopher Hom and Robert May, 'Moral and Semantic Innocence', *Analytic Philosophy*, 54:3 (2013), 293–313.
Christopher Hom and Robert May, 'Reference, Inference, and the Semantics of Pejoratives', in David Sosa (ed.), *Bad Words: Philosophical Perspectives on Slurs* (Oxford: Oxford University, 2018), 108–31.
Robin Jeshion, 'Expressivism and the Offensiveness of Slurs', *Philosophical Perspectives*, 27 (2013), 231–59.
Renée Jorgensen Bolinger, 'The Pragmatics of Slurs', *Noûs*, 51:3 (2020), 439–62.

Ernie Lepore

R. Kennedy, *Nigger: The Strange Career of a Troublesome Word* (New York: Pantheon, 2002).

J. Matisoff, 'The Languages and Dialects of Tibeto-Burman: An Alphabetic/Genetic Listing, with Some Prefatory Remarks on Ethnonymic and Glossonymic Complications', in J. McCoy and T. Light (eds), *Contribution to Sino-Tibetan Studies* (Leiden: Brill, 1986), 3–57.

Elin McCready, 'Varieties of Conventional Implicature', *Semantics and Pragmatics*, 3 (2010), 1–57.

Eleonore Neufeld, 'An Essentialist Theory of the Meaning of Slurs', *Philosophers' Imprint*, 19 (2019), 1–29.

Geoffrey Nunberg, 'The Social Life of Slurs', in Daniel Fogal, Daniel Harris, and Matthew Moss (eds), *New Work on Speech Acts* (Oxford: Oxford University Press, 2018), 237–95.

Andrew O'Hehir, 'So Much for Youth Apathy: Student Radicalism Escapes the '60s At Last', *Salon*, 2020. Available at: https://www.salon.com/2015/11/17/so_much_foryouth_apathy_student_radicalism_escapes_the_60s_at_last/.

Christopher Potts, *The Logic of Conventional Implicatures* (Oxford: Oxford University Press, 2005).

Christopher Potts, 'The Expressive Dimension', *Theoretical Linguistics*, 33:2 (2007), 165–98.

Philippe Schlenker, 'Expressive Presuppositions', *Theoretical Linguistics*, 33:2 (2007), 237–45.

Una Stojnic, 'Just Words: Intentions, Tolerance, and Lexical Selection', *Philosophy and Phenomenological Research*, 105:1 (2022), 3–17.

Timothy Williamson, 'Reference, Inference, and the Semantics of Pejoratives', in Joseph Almong and Paolo Leonardi (eds), *The Philosophy of David Kaplan* (Oxford: Oxford University Press, 2009), 137–58.

Games, Norms, and Utterances

MIHAELA POPA-WYATT AND JEREMY L. WYATT

Abstract

A body of work proposes that social-norm change can be explained in terms of game theory. These game theoretic models, however, don't fully account for how and why utterances are used to change social norms. This paper describes the problem and some of the solution elements. There are three existing, relevant, game-based models. The first is a game theoretic model of social norm change (Bicchieri, 2005, 2016). This accounts for how individuals make decisions to adhere to or violate norms, based on empirical expectations of how others will behave. The second is the idea of a conversational game (Lewis, 1979) and its extensions. This posits that speech acts are accommodated in a conversation to make what is said correct play. This feature can explain how some speech acts, such as slurring utterances, change the dynamics of a conversation. The third is a theory of pragmatic inference, known as Rational Speech Act theory (Goodman and Frank, 2016). This is a computational theory of pragmatics, of how listeners interpret utterances and how speakers construct utterances that can be understood. This paper proposes, without setting out the full formal model, that elements of these three theories need to be incorporated together into a game theoretic model of how utterances change long-term social norms.

1. Introduction

All social activities are governed by social norms – informal rules which guide our behaviour. Social norms are not static but change over time. The mechanisms of social norm change have been extensively studied. As part of this, a substantial body of work models social norms using game theory. There are, for example, game theoretic models which account for social norm adherence, violation, and change. These account for a variety of evidence concerning human behaviour. One type of social activity is dialogue. We engage in dialogue to entertain, to inform, and to achieve individual or social goals. Because it is a social activity, dialogue is therefore also a norm-governed activity. There are numerous theories of dialogue, including those that are philosophical, computational, and linguistic in their roots. A number of these theories are also game theoretic. In such models, the atomic move in the dialogue game is an utterance. Separately, we know that utterances, whether taken on their own or as part of a larger structure, are used to alter social norms. A good example of social norms evolving through public dialogue is the manner in which social and political speech evolves over time to become, for example, more or less inclusive, racist, or sexist. But dialogue does not just alter norms of speech, it has an effect on the social norms governing other kinds of behaviour. For example, political speech that dehumanizes a group often precedes a sustained campaign of physical violence against that group (Tirrell, 2012).

The problem addressed here is how utterances bring about such changes in social norms. There are two questions. First, why does a speaker make an utterance that (seeks to) alter a social norm? Second, how does that utterance contribute to altering the social norms that apply in a situation? The paper can't provide a complete answer. The paper will, however, describe which elements from three different theories should be combined to provide an answer. It will also set out some features that the combined theory must have.

As mentioned above, the main theoretical tool we will employ is game theory. There are two distinct areas of application of game theory that are relevant. One is social, another is linguistic. In social modelling, game theory has been used to explain a variety of social phenomena: social norm change (Bicchieri, 2005; Bicchieri and Mercier, 2014), the fair distribution of resources (Binmore, 1994b, 1994a; Sterelny, 2021), the emergence of oppression (O'Connor, 2019), and the emergence of social contracts through signalling (Skyrms, 2002). On the side of language, the idea of conversation as a game has a long standing in the philosophy of language, having been first introduced by David Lewis (1979). Moreover, game theoretic models have been used to model pragmatic inference in the form of the theory of Rational Speech Acts (Goodman and Frank, 2016). We can provide initial answers to our two questions by drawing on three of the above: game theoretic models of social norm change; the theory of conversational games; and the theory of Rational Speech Acts. In particular, this paper identifies requirements for a combined theory that can answer the questions.

The remainder of the paper is structured as follows. First, we give some example utterances that illustrate how speech can alter social norms. Second, we describe the idea of conversational games and recent steps to extend this theory to model social norm change. Third, we describe the essence of Bicchieri's game theoretic model of social norm change. In each section, we will identify gaps in the theories. Fourth, we describe the relevant ideas from Rational Speech Act theory. Finally, we sketch how we might fill in the gaps left over.

Games, Norms, and Utterances

2. Data

As mentioned above, utterances have an interesting property, which is that they can be used to do things as well as convey information. Take the following utterance:

(1) 'The fake news media isn't my enemy, it's the enemy of the American people.'

This was a Tweet by the then US President, Donald Trump. The intent of the utterance is clear. The aim was to sow distrust in, and animosity toward, sections of the media in the minds of both undecided and already supportive audience members. In this way, the utterance has the goal to disable that section of the media as an effective public voice and scrutineer of his presidency.

A second example is a dialogue excerpt from the film 'In the Heat of the Night'.

(2) **Gillespie:** 'And just what do you do up there in little old Pennsylvania to earn that kind of money?'
Tibbs: 'I'm a police officer.'

Prior to this utterance, Tibbs, who has been arrested on suspicion of murder, is being interrogated by the local police chief, Gillespie. Gillespie does not know that Tibbs is, in fact, a homicide detective. In this excerpt, Gillespie enquires as to how Tibbs came to have more than two hundred dollars in his wallet. The key utterance is the line from Tibbs stating that he is a police officer. This utterance equalizes the power status of the two men, which began as unequal, Gillespie having used the racist derogative 'boy'. It ends later with Gillespie addressing Tibbs with the honorific 'officer'.

On the face of it, these utterances appear to be very different. What is being done, however, at some level of abstraction, is related. Specifically, each utterance seeks to change the rules of the conversation, so as to disempower or re-empower a participant. Both utterances, in context, contributed to changing social norms. Trump's repeated attacks on the press have reduced trust in the media among Republican voters.[1]

---

[1] The Press Gazette reported a survey by Gallup showing that the percentage of Republicans who trusted the media fell from 32% in 2015 to 10% in 2020. See Majid (2022) https://pressgazette.co.uk/media-audience-and-business-data/trump-vs-media-freedom-of-press-distrust/, and assaults on journalists reached a high level around the 2020 US election, see

75

Mihaela Popa-Wyatt and Jeremy L. Wyatt

In contrast, the utterance in the film 'In the Heat of the Night' was one of several scenes where a black character was established as having equal power to the white characters. The Mr Tibbs character, with this line, makes himself the equal of the Chief Gillespie character. This culminates in a scene where the character of Mr Tibbs returns a face slap given by a powerful and racist white man. This has been called 'the slap heard around the world'. It was reportedly met with cheers (from many black audience members) and shocked cries of 'Oh!'(from many white audience members) in film theatres in the USA on the film's release and is regarded as a landmark social moment. So, the utterance not only changed the conversational dynamics in the scene but was part of a portrayal that changed social norms in America.

In the next section, we will introduce work on conversational games that goes some way to explaining what is happening within a conversation where such a dialogue move is being made. However, we will also argue that this framework cannot alone explain how the utterances cause long-term social change.

3. Conversational Games

Utterances are not stand-alone entities. They are sequenced to form monologues or conversations. From one perspective, an entire social life is simply a sequence of conversations. For our purpose, it is important to emphasize that each utterance influences subsequent utterances in the conversation and each conversation has the capacity to influence future conversations, and future social interactions. We also noted that conversations are norm-governed activities, just like other social activities. We now consider some of the effects that utterances have. This first entails summarising two independent ideas: speech acts and conversational games. We will then combine them to explain the effects of interest.

It is a well-known property of utterances that they don't merely convey information. They can also be used to perform actions or speech acts (Austin, 1975). An example of a speech act is a *performative* such as the utterance 'I now pronounce you man and wife'. This alters the world by creating a binding contract of marriage between two people. Other examples include 'We find the defendant guilty',

---

https://pressfreedomtracker.us/, where tracking started in 2017 (last accessed on 28 December 2023).

Games, Norms, and Utterances

'I name this ship the Queen Elizabeth', and 'I bet you five dollars that it will rain tomorrow'. In each case, the world has changed and there are different norms that apply after each utterance has been made. So, certain utterances can directly alter the social norms which apply in a given context.

Turning from stand-alone utterances to full conversations, an entirely independent observation is that conversations have similarities to games. The term *conversational game* is due to David Lewis (1979), who pointed out that, similarly to a baseball game, a conversation has a score and a scoreboard. This is a way to keep track of the moves in the game and their consequences for the state of play. Each time an utterance is made, the conversational score is updated. Lewis identified a peculiar feature of conversational games, which is that the score updates to make what is said correct play. For example, if I say 'I took my dog for a walk this morning', it puts onto the conversational score, via presupposition, the new information that I have a dog. This is accommodated as correct play and it would be thus inappropriate to ask me later if I have a dog. Another feature of the conversational game is that it evolves according to the rules or norms of conversation. Which conversational norms apply in a particular conversation depends on the participants and the social context in which the conversation takes place. For example, the norms of polite conversation will be different if meeting a VIP than meeting a friend in the pub.

We can usefully combine these two ideas: speech acts and conversational games, to account for the fact that speakers can change the social norms that are salient to a conversation. Mary Kate McGowan (2004) proposed the idea of a particular type of speech act, called a *'conversational exercitive'*. A conversational exercitive is a particular utterance which updates the conversational score so that new norms apply. It changes the permissibility facts in ways that may go unacknowledged by the participants in a conversation. In the example from 'In the Heat of the Night', when Mr Tibbs says 'I'm a police officer', he makes salient the social norms according to which persons of particular professional standing address one another. These social norms now guide the conversation, taking over from social norms determined by his status as a criminal suspect and a black man in the southern states. This changes the power dynamic in his favour: from low status to high status.

The idea of the conversational exercitive has also been used to explain how slurring utterances are offensive and derogatory (Popa-Wyatt and Wyatt, 2018). When addressing a target with a slur, the speaker's purpose is to grab power by changing the social norms governing the conversation. The mechanism is a conversational

Mihaela Popa-Wyatt and Jeremy L. Wyatt

exercitive within a conversational game that assigns a low-power role to the target on the basis of a reference to a low-power historical role held by members of the same group, be that group defined on the basis of gender, nationality, ethnicity, sexuality, religion, disability or another characteristic. This role assignment provides a cognitive shortcut. By using a pre-existing social role and importing it into the conversation, the speaker indexes a suite of oppressive social norms associated with the low-power social role that has been assigned. As we shall see, this role assignment exploits the way that the human brain makes decisions about whether to violate or adhere to a particular norm.

This notion of role assignment is not specific to situations involving power changes. We inherit our roles in discourse from one or more of the many social roles that we each possess in everyday life. If I am a mother and I have a job as a teacher, the norms that come into play when I speak to my child are different to those that are activated when I stand in front of a classroom. We perform a role assignment every time that we introduce ourselves or give someone salient information about our background. We also shape people's views of the social role we fulfill by the way that we interact with them. Finally, and most importantly, the role conveys a great deal of information about the social norms which apply, for remarkably little effort. If I tell you that Jenny is a neurosurgeon with a husband and two children, she lives in California and likes golf, you will have instant access from those five roles to numerous social norms. Whether you attend her clinic, play golf with her, or meet her at a school event, you will have expectations about her behaviour, and possess heuristics to guide yours.

However, there are limitations to the power of the conversational exercitive. If a role assignment carried out by an utterance is a conversational exercitive, then its effects are, by definition, restricted to the conversation. This is because the exercitive act is the illocutionary act and the utterance constitutes the act. Thus, this mechanism cannot, technically, explain effects that persist beyond or occur after the conversation. To illustrate the problem this causes, we consider a modified example of a locker room conversation first noted by McGowan (2004, 2009, 2019). Suppose that the speaker (let's call him Steve) refers to a woman he dated the previous evening (Sue) in a locker-room conversation with his friend (Bob):

(3)   **Steve:** '*I banged that bitch last night.*'
        Bob: '*She got a sistuh?*'

Now imagine that Bob sees Sue later and engages in a subsequent conversation. Because of the previous conversation, Bob now treats Sue differently than he would have done. This is because his beliefs about her role, and thus as to which social norms apply, have changed. In particular, he will be more inclined to see her as a sexual object and treat her accordingly. So the first conversation had an effect on the second conversation. But the first conversation is over, so there is no score from the first conversation still in existence. So how were the changes propagated? The answer is that Bob carried modified beliefs (be they consciously or unconsciously held) away from the first conversation with Steve. His beliefs will have been determined in part by the role assignment that was made. But these belief changes were not altered automatically by the speech act, since Bob's beliefs are not in the conversational score. Instead, Bob's belief changes are a perlocutionary effect of the role assignment.

A proposal for how those belief changes are made using Bayesian belief updating has been made (Popa-Wyatt, 2024). This proposes that, when a conversational role is assigned, an audience member reasons about hypothesized explanations. One hypothesis is that the role has been assigned incorrectly. Another hypothesis is that the role assignment is correct, and that the target really does possess that social role, from which the conversational role inherits. The Bayesian belief updating rule reasons about the probability of each hypothesis.

So, one way that we can change norms is by re-purposing existing norms to new cases. Role assignment, such as labelling the press the 'enemy' of the American people, is perfect for this. The role is a cognitive shortcut, creating an association between the media and all of the social norms associated with an enemy in the mind of the audience. This begins to answer our second question: 'how does an utterance contribute to altering a social norm that applies in a situation?'. However, it still leaves open the first question: 'why does a speaker make an utterance that (seeks to) alter a social norm?' To answer this, we will need to understand better the game theoretic model of choice between norm adherence and norm violation.

4. Game Theory and Social Norms

As mentioned above, social norms are the collections of informal rules that govern our social behaviour. Social norms are not universal but arise within groups as methods for regulating in-group behaviour. These norms can be sub-optimal from both an individual and a social perspective. Each of us learns social norms by observing the behaviour of others. Social norms change over time.

There are multiple accounts of how individuals choose whether to adhere to or violate a particular norm in a particular context. A rational choice account is one in which individuals fear fixed social penalties for norm violation and act so as to balance potential penalties and benefits (Coleman, 1994; Axelrod, 1986). This model, however, does not fit with all the available behavioural data. The rational choice model assumes that the decision to adhere to or violate a norm is made in isolation. This is not the case. Instead, norm adherence depends on two kinds of expectations that the individual has (Bicchieri, 2005; Bicchieri and Mercier, 2014). The first type are '*empirical expectations*', i.e., first-order beliefs the individual has about whether others in their group will also adhere to the norm. The second type are '*normative expectations*', i.e., second-order beliefs about whether other group members believe that the individual should also adhere to the norm.

Bicchieri introduced a model of a mixed-motive game that allows a group of players to find a Nash equilibrium balancing these forces (Bicchieri, 2005; Bicchieri and Sontuoso, 2020).[2] In this game, individuals have an expected utility for each possible action (adhere or violate). This expectation is calculated using probabilities that players will adhere to or violate the norm in question. These probabilities are estimated from observations. The game is mixed-motive because the utility combines the material payoff (which typically rises if the norm is violated) and a penalty capturing a psychological cost – or guilt – derived from the maximum cost that another player will incur due to norm violation. Using observations of norm violations to determine subsequent norm adherence yields a better fit to the behavioural data than the rational choice model (Bicchieri and Xiao, 2009). In particular, it fits empirical evidence that shows that there is an asymmetric effect of observed behaviour. In experiments with human subjects, norm adherence declines substantially if the participants observe others violating a norm, whereas norm adherence does not increase substantially if the participants observe other participants adhering to the same norm.

We propose that the mixed-motive aspect – the formulation of the psychological costs of norm violation – can be used to capture why

---

[2] A Nash equilibrium is a state in the game such that moving out of equilibrium would entail a worse pay-off, so no agent would benefit by changing, given that all other agents don't change (Osborne *et al.*, 2004).

Games, Norms, and Utterances

speakers sometimes make utterances that violate social norms. To understand this claim better, let's return to consider the example of Trump's verbal attacks on the media. We'll start with a common-sense explanation of the speaker's motivation and then assess where the game theoretic model requires extension, so as to provide a formal model of that speaker's motivation.

Let's suppose that a speaker wishes to disable a section of the media that they consider unfavourable. Their long-term goals are to sow distrust of, intimidate, cause physical harm to, reduce the audience of, and eliminate scrutiny by that section of the media. In this case, the social norms that the speaker seeks to erode are the social norms of civility, of listening to different viewpoints, and of non-violence in civil society. The speaker also aims to undermine beliefs in media neutrality. Note that the speaker need only erode those norms as applied to the target. This means that norm change by role assignment can be effective. Utterances clearly contribute to this, such as assigning the media the role of an enemy; an enemy who wants to destroy cherished institutions; and an enemy who is lying to achieve their aims. Other utterances would include encouragement to harm individual journalists; to publicly violate norms of politeness when addressing questions; and to verbally threaten those who ask questions. Thus, we can see that, working backwards from the goal of disabling the target, it is rational to make utterances of this nature. The use of role assignment also creates a cognitive shortcut, enabling audience members to use the principle of least effort when making the decision to adhere to or violate the norm (Allport, 1954).

How can this be modelled? What ingredients do we already have? Which ones are still missing? First, let us imagine applying a mixed-motive game directly to the conversation in which an utterance takes place. In this mixed-motive game, the individual would subtract the psychological costs of norm violation from the material benefit. This would require that both the psychological costs and the material benefits can be estimated. Let us focus on estimating the benefit. The speaker needs to be able, first, to define the goal at which they aim. Does that goal state lie within or beyond the conversation?

Our proposal is that speakers aim at a goal for the conversation and place a value on that goal, after having derived that conversational goal from a societal goal. So this, requires that there is a relationship between conversational goals and societal goals. It is not clear how exactly to fill that goal definition gap. There are other gaps. A simple, mixed-motive game is a one-step decision process, with a single round of play, whereas a dialogue is a multi-step process. An utterance made now will, via the conversational score, affect the dialogue many moves into the future. This is important in a model of norm violation in conversation because I might choose to suffer psychological penalties now (social disapproval) in order to yield a material benefit many steps into the future (disablement of my critics). Yet another gap is that the mixed-motive game is not a model of the conversational dynamics. Nor is it a model of how speakers and listeners generate and reason about sequences of utterances. All it does is provide a way to weigh, across candidate utterances, the pre-calculated long-term benefits and the short-term psychological costs. It doesn't provide a means to estimate the long-term benefits, but merely to employ those estimates.

In this section, we have identified one appealing feature of mixed-motive games for modelling social norm violation: the use of psychological costs estimated based on the observed behaviour of other players. We have also identified several missing elements: multi-step decision making, conversational score updating, and goal definition. We refer to these three gaps as the decision gap, the interpretation gap, and the motivation gap. We now turn to a theory that can provide one of these missing elements. This is a theory of pragmatic inference.

5. Rational Speech Acts

The Rational Speech Act (RSA) framework is a probabilistic – specifically a Bayesian – theory of pragmatic inference. At its core, RSA operates on the principle that speakers are rational agents who aim to be informative, relevant, and efficient in their communication. Listeners, in turn, use these principles to infer the speaker's intended meaning. Starting from a small number of axioms, RSA models both how speakers select utterances and how listeners interpret those utterances. There are significant limitations of RSA. For example, it has been used largely to model the interpretation of single utterances. Nevertheless, it has some utility for our enterprise.

In the RSA framework, the listener maintains a probability distribution over possible interpretations of an utterance. They update this distribution using Bayesian inference that incorporates recursive reasoning to derive the speaker's and the listener's mental models of each other. Specifically, the model incorporates: (i) a model of a literal listener based on the possible semantic interpretations; (ii) a model of a pragmatic speaker that assumes the model of the literal listener; (iii) a

Games, Norms, and Utterances

model of a pragmatic listener that assumes the model of the pragmatic speaker. These recursively defined models can incorporate both the costs of an utterance and the prior salience, and thus the probability, of particular interpretations. The significance of RSA is that it fits a variety of human behavioural data for both listeners and speakers.

RSA can, therefore, be used as an ingredient in a model of updates to the conversational score. This is because each participant has a model of the other as a pragmatic listener and so can make updates to the commonly held beliefs. The roles of the participants also sit on the conversational score. Therefore, if a role assignment is made, a psychologically plausible way in which the conversational score updates is to use Bayesian belief updating. Indeed, the Bayesian updating scheme for inferring the social role (which is a belief of the audience member) from the conversational role (which is an element of the conversational score) was proposed by (Popa-Wyatt, 2024), as mentioned earlier.

There are multiple hypotheses or pragmatic interpretations. One is that the target has the social role corresponding to the conversational role. Another is that the target does not. However, determining that variable alone may not be enough to explain the data. To conclude that the target does not have the social role, the listener still requires an explanation of why the speaker made the utterance assigning the corresponding conversational role. Explanations vary according to the context. In the case of the locker room example as in (3), an explanation is that the speaker is bigoted. In the case of Trump's attacks on the media as in (1), it is that he is being insincere so as to gain advantage. The inference could also incorporate Bayesian reasoning to account for inferential bias arising from the degree to which the speaker is trusted by the listener (Asher, Hunter, and Paul, 2021).

This Bayesian updating rule of RSA, applied in an extended way as we propose, can fill the gap of interpretation required to account for how conversational roles are communicated and inferred, but it cannot address the gaps of motivation and decision. We will sketch a further framework for these in the next section.

6. A Sketch of Requirements

We've reviewed three theories. The first was the theory of conversational games and its extension to allow speech acts that update the conversational score so as to change the rules of the conversational game. The second was a game theoretic model of social norm violation and adherence. The third was Rational Speech Act theory, which is a theory of how utterances are chosen and interpretations of utterances are made. We proposed to use the notion of conversational exercitives from the first; the mixed-motive game with an estimation of psychological costs based on observed behaviour from the second; and the use of Bayesian updating to interpret the meaning of utterances from the third. In the latter two cases, we propose to apply the existing mechanism in a new way, so as to apply them to social norm modelling. We've also identified some remaining gaps, that a complete theory will have to fill. We referred to these as the motivation and decision gaps. Let us give a little more detail on each.

The first remaining gap we termed the motivation gap. This is the problem that, in order to intentionally make utterances that have long-term effects after the end of the conversation, a speaker needs to have a sense of what those long-term effects are intended to be. This requires that the effects are cognitively represented. When a speaker such as Donald Trump attacks the media as in (1), he does so with a clear sense of the long-term disablement it will cause and the value of that to him. But knowing what the long-term goal is, is not enough. It must also be used to derive a goal for the dialogue and a benefit for the current candidate utterance. This is the decision gap.

To solve the decision gap, we require a way for the benefit of achieving long-term social goals to be back-propagated into the current dialogue. One mechanism for this is the theory of stochastic games in which agents play a game, taking decisions in turn, each trying to achieve a long-term goal (Solan and Vieille, 2015). In stochastic games, or multi-stage games generally, participants reason about how to act by attaching rewards to those long-term goals and back-propagating those to estimate the values of actions they can take now. Computational linguists have employed this kind of game-based decision framework to model strategic dialogue planning (Asher and Paul, 2017). These formalisms can provide a framework to explain how long-term motivations are turned into decisions about what to do immediately.

References

Gordon Willard Allport, *The Nature of Prejudice* (Cambridge, MA: Addison-Wesley, 1954).

Nicholas Asher and Soumya Paul, 'Conversation and Games', in *Logic and Its Applications: 7th Indian Conference, ICLA 2017, Proceedings 7* (Springer, 2017), 1–18.

Games, Norms, and Utterances

Nicholas Asher, Julie Hunter, and Soumya Paul, 'Bias in Semantic and Discourse Interpretation', *Linguistics and Philosophy*, 45:3 (2021), 393–429.
John Langshaw Austin, *How to Do Things with Words* (Oxford: Oxford University Press, 1975).
Robert Axelrod, 'An Evolutionary Approach to Norms', *American Political Science Review*, 80:4 (1986), 1095–1111.
Cristina Bicchieri, *The Grammar of Society: The Nature and Dynamics of Social Norms* (Cambridge: Cambridge University Press, 2005).
Cristina Bicchieri, *Norms in the Wild: How to Diagnose, Measure, and Change Social Norms* (Oxford: Oxford University Press, 2016).
Cristina Bicchieri and Hugo Mercier, 'Norms and Beliefs: How Change Occurs', in *The Complexity of Social Norms* (Springer, 2014), 37–54.
Cristina Bicchieri and Alessandro Sontuoso, 'Game-Theoretic Accounts of Social Norms: The Role of Normative Expectations', *Handbook of Experimental Game Theory* (Edward Elgar Publishing, 2020), 241–55.
Cristina Bicchieri and Erte Xiao, 'Do the Right Thing: But Only If Others Do So', *Journal of Behavioral Decision Making*, 22:2 (2009), 191–208.
Ken Binmore, *Game Theory and the Social Contract: Playing Fair* (Cambridge, MA: MIT Press, 1994a).
Ken Binmore, *Game Theory and the Social Contract: Just Playing* (Cambridge, MA: MIT Press, 1994b).
James S. Coleman, *Foundations of Social Theory* (Boston: Harvard University Press, 1994).
Noah D. Goodman and Michael C. Frank, 'Pragmatic Language Interpretation as Probabilistic Inference', *Trends in Cognitive Sciences*, 20:11 (2016), 818–29.
David Lewis, 'Scorekeeping in a Language Game', *Philosophical Papers*, 1 (1979), 233–49.
Aisha Majid, 'Trump vs media: Four years of presidential press attacks charted', in *Press Gazette*, Future Of Media (2022).
Mary Kate McGowan, 'Conversational Exercitives: Something Else We Do With Our Words', *Linguistics and Philosophy*, 27 (2004), 93–111.
Mary Kate McGowan, 'Oppressive Speech', *Australasian Journal of Philosophy*, 87:3 (2009), 389–407.
Mary Kate McGowan, *Just Words: On Speech and Hidden Harm* (Oxford: Oxford University Press, 2019).

Mihaela Popa-Wyatt and Jeremy L. Wyatt

Cailin O'Connor, *The Origins of Unfairness: Social Categories and Cultural Evolution* (Oxford and New York: Oxford University Press, 2019).

Martin J. Osborne, *An Introduction to Game Theory* (New York: Oxford University Press, 2004).

Mihaela Popa-Wyatt, 'Norm-Shifting through Oppressive Acts', in Sally Haslanger, Karen Jones, Greg Restall François Schroeter, and Laura Schroeter (eds), *Mind, Language, and Social Hierarchy: Constructing a Shared Social World* (Oxford: Oxford University Press, 2024).

Mihaela Popa-Wyatt and Jeremy L. Wyatt, 'Slurs, Roles and Power', *Philosophical Studies*, 175:11 (2018), 2879–2906.

Brian Skyrms, 'Signals, Evolution and the Explanatory Power of Transient Information', *Philosophy of Science*, 69:3 (2002), 407–28.

Eilon Solan and Nicolas Vieille, 'Stochastic Games', *Proceedings of the National Academy of Sciences*, 112:45 (2015), 13743–46.

Kim Sterelny, *The Pleistocene Social Contract: Culture and Cooperation in Human Evolution* (Oxford: Oxford University Press, 2021).

Lynne Tirrell, 'Genocidal Language Games', in Mary Kate McGowan and Maitra Ishani (eds), *Speech and Harm: Controversies over Free Speech* (Oxford: Oxford University Press, 2012), 174–221.

Prejudicial Speech: What's a Liberal to Do?

MARI MIKKOLA

Abstract
This paper discusses potential responses to harmful prejudicial speech. More specifically, it considers how different types of prejudicial speech merit different responses. The paper distinguishes hate speech, discriminatory speech, and toxic speech as different *types* of speech that are prejudicial or oppressive – they are not of the same kind diverging only in their severity and explicitness. As these sorts of problematic speech are categorically distinct, the paper holds, they also demand differential remedies. The task of this paper is to consider such remedies, their potential effectiveness, and compatibility with the liberal value of free speech.

1. Introduction

Prejudicial and intemperate speech is a thorny issue in liberal societies. Freedom of speech is a central liberal value. But, if left unchecked, it permits morally and socially undesirable expressions. This raises important questions about the limits of free speech: what (if anything) should be done about prejudicial speech?[1] For a start, it is worth remembering that no legal free speech principle *de facto* admits all forms of speech. Verbal threats are not defensible on free speech grounds and outlawing them raises no free speech concerns whatsoever (they constitute crimes). Defamation is legitimately actionable by tort law because it incurs serious harms to the defamed that outweigh significant and compelling free speech interests. Still, a large of bulk of speech (at least in the USA) is afforded protected status: it is judged to advance substantial free speech interests that justify non-restriction and non-interference, even if the speech incurs some harms and/or is offensive. The interests on which the value of free speech is typically taken to hinge in philosophical discussions include: the pursuit of truth and knowledge, ensuring democratic deliberation and functioning, and fostering personal autonomy and individual progress. But do these interests justify

---

[1] Note that 'speech' here is taken to denote not just spoken words and utterances, but also signs, public recordings, written words, non-verbal symbols, and other means of expression.

Mari Mikkola

non-interference in and a laissez-faire attitude toward prejudicial speech? Must we simply accept the harms of intemperate speech within a liberal framework as the price we pay for broader freedoms? Should 'our' response simply be to tolerate the intolerable, and to fight speech with more speech in the marketplace of ideas? If not, what (kinds of) governmental or legal interventions on speech might still be unacceptably illiberal?

My view is that answers to these questions depend on the *type* of prejudicial speech in question. I will here focus on hate, discriminatory, and toxic speech. The position that I hold in appealing to different types of speech goes against prominent current views about (what I call) 'prejudicial speech' and (others call) 'hate speech'. In recent years, both in academic philosophy and in public discourse, conceptions of *hate speech* have proliferated, and the conceptual terrain has become hard to navigate. In two high-profile papers, Alexander Brown (2017a, 2017b) considers a staggering quantity of academic and public literature, and concludes that the concept of *hate speech* encompasses:

> a family of different purposes including but not limited to highlighting forms of harmful speech, flagging up socially divisive forms of speech, identifying forms of speech that can undermine people's sense of equality, articulating civility norms, and labelling forms of speech that undermine democracy; a family of types of speech including but not limited to insults, slurs, and epithets, words that express or articulate ideas relating to the moral inferiority, group defamation, and negative stereotypes or generics; a family of types of speech act including but not limited to insulting, disparaging, degrading, humiliating, misrecognising, disheartening, harassing, persecuting, threatening, provoking, inciting hatred, discrimination or violence, and justifying or glorifying discrimination or violence; and a family of characteristics including but not limited to race, ethnicity, nationality, citizenship, status, religion, sexual orientation, gender identity, and disability. (Brown, 2017b, p. 600)

Given this proliferation of what 'we' mean by *hate speech*, some philosophers (Brown included) have begun refining the definition of *hate speech* by expanding its scope to catch as many expressions as possible. These (in my terms) 'expanded' strategies are increasingly popular in philosophical work. Brown along with Katharine Gelber (2021) are two prominent recent advocates in print. My contention, however, is that we should eschew the expanded strategy and embrace a pluralist strategy (I argue for this view in more detail elsewhere, see Mikkola, forthcoming 2024). 'Prejudicial speech' – for me

– is an umbrella term that encompasses different types of intemperate speech ranging from: hate (narrowly understood) to discriminatory (more broadly conceived) to toxic (diffuse and amorphous) to some still other type(s) of speech. Importantly for my typology, this division isn't about the seriousness or harmfulness of speech, with hate speech being the most serious kind. Rather, it is about scope, palpability, and definiteness, which makes a difference to 'our' reactions to prejudicial speech. With the pluralist approach, I hold, we can forge more nuanced responses and avoid getting bogged down by an unhelpful false binary of do nothing or enforce draconian restrictions.

My task in this paper is to motivate the idea that there are different types of prejudicial speech that merit different responses within a liberal framework. There is no conception of prejudicial or hate speech supposedly carved in nature's joints – it is up to us to define them in a beneficial and fitting manner. Moreover, I hold that interventions, and even restrictions, on speech are compatible with liberal commitments to free speech. But the way this is done must be relative to the type of speech in question; as I see it, the prospect of a blanket response to prejudicial speech is extremely poor.

To make my case, I will first provide some conceptual mapping of different kinds of prejudicial speech. I will then consider what is the harm of these kinds of speech. Finally, I will consider what can be done about prejudicial speech while respecting free speech rights.[2]

2. Prejudicial Speech: Initial Conceptual Mapping

In characterising (then) recent work on hate speech, Stanley Fish (2012) notes that although everyone agrees words used directly to incite violence against a person or a group count as hate speech, there is much disagreement over the remaining (in his view) hard cases. Fish's apparently uncontentious type of hate speech mirrors the well-known US case of *Chaplinsky v. New Hampshire* (1942) that took a particular narrow class of speech to be obviously punishable without raising any free speech concerns (albeit not a case that Fish explicitly cites). This included 'the lewd and the obscene, the profane, the libelous [sic], and the insulting or "fighting" words— those which by their very utterance inflict injury or tend to incite

---

[2] Given the topic of this paper, I will discuss some example cases of prejudicial speech though I won't be mentioning (let alone using) slurs or hateful epithets.

an immediate breach of the peace'.³ In the spirit of *Chaplinsky v. New Hampshire,* David Brink develops an understanding of *hate speech* that is a narrow one. On this view, hate speech is about prohibited harassment by personal vilification, and an expression counts as such if and only if

(a) it employs fighting words or non-verbal symbols that insult or stigmatize persons on the basis of their gender, race, color, handicap, religion, sexual orientation, or national and ethnic origin;
(b) it is addressed to a captive audience [when the speech is relatively difficult to avoid];
(c) the insult or stigma would be experienced by a reasonable person in those circumstances; and
(d) it would be reasonable for the speaker to foresee that his words would have these effects on a reasonable person in those circumstances. (Brink, 2001, p. 135)

This type of speech comes apart from other types of prejudicial speech, which are less clear cut. Discriminatory speech mirrors or reflects group stereotypes and represents groups or their members as inferior by virtue of these stereotypes (p. 133). Nonetheless, it does so in putatively non-vilifying and non-invidious ways. Although discriminatory speech may be and is odious and offensive, it is said to deserve free speech protections: it may nonetheless serve a socially valuable function by contributing to public debates and by enhancing deliberative practices insofar as we can challenge the speaker and the underlying stereotypes being espoused. Examples of this type of speech might be:

- Politician in an interview endorsing bio-behavioural or biologically essentialist views to explain racialised patters of criminality.
- Professor holding that well-meaning but misguided affirmative action policies are bringing undertalented students from marginalised backgrounds to university, since such students just are 'by nature' unsuited for university education.
- Manager arguing in a meeting against promoting female candidates on account that they will be more interested in having babies than in having careers.

More recently still, there has been a prominent focus on toxic speech. Lynne Tirrell (2021) takes such speech to include derogations, epithets, and slurs. But it involves more: it is

---

³ 315 U.S. 568 (1942), https://supreme.justia.com/cases/federal/us/315/568/. Accessed 23 August 2023.

a broad and mercurial category, [...] [also including] speech that acts more chronically by gaslighting, undermining, threatening, and more [...]. Some toxic speech surreptitiously re-orients people away from their settled values and conceptions of the good. (Tirrell, 2021, p. 116)

Toxic speech is broadly understood and denotes a diffuse kind of speech that is amorphous and undermines what is good for individuals. Some examples I have previously used to illustrate this type of speech include (see Mikkola, 2021):

The Brexit-Bus:
bright red *Leave* campaign bus stating 'We send the EU 350 million pounds a week, let's fund our NHS (National Health Service) instead'.

Trump 'the Winner':
stating in an interview when facing electoral defeat in November 2020 that 'This is a fraud on the American public. This is an embarrassment to our country. We were getting ready to win this election. Frankly, we did win this election. So our goal now is to ensure the integrity – for the good of this nation, this is a very big moment – this is a major fraud on our nation'. (The same sentiments of winning and the election being fraudulently stolen have of course been expressed many times in the years that have followed.)

Corona = Agenda 21:
during a 1992 UN Conference on Environment and Development, 177 national leaders (including George Bush Sr.) signed a non-binding statement of intent aiming to take action in order to ensure sustainability given population growth. This agreement, known as Agenda 21, has been dubbed by alt-right and political extremists as a secret plot to impose a totalitarian world order in a nefarious effort to use environmentalism as a means to crush freedom. In late-2020, groups protesting against restrictions brought on by the COVID-19 pandemic carrying signs stating 'Corona = Agenda 21' were seen (at least) in Germany, Switzerland, and the Netherlands. Their message is, in short, that the corona pandemic is used by global elites to annihilate people's freedoms and to reduce the world's population to advance the elite's iniquitous ends.[4]

---

[4] Whether the protesters thought that the pandemic is a hoax used for these ends or whether the real pandemic was used for nefarious ends isn't entirely clear. But this does not make a substantive difference to my discussion of the example.

Mari Mikkola

This typology then understands prejudicial speech to range from hate speech (narrowly understood) to discriminatory speech (more broadly conceived) to toxic speech (that is diffuse and amorphous).

3. What's the Harm?

Legal free speech principles do not *de facto* typically admit all forms of speech despite liberal commitments to free expression. As Fish (1993) puts this elsewhere provocatively in a book title, *There's No Such Thing as Free Speech: And It's a Good Thing, Too*. Standardly, free speech interventions are justified, but only if the harms caused and/or constituted by some speech outweigh significant free speech interests. Hence, in thinking about the types of prejudicial speech outlined above and appropriate responses to them, the first step is to assess what those harms are and their seriousness. Initial pre-theoretical considerations might suggest the following analysis of the harms. Hate speech looks to be harmful in being offensive and insulting. Discriminatory speech, then again, is stereotyping and misleading, thereby generating harms to its recipients. And finally, toxic speech is downright false, even if non-offensive, but this suffices for it being harmful (enough). On standard liberal grounds following J.S. Mill, though, these harms can be mitigated and hence do not warrant intervention. As is well known, offensiveness is not a harm in the right kind of way according to Mill (just think of his discussion of corn dealers). Misleading and stereotyping statements can be valuable even when odious: by challenging the speaker, we can debunk the views expressed, and thus advance democratic deliberative practices. On Millian grounds, even false statements have social value in advancing truth and knowledge seeking.

Nonetheless, Mill holds that autonomous functioning and democratic self-governance demand the exercise of deliberative capacities that only develop in free societies: 'observation to see, reasoning and judgement to foresee, activity to gather materials for decision, discrimination to decide, and [...] firmness and self-control to hold his deliberate decision' (1974, p. 139). As I see it, the three types of speech under examination undermine precisely the development and/or exercise of such deliberative capacities. Importantly though, they do so in different ways; therefore, we need different sorts of responses to different types of prejudicial speech.

Let's start with hate speech. Brink takes hate speech in the narrow sense to be harmful in hampering deliberative practices: it limits its recipients' participation in deliberative exchanges and prevents recipients from getting a fair hearing when they try to participate (2001, pp. 140–1). In this sense then, hate speech is akin to defamation, where free speech interests do not mitigate harms incurred – hate speech should not subsequently count as protected speech. Examples of these sorts of harms have been gleaned via interviews with targets of hate speech (Gelber and McNamara, 2016; see also Brink, 2001; West, 2012). They include: negative stereotyping, feelings of fear, existential pain, disempowerment, withdrawal from expressive opportunities, silencing, exclusion, dehumanisation, provocation to anger, restrictions on the ability to identify with one's (ethnic, national, racial) group. These harms seemingly conflict with typical free speech interests, and specifically with (a) ensuring democratic deliberation and functioning; and (b) fostering personal autonomy and individual progress. It is consequently not obvious that 'our' commitment to free speech on the whole mitigates the harms of hate speech.

Still, Brink holds that discriminatory speech is not harmful in the same manner as hate speech. The former supposedly leaves open the possibility of deliberation, open debate, and challenging of the speaker. Furthermore, Brink holds, even if 'merely discriminatory speech' has the effects of marginalising and silencing its recipients, narrowly understood hate speech is 'generally worse' and 'comparatively easy to identify' (2001, p. 148). I agree that hate speech in the narrow sense is easier to identify than more diffuse discriminatory speech. But I disagree that it is generally worse since (I hold) discriminatory speech is arguably more prominent and widespread. This being the case, I argue elsewhere (2019) that discriminatory speech is particularly detrimental in eroding self-trust. Self-trust is an attitude we take toward ourselves because we have confidence in our epistemic abilities. As Elizabeth Fricker puts it:

> Each one of us in one's everyday life relies on one's core package of cognitive faculties – perception, proprioception, memory, intellectual intuition and introspection – reliably to deliver one true beliefs [...]. The core phenomenon of epistemic self-trust consists in one's ungrounded reliance on one's cognitive faculties reliably to yield one true beliefs. (Fricker, 2016, p. 154)

And for Karen Jones,

> intellectual self-trust is an attitude of optimism about one's cognitive competence in a domain. Self-trust manifests itself in feelings of confidence, in dispositions willingly to rely on the deliverances

> of one's methods and to assert what is believed on their basis, and in modulating self-reflection [...]. Developmentally, our intellectual self-trust is created interactively [in relation to our parents, teachers, peers]. (Jones, 2012, p. 245)

With these ideas in mind, think back to Mill's deliberative capacities noted above that seemingly appeal to self-trust: 'observation to see, reasoning and judgement to foresee, activity to gather materials for decision, discrimination to decide, and [...] firmness and self-control to hold his deliberate decision' (1974, p. 139). Moreover, recall free speech interests that are taken to justify non-interference. Democratic functioning requires free speech to facilitate deliberative exchanges, and to enable informed political decision-making. And exercising autonomy involves certain competencies, for example, the ability to act according to one's own interests. My contention is that discriminatory speech erodes the kind of self-trust needed to support these free speech interests. It is in *this* sense harmful (though probably in other ways too). Still, this harm looks to be sufficient to undermine justifications for the permissibility of discriminatory speech. Self-reporting suggests that those subject to discriminatory speech are also marginalised, put off, and silenced by the negative stereotypes expounded in the absence of hateful personal vilification. Members of underrepresented groups are excluded from deliberative practices and ignored when they try to participate without anyone employing insulting fighting words or slurs. Non-hateful stereotypical speech may then also close off further rational exchanges, prevent challenging of the views expressed, and hamper democratic cultures. By way of example, I will consider espousing stereotypes about women in philosophy. Many such examples can be found in (the now defunct) blog *What's it like to be a woman in philosophy?* (Archive of posts still available online):

> In 2000 I [a female] was interviewing for jobs for the first time [...]. I was sitting at the head of the table looking out at all the men – there was one female graduate student there, that's it. I finished my talk and the questions began. The professor who I would have been replacing raised his hand and said 'So [...] we haven't had a woman teach fulltime in the department for 40 years, why should we hire one now?' Absolute silence, no one said a word. Rather than saying something clever like, 'you clearly shouldn't as you are not ready' and leaving the interview, I stammered something about perhaps this would help their enrolment, as I would have liked to have had a female role model

when I was an undergrad. To this he replied 'Well, if we want to recruit more female students why shouldn't we just hire some hot, young guy?' I was totally flummoxed by this point and just trying not to a) yell or b) cry as I knew either of these actions would reinforce his ideas about women [...]. NO ONE at the table said a word.

At one of the first [graduate] seminars I went to, I was the only girl. I raise an objection. I'm told that I have misunderstood the point. I hadn't – the professor in charge of the seminar pointed this out twenty minutes later once all the boys had finally got round to saying what I said initially. I try to speak again later. My point is completely ignored. Two minutes later, a male makes exactly the same point. The objection in his mouth is hailed as decisive. I worry that my being dismissed and ignored is not because of my gender but because I am foolish; I worry that I don't love philosophy because almost every seminar I go to leaves me second guessing my ownbilityies.

[During my first year] I made a concerted effort to participate and make at least one good comment or question in every meeting of the pro-seminar. However, at the end of the semester when we each got a report on how we did from the two (male) professors, this is what they wrote: '[Name] was sometimes a bit quiet, and we wondered whether she was a bit disengaged.' All the other people who were in that class who I told about this agree that, on the basis of my actual participation, this was unfair.

As I see it, in these examples non-vilifying discriminatory expressions have arguably also had the effect of silencing women and rendering their contributions invisible in a manner that generates self-doubt – that is, in a manner that engenders typical hallmarks of eroded intellectual self-trust.

What about toxic speech then? Earlier examples I noted were misleading, outright false, and/or without compelling justification: they are toxic in polluting our democratic milieu sometimes in very material and concrete ways. Lynne Tirrell (2021) has recently characterised toxic speech (in the sense outlined above) as being akin to a poison or virus, where propagating it can lead to an outbreak. Recall that it is 'a broad and mercurial category' and can reorient 'people away from their settled values and conceptions of the good' (Tirrell, 2021, p. 116). The toxic and poisonous effects of this sort of speech hinge on the endorsement of the speech. Tirrell understands endorsement generally to be 'automatic, not something added; it takes special care to restrict endorsement when we must' (p. 125). Although I agree with Tirrell that toxic speech undermines what is good for individuals in perfidious ways, I think that the harm of toxic speech is to be understood differently: its contamination and contagiousness is more active than those of poisons and viruses. (I discuss this at greater length in Mikkola, 2021.)

Thinking about the sorts of examples I noted above suggests that people are actively keen to endorse misleading, false, and unjustified claims, even when they are vehemently and openly challenged. This sort of endorsement may happen 'on the spot'. But it isn't spontaneous in the sense of wholly lacking control and being without conscious thought or attention. To put it in a slogan form: endorsement does not happen to people; people make it happen. Subsequently, I hold, toxic speech corrupts and perverts well-functioning epistemic agency. This is the primary harm of toxic speech, which has many real-world secondary and material harms when people for instance act on some piece of toxic speech. Still, it is 'our' default underlying cognitive situation that enables this sort of corrupting. Our cognitive architecture is like untreated steel: without prevention and if exposed to both oxygen and water, steel will rust. Hence, we treat and coat it. When the coating is damaged, we repair and recoat it to prevent rusting. In a similar fashion, it seems to me, without a protective coating our cognitive architecture will rust too. Furthermore, prevalent and infamous toxic speech examples suggest that a sort of proper cognitive 'rust prevention' is lacking. The willingness to endorse and to embrace half-truths, falsehoods, and unjustified claims is suggestive of an underlying problem at the core of epistemic agency: it has been left exposed to the elements without sufficient protections. This is what ultimately enables the corruption of well-functioning epistemic agency.

4. What's a Liberal To Do?

To recap, I take it that hate speech is defined as directly vilifying personal harassment (for example, being subject to racist or sexist slurs). It is harmful in limiting and hampering democratic participation by often quite literally silencing and marginalising its recipients. Then again, discriminatory speech is more covert and non-vilifying but diminishing speech based on stereotyping. It is harmful in hampering the development and/or exercise of autonomy and individual progress by undercutting self-trust. Finally, toxic speech is a diffuse kind of problematic speech that is amorphous and undermines what is good for individuals. It is harmful in corrupting and perverting well-functioning epistemic agency in a covert manner given 'our' default disposition to be corruptible given our cognitive architecture.

How then might we respond to these types of speech? One initial kneejerk reaction may be: *Do nothing!* If the harms of prejudicial speech are due to our cognitive architecture or inability to withstand offensive speech, there is nothing legally to be done – we are dealing with individual problems. On the other end of the spectrum, however, the reaction may be a call to: *impose draconian speech restrictions!* Since we are so prone to intemperate speech, speech should be heavily restricted and forcefully intervened in. Perhaps we can think of something less crude though. I will next consider some such interventions and even restrictions.

4.1 Hate Speech

To begin with, it is important to note that restrictions on 'our' freedoms are not *eo ipso* illiberal. There are restrictions on the purchase, distribution, and consumption of alcohol and cigarettes; there are plenty of restrictions on driving; we have employment laws to restrict our working lives (e.g., a compulsory retirement age in some jurisdictions, restrictions on how small or large employment contracts can be irrespective of individual wishes), just to name a few. So, there is no blanket liberal prohibition on legally intervening in 'our' freedoms. But, one might say, freedom of speech is different and a special case in being a basic right. Freedom of speech and expression is conceivably more important than 'our' freedom to purchase alcohol and cigarettes. Nonetheless, free speech interests do not justify a hands-off policy regarding hate speech in the narrow sense. First, the right to free speech isn't an absolute right to say whatever one wants. There is a difference between speech in the *ordinary* sense (whatever we utter, what comes out of our mouths) and speech in the *legal* sense that falls under a legal free speech principle. Hate speech is not obviously speech in the legal sense that deserves protection. The substantive question is whether it falls under the legal sense of *speech*; and understood as harassment by personal vilification, it arguably does not. Second, the right to free speech is framed in terms of advancing democratic functioning and fostering individual autonomy and progress. But evidence suggest that these are *not* advanced by hate speech; they are rather seriously stifled and undercut. There are then compelling grounds to think that harms caused are grave enough to warrant intervention. This of course still leaves open what sorts of legal interventions to advance, and whether such interventions should fall under criminal or tort law (be considered a civil wrong). Let me say something about these options.

Criminal offenses need to satisfy the *mens rea* (guilty mind) and *actus reus* (guilty act) requirements. The precise formulation of these differs from one jurisdiction to the next, but to satisfy *mens rea* intentionality is key. For instance, one cannot accidentally rob a bank or commit murder. Unless intentionality can be sufficiently established, it is hard (even impossible) to convict someone of alleged criminal offenses. One way to establish intentionality relative to hate speech is to tie the definition of *hate speech* to the notion of *incitement*. By way of example: there is no formal definition of *hate speech* in International Human Rights Law and, therefore, most [UN] instruments refer to 'incitement to discrimination, hostility or violence' [...], 'direct and public incitement to genocide'; and 'advocacy of national, racial or religious hatred that constitutes incitement to discrimination, hostility or violence' are strictly prohibited under International Law, as they are considered the 'severest forms of hate speech'.[5]

If hate speech turns on incitement, though, some apparently hard cases of hate speech raise no free speech concerns whatsoever. Inciting someone to commit a crime is in all jurisdictions that I know of itself a crime and appealing to free speech rights is not an adequate defence. For instance, inciting others to commit racist hate crimes with one's speech isn't defensible on free speech grounds or a matter of free speech. Moreover, there is nothing illiberal about criminalising incitement to commit hate crimes with one's speech. This again demonstrates that freedom of speech isn't about the freedom to utter whatever comes to mind. Having said that, I think it is a mistake to equate *hate speech* and *incitement*. There is (and should be) a substantive difference between *saying* something that counts as hate speech and *inciting* others to commit hate crimes with one's speech. The case for criminalising the latter is straightforward, but this is not so for the former. Be that as it may, my point is to highlight that there already are legal interventions on 'our' speech – so, a view that takes speech to be sacrosanct is misplaced from the start.

Perhaps, though, we should treat hate speech like defamation under tort law: as a written or oral statement that results in damage to a person's reputation. If a co-worker distributes lies about me

---

[5] https://www.un.org/en/hate-speech/united-nations-and-hate-speech/international-human-rights-law. Accessed 16 January 2024.

that harm my reputation due to which I fail to be promoted, I can seek legal recourse and damages from that co-worker for the harms incurred. Richard Delgado (1993) proposes an independent tort action for racial insults akin to defamation, where the notion of *racial insult* he employs is in line with Brink's definition of *hate speech*. One example of a US case that seemingly would fall under this tort that Delgado discusses is *Contreras v. Crown Zellerbach, Inc* (1977).[6] The Mexican-American plaintiff alleged that his fellow employees had subjected him to a campaign of racial abuse. Hence, he further alleged that he had suffered 'humiliation and embarrassment by reason of racial jokes, slurs and comments' (Delgado, 1993, p. 89). The plaintiff was further wrongfully accused of stealing the employer's property, which allegedly damaged his employment prospects and held him up to public ridicule. This case looks like a paradigm case of defamation, where racial identity and subsequent racial insult experienced are not merely additional and peripheral to the case, but are in fact at the centre of the harms generated and experienced.

An immediate objection to these sorts of torts, however, is that the tort of racial insult is illiberal since on classical liberal views, offensiveness is not a harm in the right kind of way. The insult may be odious, but something that we must apparently tolerate in a liberal society. However, this objection isn't compelling to me for reasons that are self-evident to people advancing restrictions on hate speech. Simply put: the tort isn't about offensiveness – the point is that hate speech is damaging in a very material sense by (for instance) depriving people of employment opportunities. 'Sticks and stones may break my bones. But words shall never hurt me' just is not true (see also Matsuda *et al.*, 1993; Maitra and McGowan, 2012). Of course, practically speaking, it may be difficult to measure the damages incurred. But the same is true of more 'straightforward' defamation cases, which makes them notoriously difficult to litigate. Still, legal scholars and practitioners do not seemingly hold that *therefore* the tort of defamation should be abolished. My underlying theoretical point here is that there is nothing *per se* illiberal about this sort of legal redress as we already have various similar torts. And again, it is important to stress the non-absolute nature of free speech rights: they cannot be appealed to successfully as defences in many tort actions.

---

[6] https://law.justia.com/cases/washington/supreme-court/1977/44623-1.html. Accessed 1 July 2023.

However, one might object further that the tort for racial insults is too draconian in being a form of punitive legal redress. Hence, it is not compatible with a liberal commitment to free speech – after all, punitive measures typically involve incarceration. I find this objection uncompelling as well, though. Advocating for punitive responses is not equivalent to advocating for imprisonment. There are many ways in which we punish offenders without imprisoning them (fines or community service, for instance). Perhaps even more radically, transformative justice models might be beneficial: this involves a process where the individuals involved are given the opportunity to address and repair the harm caused. Those affected recount how an act has affected them and what can be done to repair the harm. The perpetrator is then held accountable to the individual(s) affected by way of restitution. As with any form of punishment, there are no guarantees that the outcome will be successful. But my point is to highlight that much can be done about hate speech *without* invoking the bugbears of speech bans or censorship.

4.2 Toxic Speech

Given what I take to constitute the harm of toxic speech, it might look like a good idea to limit the spread of toxic misinformation to prevent it from corrupting and perverting epistemic agency. An example of this might be sensitive media policies that some social media platforms already have. This response does speak for some straightforward restrictions on what we find in the public domain – and frankly I have no objections to such restrictions. Still *de facto* this response will have limited scope due to the nature of the internet. It will also be difficult to decide what to restrict and how, given the diffuseness and indefiniteness of toxic speech. More plausibly, then, one might think that some educational efforts or cognitive therapy are needed to better protect epistemic agency from being perverted. The example of government healthy eating campaigns is akin to what I have in mind. Given our evolutionary past, it is 'our' default to consume calorific foods. When food was scarce and work involved physical strain, this 'toxicity' was dormant. But now, if left to our own devices without public health measures, many of us would be living deeply unhealthy lives. In a similar sense, to undercut the toxicity of some speech maybe we need to advance educational programs to cultivate epistemically virtuous agency.

This response requires that we identify which sorts of epistemic virtues ought to be cultivated – which, then again, hinges on the kinds of vices involved. Epistemic vices make us bad thinkers and the corrupting influence of toxic speech is seemingly such a vice. Heather Battaly distinguishes three types of epistemic vice. First, vices may produce false beliefs, thus involving 'effects-vice'. Second, certain cognitive character traits (like closed-mindedness or intellectual arrogance) are exemplary of 'responsibilist-vice': it is a vice over which agents have cognitive control and if the agent does not work towards exercising such control, they will be blameworthy. Third, epistemic vice may involve bad epistemic motives like 'motives to believe whatever is easiest, or whatever preserves the status quo, or whatever makes one feel good, instead of motives for truth, knowledge, and understanding' (Battaly, 2017, p. 224) – thus involving 'personalist-vice'.

To undercut these vices, we need to cultivate and promote the requisite virtues. To undercut effect-vice, it seems that virtue-reliabilism is the answer. This is the view that epistemic virtues are reliable epistemic dispositions that produce fewer false beliefs and more true ones. Although this would undercut effect-vice, the concerns I have discussed in this paper raise doubts about whether we have such epistemic virtues at our disposal to begin with. After all, we look to be very susceptible to personalist-vices given how corruptible our 'hard-drives' appear to be. What we need instead is some form of virtue-responsibilism, whereby epistemic agents work to shape their cognitive traits in ways that render those traits more reliable (Montmarquet, 1992). Epistemically autonomous agency, then, involves taking responsibility and working towards undermining the influence of toxic speech (and requisite attitudes) that corrupt and pervert good epistemic functioning. I find this idea attractive, but have serious doubts about its efficacy. Those who are willing and able to take responsibility for their epistemic lives are already on board, so to speak, and already concerned about the state of their epistemic well-being. The difficult question is how can we persuade the non-believers (bluntly put) to get on board. I am increasingly pessimistic about effective interventions at a later stage after individual epistemic agency has formed. Early age interventions would be needed and, I expect, continuing educational efforts from early on can play a huge role. Of course, this suggestion presents several further challenges about the appropriate method, mode, and location for such educational efforts. Educational interventions in schools guided by national curricula may be and are seen by some as illiberal: it is not the role of the state to decide and dictate what kids get taught in schools, one might hold. Also, without a prior normative theory, it becomes difficult to distinguish 'good' from 'bad' curricula in a non-ad hoc manner. Perhaps the government-dictated curriculum contains the right ingredients. But there is little or nothing to stop the curriculum from being directed at teaching something one may find undesirable. There is much dispute that would have to be settled about what schools can and should teach, how much influence parents have and should have, and whether curriculum design should be left to the state at all (just to name a few). Still, though we may disagree about the specifics, I see no reason to think that basic educational efforts to foster virtue-responsibilism and undermine epistemic vices are *per se* illiberal.

We should also bear in mind that toxic speech often functions like subliminal messaging akin to some forms of advertisement. (In fact, the success of advertising and marketing further demonstrates precisely how corruptible we are!) On Thomas Scanlon's prominent liberal view, it is legitimate to restrict subliminal advertising messages. Hence, one might think that it is legitimate and permissible to restrict toxic speech as well without compromising our commitment to free expression. Scanlon holds that subliminal messages interfere with audience autonomy in producing beliefs and desires that the audience has no control over. Subsequently, there is an interest 'in having a good environment for the formation of one's beliefs and desires' (Scanlon, 1978–9, p. 527). In other words, audiences have a positive autonomy interest in being free from manipulation. This interest (being free from manipulation) also *prima facie* justifies educational efforts to develop the sorts of capacities that enable us to exercise autonomy. I cannot say anything detailed here about the contents of such education, which of course raises complex practical questions. Still, yet again, there is nothing *per se* illiberal about educational efforts to engender conditions that enable us to develop and exercise autonomy-capacities and Millian deliberative capacities. In a similar fashion, there is nothing *per se* illiberal about state authorities providing nutritious school meals to undercut unhealthy eating habits. One might in fact think that this is precisely what they ought to do to enable good functioning of future citizens.

4.3 Discriminatory Speech

Let me now turn to discriminatory speech. Given that it is non-vilifying, there does not seem to be a good practicable way to legally proscribe or regulate such speech. My hope would be that the sort of cognitive therapy noted above can help undercut the prevalence and influence of discriminatory speech too. But apart from that, must we simply fight it with counter-speech in the 'marketplace of ideas'? I take this proposal to be too simplistic and naïve given how speech seemingly affects us. In fact, the eroding effects of discriminatory speech undermine the idea of a self-regulating 'marketplace of ideas' wholesale. Still, since discriminatory speech turns on stereotypical attitudes and ascriptions, we can act against their influence on further attitudes and subsequent behaviour. Some social psychological research suggests that we can control stereotype activation with certain egalitarian goals (Kawakami *et al.*, 2000; Moskowitz and Li, 2011). With practice and over time, it is possible to develop an associative link between the goal to be egalitarian, and a specific target group. This is just *an* example, of course, but my general point is this: research on stereotype activation suggests that we can act against the influence of stereotypes and stereotyping. One way in which we can do so is by implementing better structural and organisational arrangements. Think about hiring and teaching practices that make use of anonymous CVs and grading to undercut stereotype activation. Or ensuring that there is organisational awareness for those occupying certain roles: for instance, that by occupying certain positions (like being a professor) one has special duties toward one's students and younger colleagues to foster inclusion. Again, there is nothing *per se* illiberal about organisational and institutional (re)structuring with the aim to promote egalitarian goals, inclusion, integration, and fairness. Of course, this may be badly executed – but that is another matter.

These interventions are more indirect by targeting the grounds of discriminatory speech, and hence substantially different from the interventions discussed above regarding hate and toxic speech. This demonstrates just how complex an issue we are dealing with. But importantly (I hold), it once more highlights that the dichotomy of *do nothing* or *impose censorship* is false. There is much that can be done on structural and institutional levels too.

5. Philosophy as Vaccine?

In an editorial of *The Scotsman* in January 2021, philosophy was compared to a vaccine against examples of toxic speech like Trump 'the Winner':

> we are heading towards a new world in which philosophy and the ability to think logically become increasingly important. To use a current metaphor, we need to vaccinate ourselves against the

virulent lies of people like Trump and the best way to do that is to teach the wisdom of Socrates and co to our children.[7]

The idea that there is an antidote to toxic speech through philosophy might look immediately appealing – at least to many philosophers. I too used to think of philosophy and the ability to think critically as being akin to a sort of vaccine (or rather, a bullshit filter) that inoculates us against the influence of the speech examples I have focused on here. I no longer share my earlier optimism. Given how easily our cognitive abilities and faculties can be perverted – or given how rustable they are – different remedies are needed. But, as I have suggested in this paper, there are various remedies at our disposal when dealing with hate, discriminatory, and toxic speech, where these remedies are consistent with a liberal commitment to free speech. There is much that can be done with a more nuanced and less knee-jerk understanding of this commitment. Still, I hold, for liberal interventions to be effective, we must give up the idea of 'the marketplace of ideas', where we can debate as equals and where the truth will triumph. In thinking about the different sorts of prejudicial speech within a liberal framework, we should not consider our limitations, flaws, and non-ideal speech situations as distortions and perversions of the ideal marketplace that (somehow supposedly) came first. Rather, they are 'our' default modes of being and should be the starting point.

References

H. Battaly, 'Testimonial Injustice, Epistemic Vice, and Virtue Epistemology', in I.J. Kidd, J. Medina, and G. Pohlhaus Jr. (eds), *The Routledge Handbook of Epistemic Injustice* (NY: Routledge, 2017), 223–32.

D. Brink, 'Millian Principles, Freedom of Expression, and Hate Speech', *Legal Theory*, 7 (2001), 119–57.

A. Brown, 'What is Hate Speech? Part 1: The Myth of Hate', *Law and Philosophy*, 36 (2017a), 419–68.

A. Brown, 'What is Hate Speech? Part 2: Family Resemblances', *Law and Philosophy*, 36 (2017b), 561–613.

---

[7] https://www.scotsman.com/news/opinion/columnists/donald-trump-philosophy-antidote-dangerous-liars-us-president-scotsman-comment-3090608. Accessed 16 January 2024.

Prejudicial Speech

R. Delgado, 'Words that Wound: A Tort Action for Racial Insults, Epithets, and Name Calling', in M. Matsuda, C.R. Lawrence III, R. Delgado, and K. Crenshaw (eds), *Words that Wound: Critical Race Theory, Assaultive Speech, and the First Amendment* (Boulder, CO: Westview Press, 1993), 89–110.

S. Fish, *There's No Such Thing As Free Speech: And It's a Good Thing, Too* (NY: Oxford University Press, 1993).

S. Fish, 'Going in Circles with Hate Speech' (2012), *New York Times*, https://opinionator.blogs.nytimes.com/2012/11/12/going-in-circles-with-hate-speech/. Accessed 19 June 2021.

E. Fricker, 'Doing (Better) What Comes Naturally: Zagzebski on Rationality and Epistemic Self-Trust', *Episteme*, 13 (2016), 151–66.

K. Gelber, 'Differentiating Hate Speech: A Systemic Discrimination Approach', *Critical Review of International Social and Political Philosophy*, 24 (2021), 393–414.

K. Gelber and L. McNamara, 'Evidencing the Harms of Hate Speech', *Social Identities*, 22 (2016), 324–41.

K. Jones, 'The Politics of Intellectual Self-Trust', *Social Epistemology*, 26 (2012), 237–51.

K. Kawakami, J. Moll, S. Hermsen, J. Dovidio, and A. Russin, 'Just Say No (to Stereotyping): Effects of Training in the Negation of Stereotypic Associations on Stereotype Activation', *Journal of Personality and Social Psychology*, 78 (2000), 871–88.

I. Maitra and M.K. McGowan (eds), *Speech and Harm: Controversies over Free Speech* (Oxford: Oxford University Press, 2012).

M. Matsuda, C.R. Lawrence III, R. Delgado, and K. Crenshaw (eds), *Words that Wound: Critical Race Theory, Assaultive Speech, and the First Amendment* (Boulder, CO: Westview Press, 1993).

M. Mikkola, 'Self-Trust and Discriminatory Speech', in K. Dormandy (ed.), *Epistemology of Trust* (NY: Routledge, 2019), 265–90.

M. Mikkola, 'A Distortion or "Our" Default?', *Aristotelian Society Supplementary Volume*, 95 (2021), 143–62.

M. Mikkola, 'Discriminatory vs. Hate Speech: Wherein Lies the Difference?', in M. Popa (ed.), *Oppressive Speech and Society: Philosophical Perspectives* (NY: Routledge, forthcoming 2024).

J.S. Mill, *On Liberty* (London: Penguin, 1974).

J. Montmarquet, 'Epistemic Virtue and Doxastic Responsibility', *American Philosophical Quarterly*, 29 (1992), 331–41.

G.B. Moskowitz, and P. Li, 'Egalitarian Goals Trigger Stereotype Inhibition', *Journal of Experimental Social Psychology*, 47 (2011), 103–16.

Mari Mikkola

T. Scanlon, 'Freedom of Expression and Categories of Expression', *University of Pittsburgh Law Review*, 40 (1978–9), 519–27.
L. Tirrell, 'Discursive Epidemiology: Two Models', *Aristotelian Society Supplementary Volume*, 95 (2021), 115–42.
C. West, 'Words That Silence? Freedom of Expression and Racist Hate Speech', in I. Maitra and M.K. McGowan (eds), *Speech and Harm: Controversies over Free Speech* (Oxford: Oxford University Press, 2012), 222–48.

What Is It to Be Responsible for What You Say?

EMMA BORG

Abstract

In asserting something I incur certain kinds of liabilities, including a responsibility for the truth of the content I express. If I say 'After leaving the EU, the UK will take back control of c. £350 million per week', or I tell you that 'The number 14 bus stops at the British Museum', I become liable for the truth of these claims. As my audience, you could hold me unreliable or devious if it turns out that what I said is false. Yet this socio-linguistic practice – of acquiring and ascribing 'linguistic liability' – is complicated, especially given philosophical distinctions between the various different kinds of contents people can express (am I liable, for instance, for the claim that the number 14 bus stops at the British Museum *today* or only *usually*?). This paper explores the different kinds of contents speakers might be taken to express, arguing that our practices around linguistic liability (including in legal disputes) reveal a crucial role for a notion of context-independent, literal meaning attaching to words and sentences. These practices thus vindicate what philosophers tend to term 'minimal semantic content'.

1. Introduction

In 2017 US President Donald Trump stated that the crowd at his inauguration appeared to stretch 'all the way back to the Washington Monument'. Later Trump's Press Secretary, Sean Spicer, doubled down on this claim, telling reporters that 'This was the largest audience ever to witness an inauguration – period'. Many press outlets, however, disputed these statements. An article in the UK newspaper *The Guardian* (22 January 2017), for instance, reproduced photographs from the event and concluded that 'the evidence certainly seems to challenge Trump's assertion', while a *New York Times* piece the following day went further, stating that Mr Spicer's claim was 'clearly shown to be false' by the photographs.

Setting aside the political dimensions of these exchanges, the events lay bare a fundamental aspect of our linguistic practices: hearers assume that speakers aim to assert the truth and that speakers can be held culpable if what they say turns out not to be true. This connection between assertion and truth seems fundamental to our linguistic practices: it is only because an audience can assume that the speaker is aiming to assert what is true that hearers can use linguistic testimony to inform them about, and direct their interactions with, the world. If I want a cookie and you say 'There are cookies in the jar', I can act on what you say, using it to direct my cookie-hunting actions, only because I assume that you are telling the truth.

The interplay between meaning, communication, and truth is also fundamental to a number of philosophical theories. For instance, the Oxford philosopher of language Paul Grice held that, for communication to be possible at all, interlocutors need to be able to assume that their conversational partners are *cooperative*, i.e., that they are aiming to convey appropriate and true information (Grice, 1989). More recently another Oxford philosopher, Tim Williamson, has argued that truth provides the 'norm of assertion', whereby a speaker can only assert what they know to be true (Williamson, 1996). However, although the requirement to assert what is true seems philosophically and practically fundamental, on closer inspection the requirement turns out to be more complicated than we might initially have supposed. For in order to hold a speaker responsible for the truth of what they say there are two things we first need to know:

(1) What did the speaker say (i.e., what content did they assert)?
(2) What kind of responsibility is in play?

Answering these two questions, however, at least from the theoretical point of view, is far from straightforward. The aim of this paper is to explore this complexity and show how a proper understanding of our practices of holding speakers responsible for what they say can help to advance an entrenched philosophical dispute.

I start, in §2, by examining question (1), asking what kinds of content a speaker can be held to express in uttering what they do. As we will see, the three most plausible answers here line up with three different approaches in philosophy of language: first, so-called 'semantic minimalism' (which, as we will see, claims that well-formed declarative sentences express genuine, truth-evaluable content without significant appeal to the context in which they are uttered), second 'contextualism' (which holds that the key meanings are somewhat contextually enriched contents, ones which capture the content implicit in what a speaker says), and finally an approach drawn from the work of Paul Grice which focuses on what a speaker conversationally implies by what they say. One immediate question, however, concerns the relationship between these three different approaches: are they competitor accounts, or alternatively are they all needed for a complete account of what a speaker says? That is to say, do we really need to posit all three kinds of content which

What Is It to Be Responsible for What You Say?

the three different accounts posit, or is a more philosophically parsimonious approach possible? In this vein, advocates of contextualism have long argued that we can do without the kind of content proposed by semantic minimalists, that sentences stripped of contextual input do not (generally or perhaps ever) express a complete or worthwhile content. Furthermore (again, as we will see), minimalist content might be thought to rest on shaky foundations anyway since it requires the notion of context-insensitive word meaning, which itself looks pretty problematic. Trying to respond to this latter worry on behalf of the minimalist will push us, in §§3–4, to examine the notion of word meaning and the ways in which people arrive at an understanding of the content their words express. I'll suggest that words can be thought to have standing, context-insensitive meanings and that (given the right combination of subjective and objective approaches to linguistic meaning) those meanings are ones interlocutors can grasp. Thus, I'll argue that the existence of minimal *sentence-level* content should not be rejected on the basis of worries about minimal *word* meaning. In §5 I turn to question (2) and argue that (contra contextualist objections) minimalist content (the content delivered by putting standing word meanings together in grammatically acceptable ways) is in fact *required*, since it plays a crucial role in our practices of assigning and accepting linguistic responsibility. Getting clear on the kinds of linguistic responsibility in play (answering question (2)) turns out, I argue, to vindicate the minimalist's claim concerning the need for minimal content.

2. What Does a Speaker Say?

Consider the following toy exchange:

Abbie: Do you want to have lunch?

Bishma: I've eaten.

To decide what content Bishma is responsible for expressing here, we need to know what he has said. Yet it seems different answers to this question are possible. A first option would be to focus on the words Bishma has uttered and take him to be expressing the content that results simply from putting words with just these meanings together in just this order. So, it seems that Bishma might be taken to have asserted simply the claim that *I, Bishma, have eaten*. Notice that this minimal claim is true just in case Bishma has eaten *something* at *some time* in the past, it doesn't tell us anything further about what or when he's eaten (to see this, think about an utterance of 'I've eaten camel', where it's clearer that the speaker need not be committing to eating within a particular timeframe, see Sperber & Wilson, 1986, 189–90, or 'I've just eaten' which specifies a timeframe apparently without committing to a kind of thing eaten). If we understand Bishma as making this minimal assertion, it will turn out that he is a reliable and responsible speaker so long as he has eaten something at some point in the past, even if he hasn't eaten anything recently (i.e., in the run up to lunch today).

Alternatively, however, we might look to the wider context in which Bishma says what he does and treat some of those contextual features as affecting what Bishma says. For instance, given the context of Abbie's query about lunch, we might hold that Bishma asserts a richer content, something along the lines of *I have eaten lunch today* or *I have eaten recently*. Philosophers often label this kind of contextually enriched content an *explicature,* since it apparently makes explicit content that is implicit in the original utterance. In the above context, Bishma certainly doesn't convey the unrestricted claim that he has merely eaten at some time in the past, rather 'eaten' seems to convey the more contextually relevant idea that the speaker has *eaten recently.*

Third and finally, it seems we might look to an even more context-sensitive kind of content, focusing on the kind of move Bishma intends to make in the conversation. Assuming (as Grice suggested) that we view Bishma as aiming to be a cooperative conversational partner, it seems that we are entitled to assume that he is trying to provide an answer to Abbie's question. However, neither the minimal content (*Bishma has eaten*) nor the explicature content (*Bishma has eaten recently*) directly provides such an answer. We can, however, use the latter content to infer an answer: if Bishma has eaten recently it is reasonable to infer that *Bishma doesn't want lunch.* Thus we could hold that what Bishma says is a (polite) declining of the offer of lunch. Following Grice, philosophers tend to label this third kind of content an *implicature,* for it captures content that is merely implied by Bishma's utterance in this context. Implicature content is (usually) extremely context dependent: there are very many contexts in which an utterance of 'I've eaten' would not express a rejection of a lunch offer, but at least in the above context saying 'I've eaten' can be heard as saying *I won't have lunch with you.*[1]

---

[1] A possible exception to the greater context-sensitivity of implicatures is Grice's category of Conventional Implicatures where words themselves

What Is It to Be Responsible for What You Say?

Depending on how much we allow considerations drawn from the context of utterance to influence our judgements, then, it seems that there are three distinct candidates available to play the role of what is said:

Minimal contextual input	Medium contextual input (explicature)	Maximum contextual input (implicature)
Bishma has eaten.	Bishma has eaten *recently*.	Bishma doesn't want lunch.

These three options line up with the contents focused on by three different philosophical schools of thought. The idea that there is an important, truth-evaluable level of content which can be recovered simply by looking to the words a speaker produces and the way they are put together (plus some very limited contextual input, such as determining the referent of 'I' in our toy example) is argued for by a position known as 'semantic minimalism' (see, e.g., Borg 2004, 2012). According to semantic minimalism, looking just to word meaning and grammatical structure yields a genuine, truth-evaluable content (i.e., a content which makes a claim which, when held up against the world, can be assessed for truth or falsity) and it is a level of content to which speakers and hearers are sensitive. However, advocates of minimalism also acknowledge that this kind of content is not usually the content which speakers express, or are taken to express, in communicative exchanges. Instead, minimalists allow that, during the cut and thrust of communication, the key content is more often some sort of pragmatically enriched content (i.e., explicature or implicature content).

Given this concession, however, so-called 'contextualists' (or 'pragmaticists') – those who focus on explicature content – have argued that there is no need to posit minimal content (see, e.g., Levinson, 2000, p. 231; Carston, 2008, p. 366). Contextualists suggest that word meaning plus structure (sometimes or perhaps always) yields only a partial, indeterminate meaning, one which hearers are licensed to

---

are held to convey a further implicated content. For instance, Grice held that 'but' literally means the same as 'and', with both expressing a simple conjunction, yet every utterance of 'but' carries a conventional implicature to the effect that there is some contrast between the two conjuncts (as in 'She was poor but honest'), see Grice (1989). However, the category of Conventional Implicatures has proved controversial (see Bach, 2006).

enrich (or modulate in other ways) in order to arrive at a content which is better suited to the communicative exchange which is taking place. A very influential approach along these lines is 'Relevance Theory' (proposed by Sperber and Wilson, 1986; Carston, 2002) which holds that the content encoded in the words speakers' utter rarely (if ever) delivers the kind of complete, truth-evaluable content for sentences envisaged by semantic minimalists. Instead, they hold that hearers need to look to the context of utterance to retrieve a more relevant interpretation of the speaker's utterance (where 'relevant' is understood in a technical sense, as the interpretation which yields the most cognitive effects for the least processing effort). So, returning to our example above, the content recoverable just on the basis of word meaning and structure alone (*Bishma has eaten*) is held to be either incomplete (it can't be assessed as true or false as it stands) or irrelevant. Thus, hearers are required to recover a more relevant, enriched content, such as *Bishma has eaten recently*.

The contextualist idea that we don't need to be concerned with the claims made by sentences, independently of what they convey in particular communicative contexts, is reinforced by recognising that advocates of semantic minimalism face two significant problems:

i. If minimal content is what we get by paying attention to the literal meaning of words (and the way they are put together), then, in order to grasp the minimal content of a sentence we first need to know the literal content of the words it contains. Yet determining the literal, standing meaning of a word (and indeed whether such a thing exists at all) turns out to be a vexed issue.

ii. As noted above, advocates of minimal semantics accept that minimal content is not generally the content which hearers are concerned with recovering in normal conversational exchanges. Faced with Bishma's utterance, all parties agree that it is far more likely that hearers will focus on the explicature or implicature content, rather than the minimal claim that *Bishma has eaten something at some point in the past*. Yet why, the objection then is, should we bother positing minimal content at all, if it doesn't play any important role in communicative exchanges?

I explore objection (i) – that minimal sentence level content is impossible since there is no such thing as minimal word meaning – in the next two sections but conclude that there is a workable notion of minimal word meaning which advocates of semantic minimalism can appeal to. Finally, (in §5) I turn to objection (ii), arguing that an answer to it can be found by reflecting on our practices around assigning and assuming linguistic liability.

What Is It to Be Responsible for What You Say?

3. The Problems of Word Meaning

Intuitively, the question of how we know the ordinary meaning of a word seems easy to answer: if someone is a competent user of a language, we might expect that they can just reflect on what they know about their language (provided we are asking about a word they know) in order to deliver an account of the literal meaning of the word. After all, I relied on this kind of intuitive knowledge of word meaning when I suggested above that 'I' refers to the speaker and when I simply assumed that readers would be able to supply the meaning of 'eaten' or 'lunch'. However, just as with our grasp of what is said by a whole utterance, on reflection answering questions about word meaning seems tricky. For instance, take 'lunch': roughly speaking, 'lunch' refers to a meal taken between breakfast and dinner. But can a meal eaten at 15:00 (or even later) still count as 'lunch'? And what if someone just eats a packet of crisps or has a drink (is a 'liquid lunch' still a lunch)? And even if we all agree that a sandwich eaten at 13:00 does count as 'lunch', we then need to know what counts as a 'sandwich'? If Bishma told Abbie he wanted a sandwich and was then presented with a single piece of bread with cheese on top, would his request have been satisfied? What about if he is given an egg partially between two crackers? (See Searle, 1980.) Prima facie we might expect that a grasp of word meaning should allow us to settle questions about when to apply or to withhold a given expression, but it turns out that settling these kinds of questions is far from straightforward.

One attractive response here would be to object that the kinds of questions posed above about 'lunch' or 'sandwich' are unnecessarily picky and pedantic (the kind of thing only a philosopher with too much time on their hands might worry about), with little or no practical relevance. In fact, however, we don't have to look very far to see that these kinds of disputes about word meaning, and about what speakers can or cannot be taken to have asserted, can have serious practical repercussions. To see this, I want to briefly survey two legal disputes from the UK.

3.1 The meaning of 'widow'

The first example revolves around a piece of tax legislation: Section 262 of the Income and Corporation Taxes Act 1988 stated that, in certain circumstances, '[a] *widow* shall be entitled [...] to an income tax reduction [...]'. The circumstances in which the allowance came into effect, and the nature of the allowance itself, are not important here. Instead what matters for the current discussion is to whom the legislation refers. The problems about interpreting Section 262 first came to light when a widower, one Mr Crossland, brought a complaint under the European Commission of Human Rights, alleging breach of Article 14 (discrimination on the basis of sex). The UK tax authority (HMRC) reached an out-of-court settlement with Mr Crossland (paying him £572, the amount of the requested tax relief in his case). Subsequently, however, another widower, one Mr Wilkinson, brought a similar complaint but on this occasion HMRC rejected the claim. They agreed with the complainant that Section 262 was in breach of European law outlawing discrimination on the basis of sex, but they argued that HMRC was nevertheless warranted in enacting it as a matter of statute (arguing that if the UK government wished its tax policy to be compliant with European Human Rights regulation the government itself would have to alter the offending legislation, since it was not within HMRC's powers to contravene extant UK legislation). Mr Wilkinson appealed against this decision and his case was ultimately considered at the High Court. Part of Mr Wilkinson's case at the High Court trial was that Section 262 should in fact be read as applying to him directly, since the term 'widow' in this context should be read as meaning *widows and widowers* due to Section 6 of the Interpretation Act 1978, which states that 'unless the contrary intention appears [...] words importing the feminine gender include the masculine'.

The High Court, however, rejected all aspects of Mr Wilkinson's appeal, including this interpretative claim. The Court pointed out that draftsmen had no difficulty in finding gender neutral terms elsewhere, where there was a clear intention that passages should have the more inclusive reading. Furthermore, other sections of the Income and Corporation Taxes Act 1988 which were intended to apply to both widows and widowers explicitly stated this. Given these facts, Lord Hoffman (for the Court) stated that '[T]here is no way in which any reasonable reader could understand the word "widow" to refer to the more general concept of a surviving spouse'.[2] Section 262, then, the Court decided, had to be read in a way which placed it in contravention of European law (a fact which led to it subsequently being revoked).

[2] Wilkinson, R (on the application of) v. Inland Revenue [2005] UKHL 30 (5 May 2005), http://www.bailii.org/uk/cases/UKHL/2005/30.html.

What Is It to Be Responsible for What You Say?

3.2 The meaning of 'wife or husband'

The background to our second case, from 2002 (so pre-dating the legalisation of gay marriage in the UK), is that a landlord, Ghaidan, was granted repossession of a flat on the death of the tenancy holder (Wallwyn-James). This repossession order was granted even though the flat was occupied by Wallwyn-James' long-term homosexual partner, Godin-Mendoza. Had Wallwyn-James been survived by a partner of the opposite sex repossession would not have been ordered, as the right to assume a tenancy of those living with a deceased tenancy holder 'as wife or husband' was protected in law. Godin-Mendoza appealed his eviction, arguing that a ruling that homosexual relationships were not covered by UK tenancy laws was in breach of European Conventions. The High Court supported Godin-Mendoza's appeal, ruling that the key phrase in tenancy law – 'as his or her wife or husband' – should be taken to mean 'a relationship of social and sexual intimacy exemplified by, but not limited to, the heterosexual relationship of husband and wife'. In this case, then, the court ruled that the phrase 'wife or husband' was to be understood in the wide sense of *anyone performing the role typical of a wife or husband*.

At least *prima facie* this ruling seems in tension with our first case, where the judgement was that 'widow' could not be understood in the wider sense of 'surviving spouse', but, regardless of this apparent tension, what both cases make clear is that questions concerning the literal meaning of our words can have significant practical repercussions (indeed, as we will see below in the case of Derek Bentley, sometimes they can have the most dire of real-world repercussions).[3] So, regardless of the prospects for the philosophical approach of semantic minimalism, it seems that we need a notion of ordinary, literal word meaning (to help settle disputes like those surveyed in this section) and thus it would be good to have a firmer grip on how decisions about the ordinary meaning of an expression are, in fact, made. I explore this issue in the next section.

4. Methods for Determining the Literal Meaning of a Word

The idea that words carry ordinary, literal meanings seems appealing (as it is needed to settle disputes like those canvassed in the previous section, as well as for other reasons, such as explaining how children

---

[3] For an argument that the two verdicts are not in fact in conflict, see Hoffman's judgement on the case discussed in section 3.1.

learn a language, where the knowledge they acquire allows them to express and comprehend an indefinite number of novel word combinations on the basis of limited cognitive resources, see Borg, 2004). However, even if we assume that words do carry this kind of content, there remains an epistemic question about how language users come to know or can decide what the literal meaning of a word actually is. The most common methods for answering questions of word meaning are (as alluded to above) *subjective*: we simply ask what, as a speaker, we intended to mean by uttering some word or, on the other hand, we consider what we, as a hearer, take to be conveyed by the word the speaker produced (as Lord Hoffman apparently did when he pronounced on the meaning of 'widow'). Subjective approaches are by far the most common route for settling questions of word meaning but they can be problematic. For whenever the meaning of a word is contested and intuitions about word meaning diverge (as when we ask, 'What constitutes "lunch"?' or 'Can "widow" mean *surviving spouse?*') purely subjective routes leave us with no way to resolve disputes. A further worry is that subjective approaches face the challenge of 'humpty dumptyism' – so-called in recognition of Lewis Carroll's character of Humpty Dumpty in *Through the Looking Glass*, who stated that 'When I use a word it means just what I choose it to mean – neither more nor less'. Yet, clearly, we don't want speakers to be the final arbiters of what their words mean in this way (no matter how much I want to, I can't mean *dog* simply by saying 'cat').

In difficult or contested cases, then, it is common to appeal to more objective arbiters of word meaning. For instance, in both ordinary and legal cases, it is common for parties to consult dictionaries, where the definitions of meaning given in these works are taken to be authoritative. Once again, however, it seems that dictionary definitions can't be the whole story. For one thing, definitions may differ across different dictionaries (meaning that, in legal disputes, defence and prosecution teams often each have their own preferred dictionary). Secondly, dictionaries are unlikely to settle the kind of fine-grained interpretative issues that we saw arise in §3 (a dictionary is unlikely to tell us, for instance, whether a packet of crisps eaten at 15:00 falls within the extension of 'lunch').

Recognition of these limitations has led researchers to explore further kinds of objective approaches. For instance, so-called 'experimental philosophy' has investigated the use of experimental techniques to help identify the ordinary meaning of words, such as giving speakers questionnaires probing their views on the meaning of a target word or showing them short vignettes and asking whether a

What Is It to Be Responsible for What You Say?

target word would apply in the described situation or not (and then providing statistical analyses of the answers provided); see, e.g., Tobia (2020).[4] However, experimental techniques are often not practicable since they are time-consuming and expensive. Furthermore, a significant degree of expertise is required to construct experimental materials that properly probe word meaning without introducing confounds. An alternative objective method which has been growing in popularity in recent years (particularly as a tool for assessing the ordinary meaning of legal terms, see Mouritsen 2012; Lee & Mouritsen 2017; 2021; Gries, 2020) is Corpus Linguistics. Corpus Linguistics studies patterns of usage in large datasets of digitised texts, using specialised automatic processing software (e.g., Sketch Engine, WordSmith Tools) to reveal these patterns. Typical analyses include:

i. Frequency and keyword analysis.
ii. Collocations (words that appear together with the target word at above chance levels).
iii. Concordances (sample lines of text containing the target word).

To close our exploration of how we might uncover minimal word meaning, then, I want to look in a little more detail at how this kind of approach might help us get a grip on word meaning in a difficult case.

4.1 A corpus linguistics case study: 'hate speech'

The term 'hate speech' originated with legal theorists in the 1980s (primarily in the context of discussions about South Africa) to categorise harmful racist utterances. Many jurisdictions now have hate speech laws (though not all explicitly use the term); e.g. the UK Public Order Act 1986 – commonly considered a piece of hate speech legislation – states that 'A person who uses threatening, abusive or insulting words or behaviour, or displays any written material which is threatening, abusive or insulting, is guilty of an offence if—

(a) he intends thereby to stir up racial hatred, or
(b) having regard to all the circumstances racial hatred is likely to be stirred up thereby'.

[4] Although experimental philosophy as a school of thought is a relatively new approach, this kind of approach to word meaning has its roots in earlier work, in particular Austin's 'Ordinary Language' philosophy can be thought of as an early precursor (see Hansen, 2018).

Emma Borg

The expression 'hate speech', however, is now also widely used in public discourse (Brown, 2017, p. 424). Yet, this raises the question of whether the meaning of the term is the same in both legal and non-legal contexts. This question is important for a number of reasons: for instance, according to many theories of legal interpretation, the meaning of a legal term is a function of its ordinary meaning, thus grasping the ordinary meaning of 'hate speech' matters for questions of legal interpretation. Secondly, a key principle of a democratic system is that of 'fair notice', whereby citizens must know, or be able to easily find out, what the law demands of them. This requires that, as far as possible, words are used in legal contexts with their ordinary meanings. Finally, hate speech legislation should not lead to self-censorship of legitimate speech (Howard, 2019; 2021), i.e., it should avoid having a 'chilling effect' on legitimate speech. Again, this requires that the legal meaning of 'hate speech' coincides with its ordinary meaning. So, it is important that we are clear on the ordinary meaning of 'hate speech' and one recent suggestion is that Corpus Linguistics might help advance understanding on this matter.

To assess this claim, Lepoutre *et al.* (2023) ran a pilot corpus study to look at how 'hate speech' is used outside the legal realm. The study relied on two corpuses:

1. A general corpus (English Web 2020: enTenTen20): containing c. 38 billion words, drawn from English language internet domains 2019–2021. Main genres contained are blogs, discussions, and news articles, with some limited representation of legal sources.
2. A specialised 'hate speech' corpus: 255 news reports about hate speech related events, consisting of 164,183 words (retrieved from the Nexis database Lexis Library News, dating from 1990 to 2021). A range of UK media outlets, including 'serious press' and tabloids, national newspapers (e.g., *The Daily Mail*) and smaller regional ones (e.g., *The Belfast Telegraph*) were included.

Within (1) and (2), Lepoutre *et al.* assessed:

- frequency (how often 'hate speech' and related terms appeared)
- collocations (what expressions 'hate speech' appeared alongside)
- concordances (sample lines of text containing the term 'hate speech')

The analyses revealed that there has been a *huge* growth in the use of 'hate speech' terminology; e.g., in the Lexis Library News database

What Is It to Be Responsible for What You Say?

for British newspapers, in 1990–1995 there were 46 articles mentioning 'hate speech', in 2011–2015 there were 2753 articles, while in 2016–2020 this had shot up to 8024 articles. However, the phenomenal spread of the term was not the only finding of note. For instance, results showed that the public understanding of 'hate speech' is *wider* than the legal definition in the UK (e.g., it includes hateful speech based on gender, which UK law does not classify as 'hate speech'). On the other hand, however, the public use of 'hate speech' also seemed *narrower* than the legal definition in other respects (e.g, there was no evidence of hateful speech by a powerless minority against a powerful majority being classified as 'hate speech', although such speech could fall under the legal definition). Lepoutre *et al.* also found that the ordinary meaning of 'hate speech' involves more than 'offensive speech', with ordinary speakers often linking it to *incitement*. It seems that these empirical findings could play an ameliorative role. For instance, recognising that the public already classify problematic gender-based speech as 'hate speech' supports recent moves by the UK government to extend the legal definition in this direction, while the realisation that ordinary speakers do not simply classify all offensive speech as 'hate speech' helps to mitigate concerns about the chilling effect of hate speech legislation.

To conclude, then, whilst it seems that no single method for investigating ordinary word meaning is likely to provide a complete answer to questions about the ordinary meaning of our words, in contested cases it does seem that objective methods, like corpus analysis, may help to improve our understanding (Lee & Mouritsen, 2021, p. 358). When questions about the standing meaning of a word are raised, a mixture of subjective and objective methods should be used in order to triangulate on the most plausible analysis of the expression's ordinary meaning. Given this range of methods, though, I want to suggest that the first worry raised for minimal semantics (in §2) – that we don't have a way to determine literal, or minimal, word meanings – can be rejected.

However, this still leaves the second worry pending. Recall that the second objection to minimal content was that the literal, context-independent meaning of sentences was irrelevant as far as questions of communication were concerned. Even if there is a case to be made for needing to know about the ordinary, literal meaning of *words* (in order to resolve problem cases like the ones considered in §3), it is unclear that this will provide any support for the semantic minimalist's claim that we need to be concerned about minimal *sentence* contents (the contents that emerge just from putting words with those meanings together in that particular grammatical structure). If the

Emma Borg

contents which really matter for communicative exchanges are the contextually enriched contents of utterances (e.g., in our example of 'I've eaten' from §2, contents such as *I've eaten recently* or *I don't want to have lunch*), why, the objection remains, should we bother trying to discern some more context-free content? This brings us back to the question of the explanatory worth of minimal content and the answer I want to give is that the minimal contents generated by the literal meaning of words (plus sentential structure or grammar) matter because they are needed to answer certain questions that arise about linguistic liability.

5. Linguistic Liability

As noted at the outset, it seems that we have a practice of taking speakers to be responsible for the truth of what they assert. That is to say, speakers are generally held to have 'linguistic liability' for the contents they express – they can be held liable for what they say. However, as argued in Borg (2019) and Borg & Connolly (2022), it seems that our practices of acquiring and assigning linguistic liability are multifaceted. Specifically, it seems that there are two distinct varieties of linguistic liability:

i. Strict linguistic liability: a binary notion whereby a speaker either is or is not held liable for the *literal content* of the sentence, s, she uttered.
ii. Conversational linguistic liability: a matter of degree whereby a speaker is held more or less liable for some *non-literal content* via her utterance of s.

Compare two utterances of the sentence 'The train leaves at 11am': in the first scenario, imagine that a friend in Oxford has just asked me if I'll join him for lunch and I reply by saying 'I'm going to London today. The train leaves at 11am'. In the second scenario, imagine that I've phoned National Rail inquiries to ask about the next train to London today and an employee tells me 'The train leaves at 11am'. It seems that the kinds of liability operative in these two situations differs. In the first scenario, it seems that only conversational liability is in play – I'm trying to say that my train leaves at a time which makes having lunch together impossible, thus my hearer is unlikely to feel aggrieved if he finds out that the train I'm catching actually leaves at 10.56am or 11.03, or any other time roughly around 11am. On the other hand, however, when I speak to the rail employee, the standards of liability are much stricter. This time I'm entitled to hold the

What Is It to Be Responsible for What You Say?

speaker to the truth of what they literally say – if I arrive at the platform at 10.57 only to see the train departing, as it was actually scheduled for departure at 10.56, it seems I have every reason to feel aggrieved. In the above chat amongst friends about their lunch plans, liability goes along with the contextually enriched content, but in the exchange with the rail worker liability rests with literal content.

As with our earlier discussion of literal word meanings, this philosophical distinction is of more than merely academic interest. It is relevant both in ordinary exchanges like the ones above and in higher stakes disputes. For instance, consider the infamous 2012 'Twitter Joke Trial' (Chambers v Director of Public Prosecutions 2012). The background facts of this case were that a 26-year-old UK citizen, Paul Chambers, on learning that an airport from which he was due to travel was closed due to heavy snowfall, responded on Twitter with: *'Crap! Robin Hood airport is closed. You've got a week and a bit to get your s**t together otherwise I'm blowing the airport sky high!'*. Five days later, the duty manager of airport security read the tweet and communicated it to the police. Chambers was duly charged with, and subsequently convicted in a Magistrates Court of, 'sending a message of a menacing character' contrary to the Communications Act 2003. Chambers appealed this conviction, which was at first upheld in the Crown Court but eventually quashed at the High Court. At each stage of this case, we can see hearers' sensitivity to strict versus conversational liability. For instance, the airport security had a clear protocol for terrorist threats which required them to report any such material to the Ministry of Defence. The fact that they did not report Chambers' tweet in this way, when the literal content of 'I'm going to blow the airport sky high' would undoubtedly qualify as such a threat, shows that they did not apply standards of strict liability: they did not take Chambers to be liable for the literal content of his utterance. On the other hand, the fact that they still reported the tweet to the police shows that they thought Chambers could be held strongly conversationally liable for some non-literal threatening content, a judgement that was upheld by both the Magistrate and the Crown courts (where judges asserted that the tweet was 'clearly menacing'). The High Court, on the other hand, whilst agreeing that Chambers was not liable for the strict literal content of his utterance, also judged him not to be conversationally liable for any threatening content, stating that 'the more one reflects on it, the clearer it becomes that this message did not represent a terrorist threat, or indeed any other form of threat [...]. The language and punctuation are

Emma Borg

inconsistent with the writer intending it to be or to be taken as a serious warning'. If we want to explain the basis of these various different judgements in the Twitter Trial we need both to recognise that different kinds of linguistic liability can be assigned and that one kind of liability judgement tracks the sort of strict, literal content proposed by semantic minimalists.

Finally, it seems that sometimes the question of whether to attribute strict linguistic liability to a speaker or instead to hold them only to a more pragmatic (including, in the case to be discussed, idiomatic) content can have the most serious of consequences. One such case concerns the prosecution (in the UK in 1953) of Derek Bentley for the murder of a policeman. Bentley, who was aged just 18 at the time of the offence, was involved in an attempt to rob a warehouse with an accomplice, Christopher Craig (aged 16). However, police were alerted during the attempted break in and the first policeman who arrived on the scene (Frederick Fairfax) was able to grab hold of Bentley, at which point Craig drew the gun he was carrying. All parties agreed that Fairfax shouted 'Give me the gun lad', at which point Bentley allegedly replied with a key phrase: 'Let him have it Chris'. Soon after Fairfax's utterance, Craig fired the gun, hitting and injuring Fairfax. A short time later he shot and killed another policeman, Sidney Miles.

At the criminal case, Bentley's legal team denied that Bentley had ever uttered the words 'Let him have it'. However, they also argued that, even if Bentley were believed to have uttered the phrase in question, the meaning of the utterance in this context would have been *Let the policeman have the firearm Chris*. On the contrary, the prosecution team argued that the correct interpretation was an incitement to violence: *Shoot him Chris*. In the end, both Craig and Bentley were found guilty of the murder of Sidney Miles under the legal rule of Joint Enterprise. Craig, as he was under 18, was sentenced to be detained at Her Majesty's Pleasure (eventually being released ten years later). Bentley, on the other hand, was sentenced to death. Bentley made an unsuccessful appeal and, despite a public outcry, he was executed by hanging in January 1953. Following a 40-year campaign by his family, however, Bentley received a posthumous pardon in 1993 and his conviction was finally overturned in 1998.

Bentley's case is clearly extremely disturbing, but it does throw into sharp relief the importance that settling questions of linguistic liability can have. Should Bentley have been taken to be responsible for the conversational, idiomatic content (*Shoot him*) or instead for a literal interpretation (along the lines of *give it – the salient object – to the policeman*)? And what factors could, or should, jurors have looked to when considering this question? While the conditions which dictate the appropriateness of either strict or conversational liability attributions are no doubt highly complex and hard to state (see Borg & Connolly, 2023), and we might well query whether the jury in this case got things right, what cases like this one demonstrate is the need for ordinary interlocutors to clearly distinguish different kinds of linguistic liability and for researchers to work to clarify how the standards of linguistic liability get decided in different contexts.

Along with more everyday practices (such as understanding the differences between lying, misleading, and merely loose talk, see Borg, 2019) these legal cases demonstrate that:

- Ordinary speakers are adept at making different kinds of liability judgements, where these judgements are sensitive to different kinds of content.
- Some judgements of linguistic liability are strict and strict judgements require a grasp of minimal content.

Contra the irrelevancy objection to minimal semantics (raised as objection (2) in §2), then, it seems clear that, from both a practical and a theoretical perspective, we do need to recognise minimal content. While it may not capture the content that is most commonly at play in communicative exchanges, we need to keep track of the content a speaker expresses simply on the basis of the literal meaning of their words and the way those words are put together because, at least sometimes, this is the content which speakers acquire liability for. Our practices around assigning and accepting linguistic liability, then, provide a clear explanatory role for minimal content. When Donald Trump said that the crowd for his inauguration stretched 'all the way back to the Washington Monument' the journalists reporting him held him to a standard of strict linguistic liability, holding him responsible for the truth of what he literally said, a content shown to be false by photographic evidence that the crowd stopped far short of the Monument.

6. Conclusion

Generally, we hold speakers to be responsible for the truth of what they say. This practice is crucial to the role that language plays in our lives, for without it we would be unable to use the testimony of others to direct our interactions with the world and to further our understanding. However, although from a practical perspective we usually have little problem fixing on the contents to which we should hold speakers committed, from a theoretical perspective things are less clear. For to hold someone responsible for what they say, we first need to know:

1. The content of what they say.
2. The sense of responsibility in play.

The most common methods for assessing (1) are subjective: generally, it is intuitively clear what a given speaker should be held to have said in a given context. As we have seen, however, a simple appeal to subjective intuitions may be inadequate in difficult or contested cases. Once we start wondering about what exactly a word means, and what worldly states of affairs it does or doesn't apply to, it can begin to seem that we lack appropriate resources for settling these questions. In response, I suggested (§4) that we should investigate the options for more objective routes to word meaning, looking not just at what one or two interlocutors might suggest about word meaning but surveying assumptions about meaning across a population (e.g., via running experiments about ordinary meaning or conducting corpus analyses). Although no one method is likely to prove decisive, by gathering evidence about what a wide sweep of ordinary language users think about the meaning of some contested term, we can help to balance out the idiosyncrasies and peculiarities of individual language users, arriving at robust analyses of the ordinary, standing meaning of our words.

Furthermore, getting clear on ordinary, literal meaning matters because some perfectly standard practices around assigning liability *depend* on this kind of content. We sometimes take speakers at their word: we apply standards of *strict linguistic liability* and (contra the contextualist objection that minimal semantic contents have no explanatory role to play) this requires hearers to be sensitive to the content that emerges from the literal meaning of words plus the grammatical structure of sentences. I suggest, then, that understanding the different ways in which someone can be held responsible for what they say reveals the explanatory need for minimal content (even whilst we recognise that in the cut and thrust of communication it is often non-minimal content which is to the fore).

Acknowledgement

Research for this work was supported by a Leverhulme Trust Major Research Fellowship MRF-2019-031.

What Is It to Be Responsible for What You Say?

References

Kent Bach, 'The Top Ten Misconceptions about Implicature', in Betty Birner and Gregory Ward (eds), *Drawing the Boundaries of Meaning: Neo-Gricean Studies in Pragmatics and Semantics in Honor of Laurence R. Horn* (Amsterdam: John Benjamins, 2006), 21–30.

Emma Borg and Patrick Connolly, 'Strict and Conversational Linguistic Liability: Some Empirical Observations', in Ernest Lepore and David Sosa (eds), *Oxford Studies in Philosophy of Language* (Oxford: Oxford University Press, 2022), 1–22.

Emma Borg, *Minimal Semantics* (Oxford: Oxford University Press, 2004).

Emma Borg, *Pursuing Meaning* (Oxford: Oxford University Press, 2012).

Emma Borg, 'Explanatory Roles for Minimal Content', *Noûs*, 53:3 (2019), 513–39.

Alexander Brown, 'What is Hate Speech? Part 1: The Myth of Hate', *Law and Philosophy*, 36:4 (2017), 419–68.

Robyn Carston, *Thoughts and Utterances* (Oxford: Blackwell, 2002).

Robyn Carston, 'Review of *Minimal Semantics*', *Mind & Language*, 23:3 (2008), 359–67.

Paul Grice, *Studies in the Way of Words* (Cambridge, MA: Harvard University Press, 1989).

Stefan Gries, 'Corpora and Legal Interpretation: Corpus Approaches to Ordinary Meaning in Legal Interpretation', in Malcolm Coulthard and Alison Johnson (eds), *Routledge Handbook of Forensic Linguistics,* 2nd edition (London: Routledge, 2020), 628–43.

Nathaniel Hansen, '"Nobody Would Really Talk That Way!" The Critical Project in Contemporary Ordinary Language Philosophy', *Synthese*, 197:6 (2018), 2433–64.

Jeffrey Howard, 'Dangerous Speech', *Philosophy & Public Affairs*, 47:2 (2019), 208–54.

Jeffrey Howard, 'Terror, Hate, and the Demands of Counterspeech', *British Journal of Political Science*, 51:3 (2021), 924–39.

Thomas Lee and Stephen Mouritsen, 'Judging Ordinary Meaning', *Yale Law Journal*, 127:4 (2017), 788–879.

Thomas Lee and Stephen Mouritsen, 'The Corpus and the Critics', *University Chicago Law Review*, 88:2 (2021), 275–366.

Emma Borg

Maxime Lepoutre, Sara Vilar-Lluch, Emma Borg, and Nat Hansen, 'What is Hate Speech? The Case for a Corpus Approach', *Criminal Law and Philosophy*, (2023).

Stephen Levinson, *Presumptive Meanings: The Theory of Generalized Conversational Implicature* (Cambridge, MA: MIT Press, 2000).

Stephen Mouritsen, 'Hard Cases and Hard Data', *Columbia Science & Technology Law Review*, 13:1 (2012), 156–205.

John Searle, 'The Background of Meaning', in John Searle, Ferenc Keifer, and Manfred Bierwisch (eds), *Speech Act Theory and Pragmatics* (Dordrecht: Reidel, 1980), 221–32.

Dan Sperber and Deirdre Wilson, *Relevance: Communication and Cognition* (Oxford: Blackwell, 1986).

Kevin Tobia, 'Testing Ordinary Meaning', *Harvard Law Review*, 134:2 (2020), 726–806.

Timothy Williamson, 'Knowing and Asserting', *The Philosophical Review*, 105:4 (1996), 489–523.

On Discussing What We Should Do

JANE HEAL

Abstract

Many of the good things which make human life worthwhile are essentially social, cannot be enjoyed by one person unless they are enjoyed together with others. And it is obvious that thinking in terms of the first-person plural, we/us, plays a large part in everyday life as people consider puzzlements ('What should we do?') and remark on the success of what they decided on ('That worked out really well for us!'). Analytic philosophers should accept this at face value, recognising that human beings are often co-subjects with each other, that there is irreducible plural intentionality. The paper explores how the existence of plural intentionality manifests itself in our concepts and ways of proceeding and how attempted 'analysis' of what goes on as the assemblage of many interlocking instances of singular intentionality distorts and misleads.

1. Introduction

There are good things which a person cannot enjoy except together with other people who also enjoy them. Let us call these 'essentially social goods'. One small-scale example is being a member of a successful domestic partnership. You cannot be happily partnered all on your own. Those who are trying to realise or sustain an essentially social good may be uncertain of or disagree about the way forward. And then they are faced with the question 'What should we do?' This paper is about how to conceptualise this question and, relatedly, the nature of the discussion which is needed to address it.

A great deal of what goes on in everyday life, its puzzlements, reflections, decisions, actions, and enjoyments, is naturally reported by sentences with plural subject terms. 'We didn't know whether to do such and such. But we reflected on it and decided to do it. And it worked out well for us. We really enjoyed it.' On the surface, remarks such as these record instances of what we may call 'plural intentionality', people being co-subjects of puzzlements, reflections, decisions, actions, and enjoyments.

But much of our tradition since the 17th century, in philosophy of action, mind, and value, assumes that in understanding intentionality the first-person singular has priority. It takes for granted that 'What should I do?' must be the fundamental practical question in life and

Jane Heal

that all intentional goings on belong, fundamentally, to singular subjects. This assumption generates pressure to deny that everyday remarks containing the plural term 'we/us' can be taken at face value, as brief and accurate reports of instances of irreducible plural intentionality. Rather (suggests this familiar habit of thinking), they are to be construed as convenient (perhaps in practice unavoidable) shorthand for talking about what would be more accurately (if far more lengthily) reported as assemblages of instances of singular intentionality.

Recent years have seen a revival of interest in the first-person plural and there has been much discussion of plural (or as it is sometimes called 'collective') intentionality, asking what is distinctively plural about, for example, our intending that we do something together. Some say that that what is distinctively plural about it is confined to what is intended, in that each of us, singly, has the intention that we should act together. Others say that what is distinctively plural is the mode, in that each of us, singly, is engaged in we-intending that we act together. Both of these ways of conceptualising matters accept the mainstream prioritisation of singular subjects for intentionality. The third option breaks free of this and says that what is distinctively plural is what does the intending, namely us, as co-subjects.[1]

This paper explores a version of the third option, focusing on the example of a partnership and using this small-scale case to get the logical structure of some ideas on the table. If there are essentially social goods at medium and large scale as well, as is highly plausible, the ideas will have ramifications for thinking about issues in social and political philosophy. But that is a further topic.

Here is an outline of what follows. The paper introduces two situations where questions about action arise. One involves two people in a partnership addressing the question 'What should we do?' and the other involves a single person on their own addressing the question 'What should I do?'. Next, and taking the questions in reverse order, it reminds us of the kind of thinking they may lead to, sketching a reflective monologue for the single person and a reflective dialogue for the partners. It considers how the subject matter and

---

[1] Raimo Tuomela and Margaret Gilbert are pioneering thinkers in this area and much of what is said by them is congenial to the approach of this paper. But engaging seriously with their work takes us rapidly into elaborate and quasi-technical debates and so risks obscuring the ideas I would like to highlight. For references to their work and much further work in this area see David P. Schweikard and Hans Bernhard Schmid (2021).

structure of the monologue reveal that the thing that is thinking the thoughts it articulates is a single persisting human being. The same strategy applied to the dialogue then reveals that the thing that is thinking the thoughts it articulates should be understood as plural, the partners together. Finally, the paper makes a few observations about what this account suggests about the role of remarks in the dialogue and so about the role of language in our lives more broadly.

2. A Disagreement

So here is one case to be considered. You and I are partners. By and large we get on well, are happy that we are together. But an occasion arises on which we find ourselves disagreeing about what to do. An opportunity opens up for us to do some tandem paragliding, an activity which would be exciting but also carries some risks. You are keen that we should do it but I am reluctant and think that we should not. To you the thrill of our seeing the landscape from above is vividly apparent. To me the possibilities of feeling vertigo, landing badly and one of us breaking a limb, are all unpleasantly prominent. Gazing at each other in dismay at our disagreement, 'What should we do?' we wonder.

The word 'should' as used here does not indicate that you and I are about to get into a debate as to 'what is morally required'. It is possible to describe a situation in which the question of our paragliding could easily be labelled 'moral'. For example, perhaps our disagreement hinges on whether we should put money in the pocket of the entrepreneur who is arranging the activity. I think this person is unscrupulous and no one should deal with his company. You take another view. But let us disregard that kind of scenario and concentrate on versions of the story where issues about 'morality' (whatever exactly that means) do not seem pressing and where our disagreement has to do with which course of action would make things go better for us, would enable us to flourish more.

3. Another Conflict

What we need to note now is that a single person may face a difficulty analogous to the one just sketched. It is not true that people have complete and privileged first-person information about what will make things go well for them. It is not the case that, when other people are not affected by the choice and 'moral' issues do not arise, then a person will find it obvious what to go for. For sure,

Jane Heal

each of us probably does have a good deal of knowledge about what would make things go well for us. But we also say things like 'I had no idea that such and such could be worthwhile for me until I tried it' or 'It was only after I lost so and so that I grasped how much I had been undervaluing it'. Remarks of these kinds show that we appreciate that we can be ignorant of and mistaken about substantive questions of what promotes our welfare. A corollary of this is that a person may be confused and conflicted about how much importance to give to this or that possible element in their lives. A person in this situation needs a better understanding of what would make things go well for them, a better grasp of what their own capacities, together with the rest of the world, offers to them.

To make this vivid, consider a different me from the earlier one. This me is unpartnered and is confronted with a first-person singular version of a choice involving excitement and risk. I have an opportunity for solo paragliding but am undecided whether or not to take it up. I longingly contemplate the excitement it offers, but I also nervously recoil at the risk of bodily injury which it brings. I dither, am unpleasantly conflicted. 'What should I do?' I wonder.

4. Two Courses of Reflection: A Monologue and A Dialogue

How might things go in attempts to answer these questions, 'What should I do?' and 'What should we do?' Here are a monologue and a dialogue, to remind us of the kinds of reflection which people may engage in as they try to understand more of what is at stake for them in the options between which they are choosing.

This is the monologue, engaged in by the singular me:

> Paragliding would be thrilling. How strange it would be to see the landscape, the traces of old villages and field systems, from above, while hanging in mid-air, supported just by the glider, being able to control it as it rides the air currents! But what if it goes wrong? What if it induces vertigo, if some silly push on the control gear leads to a crash, a broken leg? Help! Help! No! But wait. How difficult would the control be? It is said to be manageable. Backing out of other things has left regrets. Certainly it would not do to overlook risks completely. That would be silly. But perhaps practice in confronting risks might lead to being, rightly, less frightened? Then many interesting options would open up!

And this is the dialogue between you and the other me who is your partner.

On Discussing What We Should Do

You: Paragliding would be thrilling. How strange it would be to see the landscape from above, while hanging in mid-air, supported just by the glider, being able to control it as it rides the air currents! You could identify and point out interesting archaeological features.

Me: Wow! I'd never thought of that! But what if it goes wrong? What if I feel vertigo, if some silly push on the control gear leads to a crash, to your getting a broken leg? Just imagining it makes me feel very anxious.

You: Well, how difficult would the control really be? It is said to be manageable. I have a good head for heights. You've backed out of other things before and regretted it later. I know that I can be a bit rash and it would be silly not to check on risks. I appreciate your doing that. But perhaps I could help you be a bit less timid about some things? Think of what that would make possible!

5. The Monologue and Its Implicit Subject

The words in which the monologue is articulated do not include any terms referring to who will do the various activities mentioned or feel the emotions. A different monologue might start 'Paragliding would be thrilling for Laura. How strange she would find it to see the landscape from above ...'. And it could end with the monologist resolving to buy a paragliding voucher for Laura. But the absence of a term like 'Laura' means that, for making explicit the subject of the activities and emotions mentioned in the actual monologue, the only possible insertion is the first-person pronoun. 'Paragliding would be thrilling for me. How strange I would find it to see the landscape from above ...' and so on. So the first thing to note about the monologue is that for it to be about me, the thinking articulated does not need to include explicit exercise of the first-person concept. The concepts exercised in the thoughts, together with the absence of a concept like 'Laura', combine to fix that the thoughts are about how things are for me and what I should do. If the thoughts do include explicit exercise of the first-person concept, and the monologue correspondingly includes 'I/ me', the token reflexivity of the first-person marks the fact that the subject of the thoughts, in the sense of what they are about, is also the subject of the thoughts in the sense of what thinks them.

Jane Heal

What further can we say about this subject of these thoughts in both senses, the 'I' who is contemplating going paragliding?

Let us set aside radical scepticism, of the kind which takes it that we can make sense of there being thoughts which are both exercises of whatever substantive concepts make them the thoughts they are while being also, at the same time, so out of touch with the world that, except for the concept 'thinking', the substantive concepts are all empty. Instead of this scepticism we shall assume that where there are thoughts, they will, despite mistakes being made, enable whatever thinks them to be helpfully aware of a fair amount of what is going on. So we shall assume that the kinds of concepts used in the thoughts have true applications and the general conception of the world thus presupposed in the thoughts is rightly not doubted by the thinker. Given such non-scepticism, this general conception can be unpacked by exploring what is taken for granted in use of the particular concepts, including the unhesitating movements of thought which deployment of those concepts makes intelligible. Let us note also that non-scepticism requires that whatever is thinking is an occupant of the world, is part of the totality of what there is. The non-scepticism thus means that the nature of whatever is thinking will be revealed, along with the nature of the rest of the world in which it lives, by the unpacking of the presuppositions.

Applying these ideas to the monologue, one thing which is evident is that the thinker of the monologue takes for granted that it is an embodied being in a spatial world. These are the presuppositions of the possibility of its being up in the air, of its having legs which can be broken. Secondly, it takes for granted that it has existed in the past, may exist into the future, and that things can go well or badly for it. These are the presuppositions of there being things in the past which it regrets and of there perhaps being things in the future which it will regret. Thirdly, it takes for granted that it can act, to influence how things go, including with itself, so as to make things go well, at least in some respects. These are the presuppositions of its conceiving the project of making itself less timid and thereby becoming able to engage in worthwhile new activities.

In summary, the thinker of the monologue is revealed (unsurprisingly!) to be a person, an ordinary functioning human being, complex and changing but continuing to act and persist through change.

It is a familiar fact that philosophical reflection, in the analytic tradition, has trouble with this kind of complex, persisting but changing being. It supposes that we can dig into, 'analyse', the idea of a person. It equips us with, and encourages us to use, various sceptical and fragmenting tools for thinking about the kind of complexity and

On Discussing What We Should Do

change which persons exhibit. The use of the tools seems to reveal each of us to be many separable items which need to be somehow assembled and stuck together if the familiar being is to exist. To take just one example, fragmentation may be driven by the grip of the idea that what exists at one time must be separable metaphysically from what exists at another time. This idea suggests construing the existence of a person over time as the existence of a succession of separable items, person-stages or temporary selves, which are somehow bundled or linked. So in the monologue (again taking just one example of the kind of speculation encouraged) we may be led to distinguish whatever speaks at the start and is excited, from whatever expresses itself in the middle and is frightened, and also from a possible future being which is less frightened. And so on.

This is not the place to engage in sustained discussion of the metaphysics of persons and personal identity. Here I want only to offer two observations. The first is this. Irrespective of exactly what account the fragmenting strategy offers, deployment of intellectual resources in trying to think in the terms it recommends is likely to have disadvantageous consequences.

For example, entertaining the fragmented picture of each of us consisting of a sequence of 'selves' requires trying to make sense of questions such as 'How does the present self relate to the future self?' and 'Why should the present self care about any future self?'. These questions are puzzling and the answers are not obvious. If we take them to be, nevertheless, meaningful and important, then their obscurity has the corollary of making the familiar idea of the persisting person seem dubious, not an idea the thinker can call on unhesitatingly when reflecting on how things are and what to do. And that in turn brings discouragement and disempowerment in pursuing enterprises which are long-term and demanding.

To see all this in action, consider my undertaking the enterprise of making myself less timid by confronting, in ways which will surely be stressful, things which I now find frightening.

An initial puzzlement brought by thinking in fragmented terms is making sense of the enterprise and what its success could be. Before the fragmenting ideas are introduced, one aspect of the future good is envisaged as being able to think 'I did it!' on touching down from my first and enjoyable paragliding. But, on the fragmented picture, an intelligible focus for these triumphant feelings is elusive. The future self is not what confronted and worked on the fears. And how is 'An earlier self did it!' a proper focus of current triumph? Moreover, to the extent that the separateness of the future self seems intelligible, it seems to become optional for the present self to care about it. Hence any present inclination to think 'Why bother?' is strengthened, and grip and urgency drain away from the long-term and difficult project of self-change. But if determined efforts to engage in self-transformation are not resolutely pushed through, self-development and the bolder new activities will not occur. Instead what will occur are a succession of shorter-term, less difficult, activities, with the limitations on possible satisfactions which they can offer.

The claim that the present self ought to care altruistically for the future self does not seem of the right logical shape to engage with this. Rather, what might block these developments is disengagement from the fragmented picture and reversion to unhesitating use of the familiar concept of the persisting person. That allows it to become vivid to me that I am short-changing myself by my timidity. The options available to me are only two, becoming a more resolute person or chickening out again. My thinking resources flow in channels shaped by this way of conceptualising the situation and do not get diverted into side-channels shaped by conceptualisations on which the claims of any future self are up for appraisal and possible rejection.

Thinking in terms of the unified, persisting, complex and changing person also makes evident the possibility and value of a kind of reflection which is disadvantageously backgrounded on the fragmented view. This is exploration of the capacities for excitement and fear, both of them aspects of the one persisting me. What exactly am I excited by or frightened of, and why? How are the responses of excitement and fear related? Which of those responses do I find, on reflection, excessive or feeble? The result of such reflection may be a richer appreciation of the world and how my capacities for both excitement and fear, and indeed their subtle interdependencies, are among the things which enable me to live a good and interesting life.

So that is the first observation about the fragmenting strategy. Thinking in the terms it encourages is disadvantageous.

The second observation is this. What is right about fragmenting accounts, what gives them their appeal, can be acknowledged without making concessions to the metaphysical picture of 'separate existences' which they call on. One thing these accounts rightly draw attention to is that our conceptions of how things are and what is worth doing are not fully coherent. We have many muddled thoughts and conflicting impulses. Another thing fragmenting accounts remind us of is that there is no guarantee that any one of us will retain our full range of capacities for complex and integrated awareness of time and possible actions. Perhaps you or I will become more thoughtless and impulsive, lose our memories, become demented or what not. And if that happens then we will cease to be so robustly present in the world as persons who can be talked to, reasoned with, co-operated with in long-term projects, although we may still be present to be fed or given a hug. And finally the fragmenting accounts are also right to point out that we face interesting questions about the future. It is possible and sensible to ask 'How much should I care about next year and what aspects of my future should concern me?'

But, and here is the crucial point, none of these facts about us show that there is a more accurate account to be got, by the use of sceptical and fragmenting tools, which reveals each of us to be an assemblage of simpler, more robust, less conflicted items. There are other ways of thinking about the facts noted. For example, as to how much to care about the future, the fragmenting account is right that we can care too much. Being demanding and long-term is not always a mark of merit in an enterprise. Instead, it may be a mark of grandiosity or lack of insight into one's finitude. We can short-change ourselves by not relishing enough what is available right now as well as by failing to be resolute in pursuit of some long-term goal. But puzzlement about how to choose between the difficult and problematic long-term on the one hand, and the easy and straightforward short-term on the other, need not be conceptualised in terms of how much the present self should care about the future self. Instead, it can be seen as about what kinds of life are available to the one persisting me. What comes to light with the puzzlement may be an example of a kind of conflictedness, perhaps unavoidable and irresoluble, which we find ourselves liable to because we are beings who can become aware of our temporality.

In short, we can accommodate all the facts equally well if we stick with the idea that we are embodied, unified and persisting, provided we recognise at the same time that we are muddled, conflict-prone, and easily damaged. And my suggestion is that this offers a fruitful and honest way of conceptualising the situation.

6. The Dialogue and Its Implicit Subjects

So now to the dialogue. Here are the ideas to be carried forward from consideration of the monologue. Thoughts may be had by and be about an implicit subject which is not referred to by any explicit conceptual element in those thoughts. Given non-scepticism, the nature of any such implicit subject (or subjects) can be unpacked by

Jane Heal

exploring what is presupposed in the kinds of concepts used and in the unhesitating movements of thought which those concepts make intelligible. Employment of sceptical and fragmenting tools is a prominent part of our tradition but brings puzzles and disadvantages with it. And there may be alternative non-fragmenting ways of accommodating the facts to which fragmenting accounts draw attention.

If we consider the dialogue, bearing these ideas in mind, what comes to light? The dialogue does not contain the words 'we' or 'us'. But these words are what are required if the subject of some of the concepts, in the sense of what the thinking is about, is to be made explicit. To whom would the paragliding be thrilling? Us. Who would engage in the new activities made possible by my becoming less timid? We would. And so on. 'We/us' slides easily into the dialogue and has a role in making explicit its subject matter analogous to that of 'I/me' for the monologue.

So whose thinking is articulated in the dialogue? Pursuing the analogy with the monologue, the indexicality of 'we/us' gives the answer that it is our thinking which is displayed. We are the co-subjects of the reflections set out. Seen this way, the dialogue presents an instance of a distinctive and irreducible kind of intentionality, namely plural intentionality, of which the actions, enjoyments and so on to which it leads are also instances.

Could this be the right way of looking at things? A couple of remarks to clarify the question. First, by 'plural intentionality' I do not mean what is sometimes called 'group intentionality'. The question is not whether groups of people, partnerships, governments, or businesses for example, can judge, act, be held responsible and so forth. The kind of intentionality envisaged with that idea is another kind of singular intentionality, attributed to things which may be, in some sense, 'agents' but are not individual people. Its existence and nature are an excellent topic, but not the one under consideration here.[2]

And secondly, our question is not whether the thinking of two people is articulated in the dialogue. The answer to that is obvious. Of course it is. Your thinking is expressed and my thinking is expressed.

The obviousness of this fact may seem to support the idea that singular intentionality is fundamental, that what goes on is most

---

[2] For more about group agents see *Group Agency: The Possibility, Design, and Status of Corporate Agents* by Christian List and Philip Pettit (2011).

accurately understood as an assemblage of metaphysically separable instances of singular intentionality, in each of which the other person may appear as an object of thought but cannot be present as a subject.

But the availability of focusing on what I express and what you express, does not settle the question in favour of this view. Consider the analogous move for the monologue. Is thinking at different times articulated in it? Of course it is. There is the thinking at the beginning, where excitement is prominent, the thinking in the middle which foregrounds the dangers, and so on. But the availability of this way of looking at things does not settle matters in favour of viewing a person as constructed from a succession of separable selves or person-stages. On the contrary, the kinds of action which come up for consideration, how those actions are appraised, what decisions are made, the responses of apprehension or triumph which following events may evoke, are all shaped by the concept of a persisting, embodied person and presuppose the existence of such a thing. The viewpoint of the monologue is that of such a person, the 'I/me' who is its subject in both senses. That is what the reflections of the previous section aimed to make vivid.

Looking at the dialogue in this light reveals that the same is true of it, when 'we/us' is put in place of 'I/me'. The viewpoint of the dialogue is that of 'we/us'. The actions which come up for consideration are joint enterprises such as our going paragliding, our working together so that I become less timid and our doing the things which then become possible. And the reasons for undertaking these actions are that we may benefit. And it is our triumph which we will celebrate, as we say with satisfaction 'We did it!' on touching down from our first tandem paragliding.

Continuing the comparison with the monologue, we saw that the ability to occupy the viewpoint of the single persisting subject, and to reap the advantages which that brings, is undermined by attempts to reconstruct what goes on in terms of the fragmented picture. Analogous observations can be made about the co-subjects of the dialogue. It is corrosive and disadvantageous to us to set aside the idea of our being co-subjects and to focus instead on representing what goes on in the terms offered by the 'only singular subjects' view. Working in terms of the 'singular subject' view, invites me to change my focus from thinking about what might be good for us to thinking about what might be good for me considered singly. Given this approach, the fact that some development would be good for you, also considered singly, can be relevant to my decision only if I happen to care about you, which of course I may do. But, given that I am focusing on myself, it becomes possible and sensible for me to ask whether I care enough about you to do something which advantages you at a cost to myself. 'Perhaps I won't bother' I think.

And when these kinds of thoughts become preoccupying, other topics are backgrounded and overlooked. For example, we will not be encouraged to explore together what your boldness and my comparatively stronger risk aversion contribute to us. We will not come to see, with shared pleasure, what our varying viewpoints contribute to ours being a satisfactory partnership for both of us.

A final point of comparison with the monologue is seeing that the fragmenting view gets some things right, but that these things can be equally well accommodated on the co-subject view. For example, partners may disagree and quarrel. Also it is proper to ask whether the partnership is unbalanced, one partner is asking too much of the other. 'Unselfishness' is not always a virtue. Invoking it may be a way in which one partner exploits the other, may be a marker of grandiosity, or lack of realism. And there is no guaranteed way of avoiding conflicts. Some may be unavoidable, may even justifiably lead to a breakup. (This is a possibility which does not have an obvious analogue in the individual person case. Plainly the parallelism between the persisting person and the co-subjects goes only so far.) But these facts do not show that all intentionality must belong, fundamentally, to single subjects. Just as difficulties about how much to care about the future are best understood as corollaries of the fact that, for good or ill, we are temporal beings, so difficulties about different views of our shared future are best understood as corollaries of the fact that, for good or ill, we are essentially social beings. So, echoing what I said at the end of the previous section, my suggestion is that this is a more fruitful and a more honest way of conceptualising our situation than struggling on trying to give an account of things in terms of only singular subjects.

7. Language and Its Roles

The view of this paper is not that the 'analytic' strategy of trying to understand some complex and interesting thing by looking for its separable parts is always wrong. Rather, the view is that this strategy is just one among many, which may get us into trouble if used inappropriately. There are other approaches by which we may get equally or more important insights, for example looking outward to the setting which sustains the complex and interesting thing we hope to understand and so coming to see its role in the larger whole of which it is a part.

On Discussing What We Should Do

Plural intentionality, as a kind of thinking in its own right, is apt to strike analytic philosophers as strange and paradoxical, as requiring telepathy or as needing the co-subjects to become somehow identical with each other. Its seeming mysterious in these ways is bound up with a picture of intentionality which takes radical scepticism, and the related drive to fragmentation, too seriously. Starting from a different metaphysical and epistemological view, one which is in effect more pragmatist in spirit, licenses other strategies for understanding and allows us to see that plural intentionality is not mysterious at all.

The 'only singular intentionality' idea has encouraged a view of the role of individual remarks in a linguistic exchange as one person trying to influence the intentional attitudes of another. 'The speaker makes an utterance intending thereby to produce in the hearer some belief.' This is the kind of thing which is said.[3] And there may be episodes which have this shape. For example, I may try to manoeuvre Auntie Flossie into leaving me her money. In the course of this, I may talk at Auntie Flossie, trying to induce in her false beliefs about myself (that I am likeable and trustworthy) and about her other nieces and nephews (that they are unpleasant and dishonest).

But another view of the role of individual remarks comes into view if we take seriously non-scepticism and plural intentionality. With those in place, the idea of talking with other people, rather than talking at them, becomes more prominent. And talking with each other is what you and I are doing, when discussing the paragliding possibility. It is evident that we can deliberate well together only if we can call on relevant common knowledge. So one role of individual remarks in a conversational exchange must be to make active the common knowledge participants have which is relevant to their current situation. A later part of our dialogue might be this: 'Do we know whether your cousins enjoyed it?' you ask. 'Yes', I say. 'They said it was great.' This exchange should be taken at face value. What I know, but have not yet told you, is part of what we know. The role of the particular remark is to make this element of our common knowledge usable by us. Compare the singular case. 'Do I know what other people have felt about it?' I ask myself. 'Yes', I recall. 'Cousins Edie and Frank really enjoyed it.' What is not currently vivid and needs to be brought to mind is part of what I know. The role of the particular episode of recollection is to make this element of my knowledge usable now by the persisting me.

---

[3] As in the whole line of thought initiated by Grice's well-known discussion in 'Meaning' (1957).

Jane Heal

So making common knowledge usable is one key role of language. This is so, whatever the topic under discussion among the parties to the conversation, whether it is theoretical or practical, scientific, historical, political, aesthetic, or what not. The relations in which the parties stand and the nature of the topic under consideration are then among the circumstances which help the parties to shape the contributions they make.

I have focused on a particular kind of discussion, about what we should do, in a context where we find we do not have a clear objective to which we are working out some means, but where we are rather trying to agree on an objective, on what to go for. When faced with this challenging kind of perplexity about what to do, my suggestion has been that one thing we can try for is a deeper and more articulate understanding of what is at stake for us in the options offered. We can, for example, try to identify what we are certain we care about and distinguish that from what is more doubtful or less important. And we can try to understand better why we care about what we care about. For this enterprise, it may be that exchange of tentative remarks will be appropriate, ones where we try experimentally to articulate how things strike us, where we acknowledge uncertainties and are open to others' ways of looking at things.

Language is essential to the human kind of social existence. It is not a surprising modern discovery that we are social animals, having much in common with other social animals. This is something obvious, which our hunter gatherer ancestors already recognised and which has been confirmed and spelled out in detail by more recent developments in biology and evolutionary theory. But syntactically elaborate language, containing many parts of speech including the pronouns 'I/me' and 'we/us' is something which only human animals have.

Use of such a language does not create the unified, persisting, changing, essentially social beings which we are. Our primate ancestors were already such beings. But what language does provide is extension of cognitive resources, increase in things we can think about explicitly, can focus attention on, debate, value, choose between. Use of language is one of the vehicles by which we carry on our social lives, in familial, sporting, political, economic, technological, artistic, and scientific enterprises.[4]

The big picture in these aspects of our lives is one of change, of development, facing us with new and challenging situations. So for us

---

[4] The view of Charles Taylor in his 'Irreducibly Social Goods' (1997, p. 127ff.) is close to that of this paper.

perplexing questions about what we should do are all over the place. If thinking in terms of plural intentionality is a helpful way of understanding our situation then these reflections about how to conceptualise and tackle such questions may have wider application. But that is plainly another topic.

References

H.P. Grice, 'Meaning', *The Philosophical Review*, 66:3 (1957), 377–88.

Christian List and Philip Pettit, *Group Agency: The Possibility, Design, and Status of Corporate Agents* (Oxford: Oxford University Press, 2011).

David P. Schweikard and Hans Bernhard Schmid, 'Collective Intentionality', in Edward N. Zalta (ed.), *The Stanford Encyclopedia of Philosophy* (Fall 2021), accessed May 2023 at https://plato.stanford.edu/archives/fall2021/entries/collective-intentionality.

Charles Taylor, 'Irreducibly Social Goods', in *Philosophical Arguments* (Cambridge, MA: Harvard University Press, 1997), 127–45.

How To Get *About*

DAVID SOSA

Abstract

The 'Only connect!' that serves as epigraph to Forster's *Howards End* tolerates a variety of interpretations; but the very idea of a *connection*, or a *relating* of one thing with another, is conceptually deep. One form of connection is when something is *about* a thing, representing or symbolizing that thing. When we think of someone, or discuss something, we connect to them, or to it.

In his *Philosophical Investigations*, Wittgenstein asks, 'What makes my image of him into an image of *him*? [...] Isn't my question like *this*: "What makes this sentence a sentence that has to do with *him*?"' Wittgenstein thus notes the ramifications of his question: what makes her *name* hers? In virtue of what is this *thought* about them a thought about them? The issue he highlights has been with us since Plato's *Cratylus* and its history is unified by a presupposition: whatever makes it that (i) a bit of language (like a name or a sentence or any linguistic symbol) is about something is, fundamentally, also what makes it that (ii) a thought (or idea or image) is about a thing. The story of aboutness will be *uniform*, simplex, or so the presupposition has it.

But the history of the issue has been one of failure: we still don't adequately understand the nature of representation. I will propose and develop a perspective that rejects the presupposition and explains the failure: there is more than one way for a thing to be about something. Representation comes, ultimately, in varieties.

1. Introduction

Begin with E.M. Forster. Remember, in *Howards End* (1910), the brilliant imperative 'Only connect!' What sort of thing is this *connection* business? Perhaps our first paradigm of connection is found in physical proximity: when things *touch* they are connected. But even while noting that, we can already appreciate that the *significance* of the phenomenon, of connection, is not fully revealed in that form. When touch matters, it matters because it is constituting some more abstract form of connection. To make matters worse, there are questions about what *touching* could itself amount to.

So, refining our question: what could connecting be that it should matter? *Does* connecting matter at all after all? And if so, *why*? In Forster's case, the idea of connecting involved building a bridge between 'passion' and 'prose', between the beast and the monk that

David Sosa

are in us all. Without such a bridge, we are 'meaningless fragments'. Forster suggests that some special relation – a 'rainbow bridge' – between what might be conceived as initially isolated, elemental parts of our selves is required, and will suffice, for a range of deep values: beauty, exaltation, happiness, love, and salvation:

Beauty   'the bridge would be built and span their lives with beauty'
Exaltation 'and both [prose and passion] will be exalted'
Happiness 'Happy the man who sees from either aspect [the prosaic and the passionate]'
Love   'with [the connecting bridge] love is born'
Salvation 'the salvation that was latent in his own soul [...]'

Most explicitly, Forster applies his proposal to the inner workings of a *single* mind or person or soul (Mr Wilcox). But he uses that individual case as a kind of model for the connections *between* individuals and other things – including those between people and between families – that can yield the same sorts of benefits collectively as they do in the individual case.

Whether or not the individual case – the case of connections between the parts of a single person – should have any priority, we can attend directly to the sorts of connection between ourselves and other things that are ultimately the broader theme of Forster's novel and of interest to anyone. So, again, what could it be to connect?

I propose that one deep form of connection is when something is *about* something. Being about is an important variety of connecting. When we think about someone, we're connected to them. Near or far, spatially or temporally, there they are, almost miraculously, *with* us! And when we engage each other about something, for example in discussion, then we are connected to that thing, as well as (thereby) to each other. Indeed our being so engaged depends on it – otherwise we're 'talking past' each other, not in a *di*scussion.

Consider now the significance of this form of connection. Without the being about anything of a thought, the thinker is rendered *isolated*, the thought exhibits a lack of friction. And if when we talk, we are not together talking about some (one) thing, then we are not having a *con*versation, we are not in that way in community, we are to that extent not in society. This encourages the conclusion that when one thing is about another, they have connected in an important way. Notice that the examples I gave are of *thoughts* and *ideas* and then of *discussion* and *talk*. Being about things is something a mind can be involved in and is also something a bit of language can do. So let's pursue this relation of aboutness further. How does it work?

How To Get *About*

In his *Philosophical Investigations* (1953), Wittgenstein asked, 'What makes my image of him into an image of *him?*' He then wondered, 'Isn't my question like *this*: "What makes this sentence a sentence that has to do with *him?*" [...] And what makes our conversation about him a conversation about *him?*'

Notice, first, the range of ways in which we characterize the phenomenon: Wittgenstein is (translated as) speaking of images being 'of' someone and of sentences 'having to do with' things. I'm using being 'about' as the basic case. But there's also betokening, denoting, going proxy for, indicating, meaning, referencing or referring, representing, signaling, standing for, and symbolizing. And then notice, second, that like many before him and since, Wittgenstein in effect unifies questions about what makes for aboutness in the case of language and what makes for aboutness in the case of thought.

Kit Fine is explicit in his *Semantic Relationism* (2007):

> The simplest and most natural view is that there is no more to the content of my belief than there is to the content of my words [...] [it is] odd to suppose that there should be any fundamental difference in the general representational character of language and thought.

And here's Stephen Schiffer, in his *Remnants of Meaning* (1987):

> Both mental states and sentences have what is called *intentionality* or *representational content*: a particular sentence means *that worms do not have noses*, and a particular state is a belief *that worms do not have noses*. What the theorist ultimately wants, of course, is a general theory of content, a theory of linguistic *and* mental representation.

Adopting a slightly different angle, Jerry Fodor, in his *Psychosemantics* (1987), worried about whether intentionality is a natural phenomenon:

> I suppose that sooner or later the physicists will complete the catalogue they've been compiling of the ultimate and irreducible properties of things. When they do, the likes of *spin, charm,* and *charge* will perhaps appear on their list. But *aboutness* surely won't; intentionality doesn't go that deep [...]. If aboutness is real, it must really be something else.

Whether Fodor is right about the fundamentality of intentionality, notice that he, too, seems to take for granted that it is *simplex*.

Out of tune with this symphony, I will propose instead not one but *two* things for aboutness really to be! The contrasting unificatory presupposition is reasonable: there are good reasons for supposing that any account of what makes a word mean what it means must serve equally as an account of what makes a thought be about what it represents. After all, we seem to be able to put our thoughts into words. If you say something, I can believe *it*. But I nevertheless recommend that we reconsider the presupposition.

What controversy there *has* been about the relation between the linguistic and the mental case has concerned *priority*, over whether

(i) having language is a precondition of thought, so that linguistic meaning to that extent precedes the meanings of thought,
    or instead
(ii) we in effect invest our languages with the sort of semantic content that our thoughts already possess, so that thought has priority.

My proposal rejects both sides of that debate: they both presuppose that the relevant linguistic phenomenon and the case of mental meaning can be ordered, in terms of priority, along the relevant dimension. On the suggestion here, neither precedes the other: they are *independent*.

I will not, here, show how I accommodate the point about communicating our thoughts in language; but I appreciate the need to do so. To make a start on developing the view that will face that challenge, we will begin by reviewing two key philosophical texts, one by the German logician Gottlob Frege and another by the American philosopher Saul Kripke.

2. The Fregean Turn

In 'On Sense and Reference', a seminal paper first published in 1892, Frege confronted a philosophical issue: 'The discovery that the rising sun is not new every morning, but always the same, was one of the most fertile astronomical discoveries.'

The general issue was about the possibility of believing one thing without believing another, about having a thought with one significance without having another, different thought, with a different significance. Frege's Puzzle, as it's now known, was specifically about how we might already believe that Hesperus is Hesperus without yet knowing that Hesperus is Phosphorus. We discover the latter, even while already having the former belief. This sort of phenomenon is widespread: Agnes Bojaxhiu, Lev Bronstein, Lewis Carroll, Samuel Clemens, Robert Galbraith, Margaretha MacLeod, *etc.*

How To Get *About*

Is what we learn, when we learn that Cicero is Tully just what we already knew, when we knew that Cicero is Cicero? *No.* But isn't Cicero's being Tully just a matter of his self-identity, his being himself? The way the world has to be, for Clemens to be Twain is just how it has to be for that individual to be himself.

Here is one way to pose the issue. If

(i) what the sentence 'Cicero is Cicero' means is just what the sentence 'Cicero is Tully' means, and
(ii) what we have in mind, when we believe that Cicero is Cicero, is just what the sentence means,
then
(iii) we did already believe that Cicero is Tully.

Frege's solution was to introduce a new kind of semantic value... for *words*. But how could it possibly help to solve a problem about *believing* one thing and not another to add another layer to the semantic value of *words*? What does the semantics of words have to do with the prospect of one or another rational arrangement of belief? Nothing very immediate.

Frege saw a difference in the cognitive potential of minds that do and don't already believe that Hesperus is Phosphorus, and inferred that the meaning of the sentence 'Hesperus is Phosphorus' – the way that sentence is about what it is about – has to be able to explain that difference in cognitive potential. That Frege should have thought such a maneuver could help is a reflection, I think, of a presupposition: *no distinction in cognitive potential without some distinction in linguistic semantics*.

View the path I'm proposing here as an alternative, an alternative to that taken in what has come to be called 'The Linguistic Turn' (Rorty, 1967). The nature and structure of linguistic meaning is *not*, contrary to a key idea of the Linguistic Turn, a good model for thought and how it represents. Frege appreciated something deep: we need theoretical materials adequate to explain distinctions as fine-grained as can be made by an arbitrarily powerful rational mind. We need this in order to understand the nature of rational thought: inference, for example, both practical and theoretical, also coherence and incoherence, informativeness, and practical and theoretical justification. We need it to understand how there's no irrationality in believing that Phosphorus is bright even while not believing – as we might or might not put it – that Hesperus is bright.

But he remained committed to a problematic unification of the linguistic case and the case of thought: confronted by subjects whose rational beliefs differ in a familiar way, he proposed a new theory of

David Sosa

linguistic meaning. In that way, he steered us toward the linguistic turn. We should separate more sharply the way thoughts connect to reality from the way language does.

Even while sentences of the form '$a=a$' and '$a=b$' have the *same* semantics, the latter form can nevertheless be informative because the informativeness of a sentence does *not* supervene on its semantics. Even relative to a fixed background set of beliefs, different sentences – even with the same semantics – can be differentially informative.

But wait: how can this be? How can sentences with the same meaning be differentially *informative*? Neither semantically encodes information the other doesn't. Nevertheless, differential informativeness can be a result of differential *causal* effect. If one sentence can, perhaps in virtue of its form, systematically cause a true belief that another sentence cannot cause, then those sentences are apt differentially to extend our knowledge. There is nothing problematic in the idea that different sentences should produce different effects *causally*, even should they have the same semantics.

The extension of our knowledge by '$a=b$' is not necessarily a matter of our engaging a different linguistic meaning than when we encounter '$a=a$.' It does, however, entail that we're caused to get different contents in mind. The product of a testimonial exchange, for example, the resulting belief in a rational audience, is not a causal result just of their existing beliefs and of the semantics of the input utterance. *Which* sentence is used matters too.

As a general point, this is obvious: even should sentences in different languages have the very same content, they are liable to be differentially informative to monolingual speakers of those languages, respectively. But the point holds up in a more specific deployment: even should the two sentences be in the same language, and even should your interlocutor understand both sentences, they may be caused to know something in accepting a sentence of the form '$a=b$' that they could not come to know in accepting '$a=a$'. Informativeness is a causal phenomenon; and causal effect is sensitive to the specific form in which a content is transmitted.

So, as I said, I think Frege set us off on the wrong path when he presumed that if a pair of sentences can (even for a competent speaker of the relevant language) correspond to – or 'give rise to', or 'be the expression of' – different contents of belief, then they cannot have the same semantics. There's an implicit *aspiration*, not initially unreasonable, in this ultimately unsustainable insistence. But the semantics of sentences is not up to the task of articulating all relevant cognitive variability.

How To Get *About*

Frege remained committed to a problematic and still widely shared presupposition – call it 'monosemanticism': that the notion of content introduced to explain the nature of rational thought has to serve also as the semantic value of the expressions of a natural language. According to monosemanticism, the being meaningful of thoughts and the being meaningful – the having a semantic value – of linguistic expressions are fundamentally akin and correlated phenomena. That sort of monosemanticism was a good place to begin in thinking about content. It is valuable in accounting for certain apparently acceptable claims. (*E.g.*, Ally believes everything that Billy said.) But we are no longer at the beginning of thought about content. It is time to reconsider the presupposition: in its place, I recommend *polysemanticism*, according to which there are multiple varieties of intentionality – so that a cognitive state's being contentful and a sentence's having a semantic value are fundamentally different – indeed *independent* – phenomena.

One significant consequence of the polysemanticist approach is a sharper separation between the Millianism/Fregeanism issue in philosophy of language and the externalism/internalism issue in philosophy of mind. A sign of the depth of the difference between cognitive and linguistic varieties of representation is in the fact that cognitive representation is *internalist* while linguistic representation is generally *externalist*. While duplicates – though just what it is to be the duplicate of a thinking thing is moot – will have propositional attitudes that represent alike, the referents of any names tokened by any duplicate human beings – which names might well even have a Millian semantics – might not be shared. And though the best linguistic theory may ultimately make the starred sentence below *false*, we can all still understand the true thought one might have tried to voice with it.

(*) 'Lois believes Superman flies' is true
    even while
    'Lois believes Clark Kent flies' is false.

Indeed, the very idea that Millianism and externalism are kindred philosophical positions, as they are often seen, should always have been odd: whereas the coarse-grained individuation of linguistic contents produced by Millianism permits substitution under what might seem relatively *weak* conditions (weaker than those imposed by Fregeanism), externalism's finding internal state insufficient for fixing content makes it a relatively *demanding* theory of content identity (and more demanding than internalism).

David Sosa

3. Kripke's Picture

As we pursue giving up the monosemanticist presupposition, we take up next a text that appears to oppose Frege's view. I think that the arguments Kripke brings to bear against a Fregean view of the semantics of names, however adequate they might be against their actual intended target, are not compelling as arguments against a Fregean conception of the contents of *thought*. I don't, incidentally, think Kripke himself tries to use them that way.

Perhaps the single best example, for seeing this, is the notorious Gödel/Schmidt case that Kripke gives in *Naming and Necessity* (1980):

> Let's take a simple case. In the case of Gödel [...] practically the only thing many people have heard about him — [is] that he discovered the incompleteness of arithmetic. Does it follow that whoever discovered the incompleteness of arithmetic is the referent of 'Gödel'? [...] Suppose that Gödel was not in fact the author of [the] theorem. A man named 'Schmidt', whose body was found in Vienna under mysterious circumstances many years ago, actually did the work in question.[...] On the view in question, then, [...] since the man who discovered the incompleteness of arithmetic is in fact Schmidt, we, when we talk about 'Gödel', are in fact always referring to Schmidt. But it seems to me that we are not. We simply are not.

This is an important passage and I think it makes a decisive point against a certain conception of how we refer with names. Recall the character in Carroll's *Through the Looking Glass* (1871):

> 'When I use a word,' Humpty Dumpty said, in rather a scornful tone, 'it means just what I choose it to mean — neither more nor less.'

The passage from Carroll is funny because of Humpty Dumpty's pretension. In fact words do not mean just what we then choose for them to mean. And similarly the *name* 'Gödel' refers to Gödel, whatever we might have meant to do with the word. Now then, in light of the distinction enabled by our rejection of monosemanticism, what should we say about the *thoughts* of the 'ordinary person' in Kripke's case?

Kripke could perhaps have been more explicit about this. But I think he does *not* intend to be making a point about the nature of belief content. Also elsewhere, in 'A Puzzle About Belief' (1979), Kripke talks explicitly about our practices of belief *ascription*, something we do with words. But ignoring the particulars of

How To Get *About*

Kripke's texts for the moment, just ask yourself the following question: if, by explicit stipulation, the property *discoverer of the incompleteness of arithmetic* is exactly what one has in mind on a given occasion, and whatever word one then uses, what is that *thought* about? Just suppose that on a given occasion a subject's thought *is* descriptive – denying that the names have a descriptivist semantics does not entail that such thoughts are not so much as possible. A thinker is working on the incompleteness of arithmetic, for example, and forms the judgment that its discoverer was brilliant. Who is the thinker judging to be brilliant? It is *not* plausible, in this case, that the referent of the subject's thought should be the thief, Gödel. It seems rather to be about, well, *the discoverer*: Schmidt. Whatever the subject might go on to say, and whatever might then be referenced by any *words* they use on that occasion, the thinker seems to refer in thought to Schmidt.

In Kripke's example the subject uses the word 'Gödel'. And in using that *name* they make linguistic reference to Gödel. But that does not entail that they believe that Gödel is brilliant. After all, by stipulation, it's *discoverer of the incompleteness of arithmetic* that the subject has in mind, and so it's the discoverer of the incompleteness of arithmetic that they believe to be brilliant. That was Schmidt.

So there's a way to *accept* Kripke's insight about names and other linguistic devices and how they represent even while preserving Frege's insight into the way rational minds work – even should Frege himself have misdeployed that insight and left himself open to Kripke's rebuttal.

Kripke claims that we do not associate with proper names properties that we believe to pick out an individual *uniquely*. We often know that most all the properties we associate with one name are the very ones we would also associate with other names. True: we should all agree that a word's being meaningfully used to refer to something does not depend on a user's associating with that word a property that they believe to pick that thing out uniquely. On one version of polysemanticism, for example, a good 'picture' of linguistic reference is drawn as Kripke does, in terms of a network of causal relations, without appealing in any problematic way to the meaning of a user's *thoughts*.

Suppose that on a given occasion you do have in mind just the property *leading theoretical physicist* and you don't believe it picks anyone out uniquely. You would then *not* use any mental analogue of 'the' with that concept; you would use an indefinite operator, the mental analogue of 'a'. You might on a given occasion think this: *no doubt a leading theoretical physicist will be asked to serve on that*

151

David Sosa

blue-ribbon commission. But whatever definite referring you might then do with the name 'Feynman', in such a case it is not plausible that your *thought* is referring differentially to Feynman rather than to Gell-Mann. Of course, normally, if you did then use that name competently, it will be because you in fact have the property *leading theoretical physicist named 'Feynman'* (or something like that) in mind: one needn't defend a metalinguistic theory of names to think that occasionally subjects have *is in this context uniquely referred to by [N]* in mind when using a name. But that's not offered now as a general theory of the meaning of names; it is a plausible speculation about what might sometimes be in the mind of a subject using a name.

And *contra* Kripke's claim in the 'Puzzle About Belief', it does *not* seem possible to wonder whether Cicero is Tully, so to speak, if the content you have in mind, associated with the 'Cicero' term, is exactly the content you have associated with the 'Tully' term. An identity issue presented to you *as* exactly the same content, twice over, flanking an identity concept, cannot provoke uncertainty.

We do not have to be committed to a metalinguistic theory of the meaning of names in order to recognize the role of metalinguistic commitments in the transition from an attitude to its expression. A speaker will tend to communicate their belief that *an F is G* with a name 'N' only if they associate *the F* with 'N'. All of this is consistent with the most radical Millianism about the semantics of names.

If the way minds manage the task of being about things is fundamentally different from the way words manage that task, then Frege's proposal, though he pitched it as about the way language works, can be accepted as a viable claim about the way minds work. And Kripke's insights about the way language works need not be seen as incompatible with the new conception of the contents of thought.

In Kripke's example, if we have *discoverer of the incompleteness of arithmetic* in mind, and use the word Gödel, then our thought is about Schmidt and our sentence is about Gödel.

Aboutness bifurcates.

4. Conclusion

I've revisited Frege's 'On Sense and Reference' and Kripke's *Naming and Necessity* from, if you will, a polysemantical point of view. The leading ideas so far are that Frege's seminal insight actually concerns the nature of thought and its contents and that expressing that insight

How To Get *About*

in the way he did, as about the semantics of proper names, is problematic – ultimately, I believe, for the reasons Kripke gives. At the same time, Kripke's arguments are compelling specifically when applied to the form in which Frege did express his insight – they are not telling against a Fregean conception of thought content.

Once we separate linguistic semantics from the intentionality of thought, then the fact – as a Millian semantics would have it – that 'If Lois believes that Superman can fly then she believes that Clark can fly' is a true sentence of English is rendered a different *sort* of philosophical challenge. Our contrary intuition is about the possible condition of Lois's mind, about how she might rationally represent reality in thought. And the truth of such sentences does not determine the contents of her mind – if you'll allow me perhaps to misuse *words* just now in this way! – determined as *they* are by *their* meanings.

There is accordingly a sense, awkward though it may be to express, in which 'belief' reports do not report *beliefs*: my apologies, I have no better *word* and yet we all know what I mean.

Polysemanticism is a useful framework for Millianism: whether or not it is best to allow the truth of 'Lois believes that Clark can fly', the intuition that drives resistance *can* be preserved. Perhaps the most refined form in which to put the point is that the thought driving resistance to the truth of that sentence is itself just that, a *thought*. It's an intuition about Lois and whether she believes something. Without using 'that Clark can fly' to express that thought, without, indeed, using any other ordinary English sentence involving a name to specify it, we can anyway engage, in our own thought, the thought that Lois might lack. Whether to use one or another sentence in expression of her belief is a decision we will make collectively, answering to the sorts of pressure characteristic of linguistic convention. But whether Lois actually has one or another thought is not similarly a matter of convention.

Now if, in the grip of a view according to which the contents of thought are just what's expressed by ordinary sentences, we try *heroically* to discover the linguistic expression that reflects her mental circumstances, we might ourselves *say* that she 'does not believe that Clark can fly', or we might on the other hand say '*that Clark can fly*' is indeed something that 'she stands in the belief relation to'. Each of those moves can be pushed to confront well-known problems – the first will eventually have to resist Kripke's powerful arguments about the semantics of names, the second will eventually give up articulating mental differences between Lois and, say, Superman himself in terms of the contents to which they do and

David Sosa

don't stand in the belief relation to, respectively. Better, I think, to admit that any expression of her thought in an ordinary sentence is not well suited to making explicit her mental circumstance and then go on to admit even that the first admission is itself not quite well *expressed* (because it used the *phrase* 'mental circumstance'). If you understand this, you understand polysemanticism.

Sense was recruited for one job, and then given another. We think with the sort of thing a sense is introduced to be; but we don't need language to have sense in order to understand how we think that way. It would help my pitch for polysemanticism to recommend, finally, a particular form in which it might be developed.

Return to Fodor, who, recall, insists that aboutness has to really be something else. I said above that I would offer *two* things for aboutness really to be. Our philosophical mystification in the face of the phenomenon of intentionality is I think in part the product of confusion about what the relation of representation could, ultimately, *be*. Unless we think that relation is primitive, unless we think one thing's being of or about another is *not* a condition whose obtaining is in virtue of any other condition's obtaining, then we should wonder just what (other) relation might subserve it.

There are in fact two relations, with each of which we are more or less familiar, that are, though quite different from each other, *both* plausibly helpful in understanding in virtue of what one thing might be about another.

Consider for example the *instantiation* relation that holds between collections of properties and the particulars that might *instantiate* those properties. If an individual has a bunch of properties, then anything that is somehow constituted by those properties is in *one* important way distinctively related to that thing (those constitutive properties *select* it, through its instantiating them, from all the things there are). From this perspective, the relation of instantiation can be understood to ground a variety of intentionality. By getting *sphericity* in mind, for example, a subject can in a way represent *inter alia* soccer balls. By being spherical, those objects can be the intentional objects of a thought with *sphericity* as an appropriate constituent part.

But there is also, differently, the phenomenon that Grice (1957) distinguished as *natural meaning*: smoke represents fire in virtue of a systematic *causal* correlation between those phenomena. In this case the representation relation is subserved through *causal* mechanisms. *Properties* of fires can *stand in* for them representationally; but *causal correlates* of fire can do that too, if in a recognizably different way.

How To Get *About*

The aboutness of language is, I think, to be made out in terms of *causation*, compatibly with the causal 'picture' that Kripke himself proposes. The aboutness of thoughts, by contrast, is to be made out in terms of *satisfaction*, in line with the model Frege offered (though he mistakenly offered it as accounting for the reference of words).

Returning then, finally, to Forster: we *connect* in more than one way. We can think of loved ones – remembering long-lost ancestors as easily as we anxiously await offspring – and we can consider whether worms have noses or whether to seek out a saucer of mud. We do that kind of thing by getting properties in mind that the relevant individuals *instantiate*.

But we also connect in a very different sort of way, with language, by naming things and referring to them and talking about them. We do that by taking advantage of *causal* relations that have been established between the words we use and the things they (thereby) stand for.

The possibilities for beautiful and loving relationships, the prospect of a kind of exaltation, and of salvation, and the preconditions for happiness, are all accordingly in place, in more than one way. We need not be alone in the nightmare scenario postulated by the solipsist: our thoughts provide for a satisfying connection, and our language provides for yet another. If you want to get *about*, understanding its multiplex character is the beginning of wisdom.

References

Lewis Carroll, *Through the Looking Glass and What Alice Found There* (London: MacMillan, 1871).
Kit Fine, *Semantic Relationism* (Oxford: Wiley, 2007).
Jerry Fodor, *Psychosemantics* (Cambridge, MA: MIT, 1987).
E.M. Forster, *Howards End* (London: Edward Arnold, 1910).
Gottlob Frege, 'On Sense and Reference', in P. Geach and M. Black (eds), *Translations from the Philosophical Writings of Gottlob Frege* (Oxford: Blackwell, 1952). First published in *Zeitschrift für Philosophie und philosophische Kritik*, Vol. 100 (1892).
H.P. Grice, 'Meaning', *The Philosophical Review*, 66:3 (1957), 377–88.
Saul Kripke, 'A Puzzle About Belief', in A. Margalit (ed.), *Meaning and Use* (Dordrecht: Reidel, 1979).
Saul Kripke, *Naming and Necessity* (Cambridge, MA: Harvard, 1980).

David Sosa

Richard Rorty (ed.), *The Linguistic Turn* (Chicago: University of Chicago, 1967).
Stephen Schiffer, *Remnants of Meaning* (Cambridge, MA: MIT, 1987).
Ludwig Wittgenstein, *Philosophical Investigations* (Oxford: Blackwell, 1953).

Stories and Selves: A Twisted Love Story about the Meaning of Life[1]

ELISABETH CAMP

Abstract

I argue that stories are 'equipment for living' in two senses: retrospectively, they provide 'configurational comprehension' of a temporal sequence of events; prospectively, they offer templates for action. Narrative conceptions of the self appear well poised to leverage these functional roles for stories into an intuitively compelling view of self-construction as self-construal. However, the narrative conception defines selves in terms of the lives they live: a self is the protagonist in a lifelong story. And narrative structure is itself defined by 'retrospective necessity': the meaning of events within a story is given by their contribution to that story's ending. Together, this entails that life stories hold selves metaphysically, epistemically, and practically hostage to their ends. Fortunately, narratives are just one species of interpretive frame. I suggest some alternative types of frames, including identity labels and metaphors, that support configurational comprehension, action guidance, and self construction without shackling selves to their lives' ends.

1. Why We Tell Stories

It is a truth universally acknowledged that people love stories. From the *Mahabharata* and the *Iliad* to *The Rise and Fall of the Roman Empire* and *Paul Revere's Ride*, from *One Hundred Years of Solitude* to *The Handmaiden's Tale* – across times, cultures, and media; in art high and low; in myth, fiction, and history; on college applications, at family reunions and office parties – we are drawn to tell and consume stories. Indeed, the anthropologist John Niles (1999) proposes 'Homo narrans' as a more fitting label to capture our essential differentiating characteristic than *Homo sapiens*.

---

[1] This paper extends arguments in my (2011). Thanks to audiences at the 45th Conference on the Great Mother and the New Father, the Royal Institute of Philosophy, the University of Massachusetts Amherst, the New England Workshop on Metaphysics, and North Carolina State. Special thanks to Abbot Cutler, Jeanne D'Amico, Nick Adamski, Avi Steinhardt, Lucy O'Brien, Xinhe Wu, Nevin Johnson, and Isabel Uriagereka Herburger for discussion, and to Justin Khoo for very helpful commentary.

Elisabeth Camp

Why are we such inveterate makers and consumers of story? For many reasons, including the sheer imaginative pleasure of filling our minds with something other than the exigencies of the everyday. But beyond this, it's natural to ask how stories work as 'equipment for living', in literary critic Kenneth Burke (1938)'s phrase. In this section, I tease out two functional roles for stories, which relate to time and telling in different ways.

The first role is expressed by the psychologist Jerome Bruner's descriptions of stories as part of 'our armamentarium for dealing with surprise' (2002, p. 29). More specifically, Bruner (2002, p. 31) says that

> Narrative is a recounting of human plans gone off track, expectations gone awry. It conventionalizes the common forms of human mishap into genres – comedy, tragedy, romance, irony, or whatever format may lessen the sting of our fortuity. Stories reassert a kind of conventional wisdom about what can be expected, even (or especially) what can be expected to go wrong, and what might be done to restore or cope with the situation.

Translating this line of thought into Burke's equipment metaphor, we might say that stories are wayfinding instructions for navigating life. They specify recurring types of events, situations, and characters, and offer diagnostics for recognizing them. They tell us what to expect next, and offer strategies for response: reasons to select one path over another, and techniques for getting back on track.

On this model, stories' functional role is essentially prospective and practical. However, this doesn't explain why we *re*tell stories, or care so much about the details of different stories that instantiate the same basic template. We don't just tell a story until we have internalized its moral. Rather, we retrace past events repeatedly, in loving detail, even with the end clearly in mind and even when we don't expect a similar type of situation to arise again. The philosopher Louis Mink (1970, p. 554) proposes that we engage in such retrospective rumination

> Because [we] aim at producing and strengthening the act of understanding in which actions and events, although represented as occurring in the order of time, can be surveyed as it were in a single glance as bound together in an order of significance, a representation of the *totum simul* which we can never more than partially achieve.

On Mink's model, we make and consume stories because they give us a cognitive grip on a sequence of events by knitting them together into a coherent explanatory pattern. As he puts it:

> In the configurational comprehension of a story which one has followed, the end is connected with the promise of the beginning as well as the beginning with the promise of the end, and the necessity of the backward references cancels out, so to speak, the contingency of the forward references. [T]ime is no longer the river which bears us along but the river in aerial view, upstream and downstream seen in a single survey.

Thus, if Bruner treats stories as wayfinding instructions, Mink construes them as satellite maps. Just as having a map of a spatial region scaffolds understanding, recall, and reasoning in a way that even an exhaustive set of turn-by-turn navigational instructions does not (Camp, 2007a), so too does a story's 'configurational comprehension' scaffold explanation and prediction by situating events in relation to one another. Moreover, in contrast to Bruner's culturally conventional templates, Mink's 'configurational comprehensions' can be highly specific, connecting fine-grained details of the particular events they recount in complex, nuanced ways. This is especially relevant for Mink as a philosopher of history who aims to justify stories as providing a species of understanding distinct from scientific categorization and causal generalization. I think this insight about particularist explanation is profound, not just for history but for the humanities more generally (Ismael, 2017), though the nature of explanation is not my focus here.

2. What Is a Story?

In §1, we identified two roles for stories as 'equipment for living': as comprehensive configurations and as templates for action. In §3, I'll consider stories as tools specifically for constructing selves. But first, we need to get clearer about how stories function, such that they can perform these two roles. Both Bruner and Mink take stories to be useful because they offer us a structure for understanding a collection of otherwise disparate events. What is this structure? Fully addressing this question would require an extensive journey through narratology; for current purposes we need just three basic points, all following from Aristotle's famous claim that a story has a *beginning, middle, and end*.

While this observation might appear trivial, it entails a substantive relationship to time, with significant implications for what stories can do. A story is temporally bounded: it selects out a portion of the universe's vast continuum of space-time possibilities. It is also essentially about events: the sorts of things that start and stop at times and involve change. While stories also describe states, these occur as the background conditions and consequences of those events. Further, a story connects multiple events into a temporal sequence. Thus, just as maps represent by placing entities in spatial relation (Camp, 2007a) and family trees represent by locating entities in ancestral relation (Camp, 2009a), so stories represent by placing events in temporal relation.

So, stories describe *temporally bounded sequences of events*. But they don't just list events, as annals do, or even events related to a single subject, as chronicles do (Carroll, 2001; Fraser, 2021). A beginning is more than a starting point, and an end is more than a stopping point: together, they delimit a span of time as an integrated unit. More importantly, as Mink emphasizes, a story connects the described events into a configuration that renders both the events themselves and their dynamics comprehensible, by placing them in explanatory relation.

Aristotle maintained that the principle of 'narrative connection' is causal: later events are necessary or probable consequences of earlier ones. While there is something intuitively right about this, causation cannot be necessary for narrative connection, given that many satisfying stories are driven by remarkable coincidences (Carroll, 2001). Nor is causation sufficient for narrative connection on its own: a recounting of the paths of billiard balls across a table in terms of the transfer of kinetic force constitutes a narrative only in the weakest sense. Rather, recall that Mink speaks of a story's end being rendered 'necessary' by the 'promise' of the beginning and the beginning by the promise of the end, through a kind of interactive 'backward reference'.

Retrospective necessity, then, is the second crucial feature of narrative structure: a story's end provides an interpretive principle for selecting, describing, and explaining events in its beginning and middle. In the simplest case, retrospective necessity is achieved by describing one agent pursuing one goal, beginning with the goal's formation and specifying crucial causal steps to its fulfillment. This is the canonical case of teleological explanation, sometimes described as backward causation. Obviously, most stories don't hew to this simple, linear, straightforwardly causal format. However, we just need the weaker point that stories interpret a sequence of events as contributing somehow to the story's ending, where these contributions are related to agents trying to make things happen, and the ending somehow resolves those attempts.

As fictions like *Lolita* or *Ender's Game* and films like *Rashomon* and *Sixth Sense* relish demonstrating, substantively different narratives of

Stories and Selves

the same temporal interval will be generated by attributing different goals to the same agent, by shifting the explanatory focus to different agents, or by raising different explanatory questions about their actions. Different narrative frames select different events in a sequence as relevant for inclusion in a story. They warrant different descriptions of a given event, by subsuming it under different nexuses of causal 'joints and sockets' (Dennett, 1991). And they prioritize and connect events in different ways – as initiating, forestalling, foreshadowing, or otherwise motivating or impeding each other – which may not be causal or even explanatory in a more narrowly metaphysical sense. Moreover, selecting, describing, or connecting particular events in a certain way affects the appropriate selection, description, and connections among other events in a global holistic way, so that the significance of the whole both influences and is influenced by the significance of its constituent events. As a result, shifting a story's narrative focus can dramatically transform, not just which events deserve to be mentioned, but what those events fundamentally mean (Camp, 2017).

The third feature of narrative structure is that stories don't merely explain the dynamics of a bounded temporal sequence of events involving agents making and undergoing change. Those agents and events are presented as *mattering*, in a way that engages emotional and evaluative response. More specifically, stories embed a dynamic sequence of events within an emotional or epistemic cadence – what David Velleman (2003), following Frank Kermode (1967), calls the narrative 'tick tock'. Bruner's 'sting of fortuity' displays this cadence in its most basic form: we have hopes and dreams, and feel anger or grief when they are stymied. Again, obviously most narratives are not so simple: we experience emotions on behalf of a story's protagonist that they don't themselves feel, or gloat at a villain's downfall. Stories often also engage epistemic emotions, like curiosity about why the Roman Empire fell (Carroll, 2007; Fraser, 2021). The crucial point is that narrative closure – the 'sense of an ending', as Kermode puts it – involves an engaged, dynamic investment in the story's guiding concerns.

Here, then, is where we've arrived. We use stories to achieve a comprehensive understanding of a temporally bounded sequence of events, sometimes at least partly in order to guide action. Stories accomplish this by selecting, describing, and connecting those events into a coherent, holistic configuration that explains them in terms of their contribution to the story's ending, which resolves the story's operative concerns in a viscerally satisfying way. Various genres – comedy, tragedy, etc. – offer more specific templates for

161

Elisabeth Camp

types of events and characters, guiding concerns, and resolving cadences. And particular stories implement and tweak those templates by recounting particular characters encountering particular suites of obstacles and opportunities in ways that elicit particular constellations of epistemic, emotional, and evaluative cadences.

3. Stories for Selves

So far, I've been discussing stories as tools for managing our engagement with the world in general. Some theorists treat stories as 'equipment for living' in a more specific sense: as tools for building selves. A minimal version of this view follows naturally from Bruner's point that we use stories to navigate unexpected events: if we regularly use stories to guide action, and our selves are the products of our actions, then stories often play a role in creating our selves. And indeed, Bruner claims that 'self-making is a narrative art'; '[i]t is through narrative that we create and re-create selfhood' (2002, pp. 65, 85).

By itself, the core idea that we use stories to create selves might just amount to the claim that stories create selves by guiding action at critical junctures of our lives. But this invites the question of what unites the self we thereby create into a coherent whole. And given what we've said so far, a natural answer is that this unity is provided by an overarching narrative of the self's life. Thus, Marya Schechtman claims that 'a person creates his identity by forming an autobiographical narrative' (1996, p. 93); 'constituting an identity requires that an individual conceive of his life as having the form and the logic of a story [...] where "story" is understood as a conventional, linear narrative' (1996, p. 96).

By itself, the core idea might also just amount to the claim that stories are one tool within a richer 'armamentarium' for self-construction. But again, given what we've said so far, it's natural to take a further step. In §2, we saw that narrative structure is essentially teleological, in the broad sense of selecting, describing, explaining, and evaluating constituent events in terms of an overarching structure defined by 'retrospective necessity'. Stories in general need not be teleological in the narrow sense of recounting an agent's pursuit of a goal. But it is plausible that stories focused on selves will focus on the goals and concerns of those selves. Moreover, one might think that any description of actions *as* actions will be teleological in the stricter sense of explaining them in terms of an agent's intention to achieve a goal. Together, these points might seem to suggest that,

Stories and Selves

as Alisdair MacIntyre says, 'narrative history of a certain kind turns out to be the basic and essential genre for the characterization of human action' (1981, p. 208).

If we amplify the core idea in these two ways, we end up with a view on which articulating an overarching autobiographical narrative is the essential mechanism for constructing selves as agents. It follows from this amplified view that it is essential to having a self that one actualize such a life narrative. It also follows, perhaps less directly but still fairly naturally, that selves have value insofar as they do implement that identity-constituting narrative. As MacIntyre (1981, p. 203) puts it:

> The unity of an individual life is the unity of a narrative embodied in a single life. To ask 'What is the good for me?' is to ask how best I might live out that unity and bring it to completion [...]. The only criteria for success or failure in a human life as a whole are the criteria for success or failure in a narrated or to-be-narrated quest.

I want to note three things about this amplified view of stories as tools for self-construction. First, it is remarkably strong: it holds that the essential principle of a self is the explicit articulation of a narrative of a lifelong quest in pursuit of an overarching goal. While the overarching goal that drives an agent's lifelong quest may be complex and the path to its achievement indirect, failing in that quest means failing to be a self in the full sense of the term. For many of us, this is starkly counter-intuitive. We ordinarily take many selves that fail to satisfy this criterion to be successful, including 'Episodics' who live for the moment (Strawson, 2004); 'characters' who simply instantiate a stable identity across a long period; and those with cognitive deficits that prevent them from articulating an overarching quest either prospectively or retrospectively (Camp, 2011).

Second, we arrived at this amplified view through a series of plausible, if hardly incontrovertible steps: starting from the core observation that story-telling plays a central role in our ordinary practices of self-interpretation and action-guidance; noting that narrative structure is teleological in the broad sense of being defined by retrospective necessity; and adding a pair of motivations for interpreting that broadly teleological structure in a more robust way, as a lifelong quest. We also moved from a claim about interpreting selves to a claim about constituting them, justified by the implicit assumption that well-grounded interpretations reflect reality, and from there to a claim about evaluating selves.

Third, strong as it is, the conclusion is not just a philosopher's abstract concoction: it articulates an intuition that runs deep and wide. The idea of a Hero's Journey is especially prevalent in Western Romantic culture, as reflected in the long-standing admiration for figures like Alexander the Great, Napoleon, and Wordsworth. But practitioners of 'mythopoetics' including Carl Jung, Joseph Campbell, and Robert Bly have traced out variations on the basic genre across cultures. More recently, it has thrived in the neo-Jefferson American myth of the self-made man, evinced by figures like Abraham Lincoln, Booker T. Washington, Henry Ford, and Elon Musk. And it animates various self-help therapies and movements with broad contemporary popularity, like *The Purpose-Driven Life*.

4. Narrative Hostage-Taking

We stand, then, on the edge of a dark forest, having followed a fairly well-trodden path, with a hidden dragon's lair marked out just around the bend. My primary interest here is not to assess the narrative conception of self on metaphysical or normative grounds. As we noted in §3, there is ample room to worry about whether the narrative conception, in the amplified form it does and arguably needs to take to perform the explanatory work assigned to it by theorists like Schechtman and MacIntyre, is committed to an implausibly pervasive error theory about our ordinary practices of describing and valuing selves (Camp, 2011). There is also room to worry that narratives are epistemically suspect because they lead us to confabulate an unwarranted grounding basis for the emotional cadences that make them so viscerally compelling (Velleman, 2003), when really they are just epiphenomenal fictions (Dennett, 1988). I want to put these more general concerns to the side, to focus on how the narrative conception interacts with stories' ability to perform the functional roles we identified in §1.

The fundamental problem is that the narrative conception of selfhood saddles stories with an explanatory burden that compromises their capacity to perform the functional roles of configurational comprehension and guiding action. Because narrative structure involves retrospective dependence, a narrative's overall meaning is only determined, and only accessible, given the story's ending. By defining selves in terms of life narratives, the narrative conception holds the meaning and value of those selves hostage to their lives' ends, in a way that leaves radically underdetermined not just who we might become, but who we are and what we should do right now.

Stories and Selves

More explicitly, as we saw in §2, the comprehensive configuration offered by narrative is complex, holistic, and broadly teleological: it selects, individuates, and connects a sequence of disparate events in terms of their contribution to the story's ending. A constituent event can contribute to that ending in many ways: in the simplest case, by causally facilitating the protagonist's focal goal, but also by explaining or motivating the ending in non-causal ways, or by reinforcing or qualifying its broader epistemic or emotional significance. What matters is just that the complex, holistic structure for an entire life narrative depends essentially on its end. The consequence is that, as the literary theorist Peter Brooks (1985, p. 95) puts it, 'All narrative may be in essence obituary in that [...] the retrospective knowledge that it seeks [...] stands on the far side of the end, in human terms on the far side of death.'

Epistemically, this means that as we move through our lives, the narrative meanings we assign to past and present events can be no more than guesses about their ultimate contribution to our life's end. Brooks says that we read novels 'in anticipation of retrospection' (2005, p. 23). This basic point also applies to life narratives. As we might put it, in interpreting our lives just as in reading a novel or history, we are attempting to solve a multivariable equation in which the value of each particular event is constrained by the values of other events in relation to the whole, by way of their relation to the end.

But this basic similarity cloaks a significant difference. An essential condition on the anticipation of retrospection we perform while reading a fictional or historical narrative is our trust that an intentional agent has constructed or imposed a comprehensive, epistemically and emotionally satisfying structure on the narrative's constituent events. Again, we are often deeply unsure how the author will manage to build that satisfying structure; and they can manage it in many, often unexpected ways. We may also question, while reading and at the end, whether our trust is well placed. Still, the act of reading a completed narrative constitutively involves a basic level of trust that the equation does have a satisfying solution. At the most basic level, this trust imbues the story's constituent events with a minimal level of significance: we assume that if an event has been mentioned at all, it must contribute in some substantial way to the story's end.

When we transfer narrative understanding from these sorts of authoritatively authored texts to real life, the anticipation of retrospection that governs our provisional interpretations of unfolding events becomes considerably more fraught. Some people experience a basic authorial trust for real life, typically via belief in a personal God; but many do not. But absent a faith that the events of our life will ultimately be subsumed into some coherent holistic configuration, we lose even the provisional constraints on events' narrative meanings that we deploy while reading novels and histories. Indeed, unless we assume that some intentional agent has engineered a coherent ending which is already determined albeit inaccessible to us, the unfolding events of our lives can't even *have* the sort of robust, descriptively thick, and emotionally resonant meaning that narrative promises to provide until our lives have ended. And in turn, if life narratives define selves, then this further entails that stories can only bring selves into being at life's end.

The facts that the narrative meanings of unfolding events are contingent on faith that those events contribute to a satisfying ending, and that their meanings are constrained only by our assumptions about what that ending might be, also makes trouble for narratives' capacity to guide action. The basic challenge here is, in Kierkegaard's pithy (1843, p. 306) motto, that 'life must be understood backwards but lived forwards'. At any given moment, I must act based on my understanding of my current situation. A narrative conception of selfhood promises to assist in this task by individuating and prioritizing a profile of options for action for *me*, defined in terms of my particular life. But the anticipatory retrospection of narrative comprehension *in medias res* entails that this profile of options is only defined in terms of its contribution to my life's end. Thus, I can at best guess at what I should do now by guessing at an ending that is determined but as yet unknown. And the more indeterminate that ending is, the more indeterminate what I should do now becomes and the less guidance a life narrative can provide.

This indeterminacy does not undermine Bruner's less ambitious point that stories are templates for action. For Bruner, stories are conventionalized tropes that guide action by assimilating my particular situation to a more generic one, which is itself defined by its contribution to a generic ending. Thus, if I assume my life is a comedy, then it makes sense that *this* must be the 'meet-cute' with my future spouse with whom I will live happily ever after; while if I assume that it is a tragedy, then *this* must be the fateful error that ultimately unravels my career and leaves me slobbering drunk in a dank hotel. Because Bruner's 'cultural coins' don't traffic in the narrative conception's highly individualized selves, the options for action they deliver are also commensurately generic.

So, the retrospective dependence of narrative structure entails that stories can offer specific guidance for action *in medias res* only insofar as they treat life's ending as itself determinate and specific. Beyond its epistemic and metaphysical implications, this point has an important practical consequence. Precisely in order to individuate and prioritize what we should do now, narratives must foreclose other options for action, defined by other potential endings. In this sense, the very feature that makes stories powerful equipment for living also makes them constricting shackles: they highlight a particular path forward only by concealing alternative paths. Given an assumed life story, it can palpably feel like *this* is what will happen next, and so that *this* is what I must do now. If events don't then transpire as anticipated, this raises the stakes for future action: it may seem that *this* is the only remaining path for me to achieve the 'right' ending. And if my life's guiding *telos* becomes unattainable, I may feel that I am an utter failure – echoing Marlon Brando's Terry Malloy in *On the Waterfront*: 'I could have been a contender. I could have been somebody instead of a bum, which is what I am, let's face it.'

The risk is that by blinding us to alternative paths, an assumed life narrative becomes a self-fulfilling prophecy. This dynamic is particularly insidious for those who undergo trauma, like rape or war. Trauma is by definition a profound disruption of the anticipated course of events, in which a person's agency is undermined at least temporarily. This is inherently disorienting. But this acute local disruption often generates a broader narrative disruption, which compounds the initial insult by threatening to undermine the person's entire self-conception. Moreover, the traumatic event's acute local significance also makes it an especially tempting locus for a new narrative, one that imposes the additional penalty of holding the rest of the person's life and self to its intuitive narrative schema, often in the form of self-blame (Brison, 2002).

5. Antidotes to Narrative Foreclosure

In §1, I identified two functional roles for stories: configurational comprehension and action guidance. In §2, I identified the basic contours of narrative structure: a complex, holistic configuration of a temporal sequence of events, presented as mattering in virtue of their contribution to an emotionally and epistemically satisfying ending. In §3, I introduced an apparently natural extension of the core idea that stories are 'equipment for living': the view that selves are constituted by narratives of their lives. In §4, I argued that given the retrospective dependence of narrative structure, this view ends up holding selves interpretively and practically hostage to their life's endings.

Elisabeth Camp

For many people, the retrospective dependence of a life story may be benign or beneficial. Some have an abiding faith in Fate or a personal Author. Some stumble into a critical event that they take to have been highly contingent but that sets them off on a quest they fully embrace. However, we also saw in §3 that many people's lives fail to conform to a familiar narrative template, or to ever come together into any overarching structure defined in terms of a satisfying ending. For them, defining their selves in terms of their lives' stories can be disorienting or defeating.

The problem is that we do need 'equipment for living'. We need to construe an overwhelmingly complex world in a way that renders it intuitively coherent and personally meaningful; and we need to act fluently in real time in service of our personal goals and values (Camp, 2019). If narrative is our only tool for doing this, then the price of assuming a hidden ending engineered by a remote author may not be too steep to pay. Even if it dooms many of us to being erstwhile contenders, at least our lives have some meaning, insofar as there is somebody we *might* have been and something we should have done.

But must we pay that price? In this section, I suggest that the narrative conception is driven by two plausible but pernicious assumptions: that narrative is our only tool for making meaning; and that selves are defined by their lives. We can achieve a healthy flexibility for constructing selves, and rehabilitate stories as equipment for living, if we abandon these assumptions.

5.1 Kinds of Frames

Bruner, Mink, and others are right to observe that stories are among our most basic interpretive tools. Indeed, MacIntyre is arguably correct that the basic task of interpreting agents as taking action ascribes some narrative structure, however implicit and minimal. However, stories are not our only equipment for comprehending the world; and the world does not consist entirely of agents pursuing goals.

Narratives are just one species within the broader genus of what I call *frames* (Camp, 2019). As I understand them, frames are representational devices that crystallize perspectives, guiding intuitive cognition by orienting attention, explanation, and response in terms of a focal principle. We use frames to express, communicate, and negotiate perspectives across a wide array of domains, including politics, science, religion, and art. Familiar examples include mantras ('Boys will be boys'; 'It's the economy, stupid'; 'Minds are computers';

Camp, 2020); metaphors ('Juliet is the sun'; 'John is a pit bull; Camp, 2006); and identity labels ('Black'; 'queer'; 'evangelical'; Camp and Flores, forthcoming a, b).

Frames in general exhibit three key features, producing a characteristic profile of cognitive benefits and risks. First, they *schematize* intuitive cognition by offering heuristics for parsing, prioritizing, connecting, and responding to information. A frame offers a principle for deciding what matters about a domain and why: 'all you need to know' in order to get an interpretive grip on objects, individuals, and situations in that domain. The benefit is that frames focus attention on important features, preventing us from being overwhelmed by irrelevant clutter. The risk is myopic complacency: we smugly explain away or fail to notice features that really do matter, even by our own lights, but that fail to fit the frame (Nguyen, 2021; Camp, forthcoming).

Second, frames *stabilize* intuitive cognition by anchoring an open-ended perspective in a tangible vehicle. The benefit is that they enable us to coordinate interpretation across agents and times. Intuitive cognition is typically highly malleable by contextual factors; and individuals often bring significantly different assumptions to a conversation. Frames help us to get and stay on the same page, individually and collectively. Individually, a frame can help us to recall and stick to our avowed principles in the face of contextual temptation; for instance, someone trying to leave a dysfunctional relationship might remind themselves 'He's just not that into you'. Collectively, a frame can introduce a rich body of intuitive assumptions into a conversation without their needing to be explicitly articulated. The risk is rigid ossification: a frame that works well enough in some contexts can become so cognitively or communicatively entrenched that it dominates interpretation across the board (Camp and Flores, forthcoming a).

Third, frames *activate* intuitive cognition in ways that are partly, but only partly, under voluntary control. Perspectival interpretation in general is intuitive, in the sense that one's actual cognitive processes are governed by the perspective's operative dispositions unless actively inhibited. 'Getting' a frame requires actually implementing the perspective it expresses, so that one is actually, if only temporarily, disposed to notice, recall, explain, and respond to situations or individuals of the relevant kind in its terms. One can try to employ a frame, by focusing attention and activating certain thoughts and images. But as the experience of Gestalt perception palpably demonstrates, trying is neither necessary nor sufficient for 'getting'. On the one hand, one may sincerely believe that a situation should be construed in terms of a certain frame – say, 'equal pay for equal work' – without that belief being reflected in one's intuitive, detailed patterns of attention, explanation, and response. And on the other hand, a frame – say, 'children should be seen but not heard' – may intrude into one's intuitive interpretations unbidden, despite one's efforts to inhibit it. The benefit of intuitive activation is that it streamlines processing and amplifies the motivational immediacy of emotional, evaluative, and practical response. The risk is that one's visceral reactions are out of kilter with one's reflectively avowed principles.

In §§1 and 2, we saw that stories fit the model of frames, in a way that explains their functional roles: they offer focal principles for parsing, selecting, explaining, and responding to a complex body of information in an intuitive, holistic way. Stories bear retelling because activating their overarching schematic structure reinforces cognitive dispositions that support a robust, stable, intuitive understanding of its constituent events, rendering their details meaningful in a way that facilitates individual recall and collective communication. And they help us cope with surprise by explaining individual events in terms of larger structures that support fluent, flexible, open-ended prediction, and by parsing and prioritizing a profile of options for action presented in a motivationally engaged way.

At the same time, these interpretive benefits also induce frames' characteristic perils: their viscerally compelling construals blind us to details that don't fit and lure us into self-fulfilling prophecies. So far, these are just the perils of frames generally. Given that we need 'equipment for living' that streamlines and stabilizes the processing of information in light of our goals and values, it would be counterproductive to try to dispense with frames entirely (Camp 2019, forthcoming). We also saw in §4, though, that the retrospective dependence of narrative structure generates a more specific profile of risks: when life stories are tasked with defining selves, they hold those selves metaphysically, epistemically, and practically hostage to their lives' ends.

Abandoning the narrative conception's identification of selves with lives frees us to deploy other species of frames to comprehend our selves and to guide action without importing the baggage of the narrative conception. Each species of frame carries its own profile of interpretive strengths and weaknesses. None is inherently better or worse. But by analyzing how they work, we can choose among them in ways that amplify their distinctive strengths and mitigate their distinctive risks. I'll briefly mention four kinds of frame that may be especially useful for self-construction.

Stories and Selves

First, *identity labels* like 'Mom', 'queer', 'Latina', 'evangelical', or 'doctor' frame individuals in terms of social kinds, offering cultural templates for being an instance of that kind. Some of these kinds, like *doctor*, are achievements, which evoke corresponding narratives about pursuing their *telos*. Others, like *woman* or *Black*, are unchosen categories that one (typically) inhabits throughout life. And still others, like *teenager* or *mother*, are temporary, or ambiguously telic. As generic categorical terms, identity labels risk erasing the particularity of individual selves: treating someone as 'nothing but' an instance of that kind, inappropriately centering features of their identity that may actually be peripheral to them, and importing unwarranted assumptions about what further features they possess (Whiteley, 2023; Camp and Flores, forthcoming a). However, identity labels can also construct selves in more positive ways, by offering intuitive, open-ended scripts for how to perform being that kind (Butler, 1988). The risk of flattening is greatest when others apply a label for a coarse-grained, socially disempowered social kind to an individual, as with weapon uses of slurs (Camp, 2013). But when labels are self-applied, especially when they are fine-grained and flexible, they can scaffold individual and collective agency (Camp and Flores, forthcoming b).

Second, *metaphors* like 'I am a butterfly', 'I am a snowplow', or 'I am Anna Karenina' frame an individual in terms of a 'twofold' lens of similarity and difference, by highlighting features in the target that can be matched in some way to features of the frame (Camp, 2006, 2009b). Unlike identity labels, which are essentially generic and static, metaphors involve an open-ended, dynamic interaction between frame and target (Black, 1955). As a result, the same metaphorical phrase can induce dramatically distinct configurations when applied to different targets or in different interpretive contexts: thus, the metaphor of 'the sun' highlights and imputes very different features when applied to Juliet, Achilles, Louis XIV, and Richard III (Camp, 2005). Because metaphors wear their non-literality on their sleeves, they are less likely than either identity labels or life stories to ossify into rigid frames that purport to capture the whole truth about an individual. On the other hand, because metaphors are non-literal, context-dependent, and open-ended, they are less likely to offer clear, stable scripts for action.

Third, *telling details* like 'He was climbing ladders before he could talk' or 'She rolls the socks and underwear in her drawers' frame an individual by displaying a particular feature as exemplifying a broader pattern (Camp 2007b, 2019). Their actual, concrete instantiation makes telling details especially specific, vivid, and visceral; and they can be deeply evocative and resonant. However, because they leave unarticulated how to extrapolate from the presented detail to a more general structure, telling details tend to be less productive as guides for action: they neither encode schematic scripts, like identity labels and generic narratives, nor suggest open-ended filters for mapping new situations, like metaphors.

Finally, *games* crystallize modes of agency: intuitive patterns of attention and profiles of goals, along with sets of skills for achieving them (Nguyen, 2020). Because games enact schematized scripts for action, often in the form of explicit, formal rules, they inculcate ways of being and acting in an especially direct way: one actually, albeit temporarily, inhabits a certain role. However, by 'sealing off' that enactment from reality, games risk seducing us away from the gritty, confusing messiness of life (Nguyen, 2021; Camp, 2023).

5.2 Framing Selves

Noticing that there are other kinds of frames besides narrative gives us more tools for achieving configurational comprehension, guiding action, and constructing selves. Still, given that all frames are interpretively risky and that each species of frame carries its own profile of interpretive risks, we might wonder why we should think that other kinds of frames will help us escape narrative conception's problematic consequences. Maybe the problem is more fundamental, in the very idea of self-creation as an art of self-interpretation.

At a basic level, one might think that the narrative conception's core claim – that we construct ourselves by construing ourselves – is inherently paradoxical. Narrative's retrospective dependence entails that selves only ever *are* at the end of life. The individual who works to actualize that self cannot be that self, because that self does not yet exist; and yet there is someone *now* who is creating that self, by construing what the appropriate course of action for that future self to have done would be.[2] Surely telling a story can't have that kind of bootstrapping power; perhaps the selves we create through stories are just epiphenomenal fictions (Dennett, 1988).

I think the appropriate response to the general worry about the paradox of self-creation is that telling a story about one's self can have causal looping effects, affecting one's actions at a local level in a way that anchors selves in reality (Velleman, 2006). Deploying a frame to comprehend myself involves highlighting certain of my

---

[2] Thanks to Justin Khoo for pressing this worry.

existing features and downplaying others, connecting features together into explanatory patterns; and prioritizing certain goals and values within my current cognitive dispositions. Actually configuring my intuitive thinking about my self in the frame's terms at this moment directly influences my current behavior, by influencing which options for action I intuitively entertain and am motivated to perform, and habituates me into deploying those same patterns of perspectival thought and modes of agency downstream.

However, because the narrative conception defines selves in terms of life narratives, it lengthens the operative causal loops through to the end of life, in a way that renders the selves we construct through self-construal temporally precarious. By contrast, because alternative species of frame don't involve retrospective dependency, they shorten those loops, in a way that allows selves to *be* at each moment. I actually am, now, a white female philosophy professor and a mother; our Dean really is (metaphorically) a pit bull; my mother really is the kind of person who organizes her rolled-up underwear in careful columns.

Even if other kinds of frames make the idea of self-construction less metaphysically and epistemically paradoxical, they might still hold selves hostage. We might smugly deploy an inaccurate or unfitting identity label, metaphor, or telling detail to construe ourselves, all the while conveniently ignoring or explaining away less flattering features. Or we might trap ourselves in a self-fulfilling prophecy, molding our self to fit a frame that prevents us from acheiving a better possibility. Why think identity labels and metaphors do any better at liberating us from interpretive shackles than stories?

The risk of myopic complacency is the basic, besetting sin of perspectival cognition; as I said in §5.1, it is an inevitable corollary to the intuitive, flexible streamlining of cognition that perspectives bring. The most powerful antidote to myopic complacency is playful open-mindedness: trying on a range of frames in an exploratory way (Camp, forthcoming). Playfulness carries its own risks. We may end up seduced or habituated into a frame we intended to try on only instrumentally (Camp, 2017, 2023); or we may flit among frames without deeply inhabiting any, ironically distancing ourselves from the very project of authentic self-construction. At a deeper level, as María Lugones (Lugones, 1987) emphasizes, playfulness involves vulnerability: to being surprised, to being foolish, to being construed in ways one rejects by hostile and oppressive interpreters. In the wrong environments, such vulnerability can be dangerously unwise. Nor is playfulness always necessary. Many people flourish by embracing a culturally established narrative or identity label. For others, such as 'strivers' climbing the socio-economic ladder,

Elisabeth Camp

blinkering one's self-construal with a frame that doesn't fit may be a productive form of bootstrapping (Morton, 2019).

However, many people at some point in their lives feel that they lack a good frame for their selves, either because their available options are all unfitting or oppressive, or because they are too complex to fit any one story, label, or metaphor. And such cases, it can be productive to try on a variety of frames with a playful attitude. Performed in a supportive context and with due critical humility, playful framing can scaffold self-construction by highlighting neglected properties, suggesting novel connections and sources of value, and offering new scripts for action. By feeling out which properties and configurations feel most resonant within and across frames, one can cultivate a more nuanced and robust self, and glimpse opportunities for understanding and transforming one's self in heretofore unforeseen ways (Camp and Flores, forthcoming b). Such playfulness may be deeply serious: thus, Joshua Landy (2022) argues that in *The Periodic Table*, Primo Levi deploys the identity label of *chemist* as a way to reclaim his own distinctive self from the traumatic life narrative imposed by the Holocaust.

Assuming that narrative is the unique, essential mechanism for self-construction makes it easy to assume that one's job is to articulate and enact the true narrative of one's life and to treat that narrative as given and fixed. Acknowledging other kinds of frames makes it easier to liberate ourselves from taking any one frame as hegemonically authoritative. We can also take a more playful attitude toward stories themselves. Once we abandon the identification of selves with lives, we can employ shorter stories as telling details that exemplify a strand of one's identity without defining one's full self. We can also take a more flexible stance toward our entire life story, by toggling among different narratological roles. We navigate life *in medias res* as protagonists. But we can also extricate ourselves from the flow of time to adopt the role of narrator, shifting our focus to other characters, raising alternative guiding questions, and prioritizing different values. And at least sometimes, we can step into an authorial role, actively revisiting and revising the guiding genre of our life's story or the ending toward which we assume we are hurtling.

The easiest way to liberate ourselves from the shackles of an imprisoning frame is to try on an alternative one. Perhaps we will then be fortunate enough to discover a cultural template that fits, or creative enough to construct an idiosyncratic frame that we can wholeheartedly employ to comprehend our selves and guide our actions. However, some people find no single frame to be adequate to their full nuance and complexity, either at a time or over time. And for

Stories and Selves

them, the specter of disunity that motivated us in §3 to amplify the core idea of stories as tools for self-construction into lifelong narratives rises again: what coherent principle of self-constitution might we appeal to, if neither narratives nor alternative frames are available?

Although frames are valuable technologies for schematizing and stabilizing cognition, they are not essential to interpretation as such. Nor are they essential for self-construction: we can work to build and modify our selves directly, by intervening on what Iris Murdoch (1956, p. 39) calls our 'texture of being': our intuitive way of inhabiting and responding to the world.

To make sense of frameless self-construction, sculpting offers a better analogy than storytelling. Just as a sculptor must work with the affordances of the materials they have, but can still creatively transform those materials into an aesthetically satisfying object, so can we take the profile of characteristics that we are born with and have acquired through life, and creatively augment, eliminate, and modulate them to produce a coherent whole that embeds a complex configuration of disparate features into a satisfying configuration.

Thus, Nietzsche (Nietzsche 1886/1966, §290) recommends the 'great and rare art' of 'giv[ing] style to one's character' through 'long practice and daily work'. 'In the end,' he says, 'when the work is finished, it becomes evident how the constraint of a single taste governed and formed everything large and small. Whether this taste was good or bad is less important than one might suppose, if only it was a single taste!' Just as on the narrative conception, Nietzsche allows that a self is not finished until life's end. But where the narrative conception requires a knowing author who engineers intermediate events into meaningful relation by describing them in terms of their contribution to the life's ultimate end, a sculptural model allows the unifying, meaning-making principle to be actually and directly operative throughout the course of life.

We might prioritize moral and practical constraints more than Nietzsche does; in particular, I would lean more heavily on Murdoch's 'vision of morality' than on Nietzsche's 'will to power' in configuring my texture of being. However, the basic model of self-construction as incrementally sculpting a richly textured character offers a way to capture the narrative conception's core insight that self-construal can constitute self-construction. But it does this in a non-paradoxical way that allows selves to already *be* at each moment, and not merely insofar as they contribute to an eventual actualization. At the same time, unlike identity labels, a sculpting model captures the dynamic, prospective promise of *becoming*.

Elisabeth Camp

Finally, as both Nietzsche and Murdoch emphasize, it centers our primary locus of being and agency less in heroic questing and more in the 'daily work' of habituating ourselves into intuitive patterns of interpretation and action.

6. Conclusion

What do I hope you to take forward from this discussion on your life's journey? In §1, following Burke, Bruner, and Mink, we identified two functional roles for stories as 'equipment for living': configurational comprehension and guiding action. We should celebrate stories' power at performing these tasks. However, the way that stories accomplish this is by imposing retrospective necessity on a temporal sequence of events, so that beginning and intervening events are defined and explained in terms of their contribution to the story's ending. As a result, when those functional roles are coupled with a narrative conception of selves, stories end up holding selves metaphysically, epistemically, and practically hostage to their lives' ends. Our understanding and options for action become at best glimpses 'in anticipation of retrospection', dooming many people to disorientation and despair.

Once we distinguish selves from the lives they live, we are free to employ stories as one tool in a larger armamentarium of frames for self-construction. We should do so in awareness of their distinctive profiles of peril and payoff, and in the recognition that the complex configurations of our actual selves often resist reduction to any easy formula.

References

Aristotle, *Poetics*, Samuel Butcher (trans.), 3rd edition (London: MacMillan, 1902).

Max Black, 'Metaphor', *Proceedings of the Aristotelian Society, New Series*, 55:1 (1955), 273–94.

Susan Brison, *Aftermath: Violence and the Remaking of a Self* (Princeton, NJ: Princeton University Press, 2002).

Peter Brooks, *Reading for the Plot: Design and Intention in Narrative* (New York: Vintage, 1985).

Peter Brooks, *Realist Vision* (New Haven: Yale University Press, 2005).

Stories and Selves

Jerome Bruner, *Making Stories: Law, Literature, Life* (Cambridge MA: Harvard University Press, 2002).
Kenneth Burke, 'Literature as Equipment for Living', *Direction*, 1:1 (1938), 10–13.
Judith Butler, 'Performative Acts and Gender Constitution: An Essay in Phenomenology and Feminist Theory', *Theatre Journal*, 40:4 (1988), 519–31.
Elisabeth Camp, 'Critical Study of Josef Stern's Metaphor in Context', *Noûs*, 39:4 (2005), 715–31.
Elisabeth Camp, 'Metaphor and That Certain "Je Ne Sais Quoi"', *Philosophical Studies*, 129:1 (2006), 1–25.
Elisabeth Camp, 'Thinking with Maps', *Philosophical Perspectives*, 21:1 (2007a), 145–82.
Elisabeth Camp, 'Showing, Telling, and Seeing: Metaphor and "Poetic" Language', *The Baltic International Yearbook of Cognition, Logic, and Communication*, 3:1 (2007b), 1–24.
Elisabeth Camp, 'A Language of Baboon Thought?', in Robert Lurz (ed.), *The Philosophy of Animal Minds* (Cambridge: Cambridge University Press, 2009a), 108–27.
Elisabeth Camp, 'Two Varieties of Literary Imagination: Metaphor, Fiction, and Thought Experiments', *Midwest Studies in Philosophy*, 33:1 (2009b), 107–30.
Elisabeth Camp, 'Wordsworth's Prelude, Poetic Autobiography, and Narrative Constructions of the Self', *Nonsite.org*, 3:1 (2011), 1–34.
Elisabeth Camp, 'Slurring Perspectives', *Analytic Philosophy*, 54:3 (2013), 330–49.
Elisabeth Camp, 'Perspectives in Imaginative Engagement with Fiction', *Philosophical Perspectives*, 31:1 (2017), 73–102.
Elisabeth Camp, 'Perspectives and Frames in Pursuit of Ultimate Understanding', in Stephen Grimm (ed.), *Varieties of Understanding: New Perspectives from Philosophy, Psychology, and Theology* (Oxford: Oxford University Press, 2019), 17–45.
Elisabeth Camp, 'Imaginative Frames for Scientific Inquiry', in Arnon Levy and Peter Godfrey-Smith (eds), *The Scientific Imagination* (Oxford: Oxford University Press, 2020), 304–36.
Elisabeth Camp, 'Agency, Stability, And Permeability in "Games"', *Journal of Ethics and Social Philosophy*, 23:3 (2023), 448–62.
Elisabeth Camp, 'Perspectival Complacency, Perversion, and Amelioration', in Wayne Riggs and Nancy Snow (eds), *Open-Mindedness and Perspective* (New York: Oxford University Press, forthcoming).
Elisabeth Camp and Carolina Flores, '"That's All You Really Are": Centering Social Identities Without Essentialist Beliefs', in

Elisabeth Camp

Sally Haslanger, Laura Schroeter, and Francois Schroeter (eds), *Mind, Language and Social Reality* (Oxford: Oxford University Press, forthcoming a).

Elisabeth Camp and Carolina Flores, 'Identity Labels as Interpretive Frames for Building Agency', *Philosophical Quarterly*, (forthcoming b).

Noel Carroll, 'On the Narrative Connection', in *Beyond Aesthetics* (New York: Cambridge University Press, 2001), 118–33.

Noel Carroll, 'Narrative Closure', *Philosophical Studies*, 135:1 (2007), 1–15.

Daniel Dennett, 'Why Everyone Is a Novelist', *Times Literary Supplement*, 4459 (September 16–22, 1988), 1016, 1028–29.

Daniel Dennett, 'Real Patterns', *Journal of Philosophy*, 88:1 (1991), 27–51.

Rachel Fraser, 'Narrative Testimony', *Philosophical Studies*, 178:12 (2021), 4025–52.

Jenann Ismael, 'Why (Study) the Humanities? The View from Science', in Stephen Grimm (ed.), *Making Sense of the World: New Essays on the Philosophy of Understanding* (New York: Oxford University Press, 2017), 177–93.

Frank Kermode, *The Sense of an Ending: Studies in the Theory of Fiction* (Oxford: Oxford University Press, 1967).

Søren Kierkegaard, *Journalen* JJ:167, *Søren Kierkegaards Skrifter* (Søren Kierkegaard Research Center, Copenhagen 1843/1997).

Joshua Landy, 'Saving the Self from Stories: Resistance to Narrative in Primo Levi's The Periodic Table', *Narrative*, 30:1 (2022), 85–103.

María Lugones, 'Playfulness, "World"-Travelling, and Loving Perception', *Hypatia*, 2:2 (1987), 3–19.

Alasdair MacIntyre, *After Virtue: A Study in Moral Theory* (South Bend, IN: University of Notre Dame Press, 1981).

Louis Mink, 'History and Fiction as Modes of Comprehension', *New Literary History*, 1:3 (1970), 541–58.

Jennifer Morton, *Moving Up Without Losing Your Way: The Ethical Costs of Upward Mobility* (Princeton, NJ: Princeton University Press, 2019).

Iris Murdoch, 'Vision and Choice in Morality', *Aristotelian Society Supplementary Volume*, 30:1 (1956), 14–58.

Frederick Nietzsche, *The Gay Science: With a Prelude in German Rhymes and an Appendix of Songs*, Bernard Williams (intr.), Josefine Nauckhoff and Adrian Del Caro (trans.), (Cambridge: Cambridge University Press, [1886] 1966).

John Niles, *Homo Narrans: The Poetics and Anthropology of Oral Literature* (Philadelphia: University of Pennsylvania Press, 1999).

Christopher Thi Nguyen, *Games and the Art of Agency* (Oxford: Oxford University Press, 2020).
Christopher Thi Nguyen, 'The Seductions of Clarity', *Royal Institute of Philosophy Supplement*, 89:1 (2021), 227–55.
Marya Schechtman, *The Constitution of Selves* (Ithaca, NY: Cornell University Press, 1996).
Galen Strawson, 'Against Narrativity', *Ratio*, 17:1 (2004), 428–52.
David Velleman, 'Narrative Explanation', *The Philosophical Review*, 112:1 (2003), 1–25.
David Velleman, 'The Self as Narrator', in *Self to Self: Selected Essays* (Cambridge: Cambridge University Press 2006), 203–23.
Ella Kate Whiteley, '"A Woman First and a Philosopher Second": Relative Attentional Surplus on the Wrong Property', *Ethics*, 133:4 (2023), 497–528.

A New Look at the Classical Chinese *Dào* of the Relation between Word and World

CHAD HANSEN

Abstract
I argue that the absence of some of the 'greatest hits' of Western philosophy in Classical China can be explained by a Wittgensteinian take on the role of language in philosophy. One is the 'Idea Theory' of meaning which anchors Western Mind-Body dualism. Its attraction is removed when the writing reminds us that a picture does not by itself 'give life to' our language even while it plays a role of cross-linguistic communication. Another is the centrality of a law-command theory of normativity which combines with mind-body dualism to give a natural push toward monotheistic supernaturalism. Western attempts to make the 'God' impulse logical (e.g., the Ontological Argument) fail because of differences in Chinese syntax. The upshot is we need not deny Chinese thinkers the status of philosophers for their failure to share our philosophical presuppositions and resultant agenda.

1. Introduction

This paper argues for the unsurprising proposition that the language of a culture influences their philosophy of language. The surprise is that our European culture's blindingly obvious traditional theory of language was such a non-starter for ancient Chinese philosophers. Writing about the same time as Plato and Aristotle, they treated a causal-historical philosophy of language as obvious. In Western thought, the causal theory was a modern, revisionist, naturalist theory. That causal theory of language shaped Classical Chinese philosophy as thoroughly as Greek rationalist linguistic theory did Western thought.

Their theory looks modern to us because our version of that theory emerged in the 20th century as a reaction against traditional Western 'idea theory' which shaped Western mind-body dualism. There is a natural world of *material* objects and an intellectual world of *immaterial* minds and ideas. What makes Chinese theory of language difficult was not only the inherent complexity of Chinese written characters, but that Chinese thinkers did *not* present it as replacing our familiar use of mind-body dualism to fund a resemblance or picture theory of the relation of word and world.

Pictures *represent* (stand for, symbolize, refer to *etc.*) things. Words represent things. How? Western 'folk' theory says by representing the mental thing which pictures the natural material thing. Accepting that 'folk' theory entails accepting that the theory is blindingly obvious. The Chinese twist on representation seems problematic because it suggests they don't have minds and ideas. If the paradigm problem of philosophy is the relation of mind (ideas) and body (natural objects), then they are not philosophers.

The puzzle deepens when we appreciate that Chinese theory of their writing treats written words as combining pictures and indicative elements to form meaningful units—the things Western rationalists would class as abstract, mental objects, the meanings of words. Why, with a notoriously pictographic/ideographic folk theory of their written word, were Classical Chinese thinkers *not* compelled to see how obvious the *idea-thought represents object-fact* theory is to Western common sense?

Language was as central to their philosophical tradition as it was to ours. But while Western philosophy of language became a dominant field in the 20th century, the Chinese viewed their own theory of their language as pivotal during their Classical period (3rd c. BC), keying their account of humans' place in the natural world. Both traditions of philosophy had strong currents of deflationary theories of language, that dismissed language as superficial in relation to something more real and authentic. The crucial point of divergence was that Western philosophy's reality was the individual soul or mind (psyche) and Chinese reality was a natural world in which humans cooperated via historically evolved social-political structures.

2. Daos and Laws

We start with one key to the puzzle: the Chinese concept of *dào* (道 path, way). I call this a Dào in the title, but all Classical Chinese philosophy pivoted around that normative/causal concept. In the earliest historical text, Confucius's *Analects,* that core concept structured the schema for understanding natural guidance. On the other side of the Himalayas (from India to Egypt) the metaphor with a similar gravitational pull on thought was a social practice: kings making *laws* (and punishing *disobedience*). These two different conceptual frames structured our respective philosophies of language.

A New Look at the Classical Chinese *Dào*

On one side, we had *ways* of speaking and writing, on the other, someone authored or agreed on *rules* of grammar and spelling.

The metaphysical outcomes were stark. The Western side had *concepts, ideas,* and *meanings* to help explain how to use *words* but also had intellectual world counterparts of grammatical sentences such as thoughts, beliefs, opinions, and a world built of facts, events, and actions. The norms involved the 'logical/syntactic' fitting of grammatical sentences to these sentence-like bits of reality. The Ionians and Greeks discovered *laws* of logic and the concept of a proof (Pythagoras's theorem) to understand how to guide our use of sentences, and thus how to *think* and *believe*.

This Western account of words, minds, and the *sensible* world we call semantics. It grounds the Western mind-body dualism, the theory of minds and ideas. Our theory of knowledge involves getting the semantic mapping right, representing, picturing the world accurately. Beliefs, thoughts, and the sentences that *express* them will count as *known* only if they are true, i.e. map accurately onto facts or events. And our normative goal is not only to make *true* our *beliefs* and *assertions*, but to make true the *laws* of moral conduct or behavior. Philosophers know to invoke a plethora of other conditions, qualifications, and clarifications of this orientation. It fills two millennia of Western thought around this core Western 'common sense' view of knowledge of reality.

Looking at Ancient Chinese thought, a familiar reaction is that it is not philosophy. It doesn't struggle with the relation of mind and body which is the essence of metaphysics. It doesn't have a discipline of logic. It didn't have an *obvious* counterpart of truth until after the spread of Indian Buddhism from the other side of the Himalayas, so it's not recognizable as epistemology. At most it deals recognizably with ethics but lacks the rest. It is merely wise humans moralizing.

What is less noticed in this clash of philosophical civilizations are the two related contrasts we address here: the absence of the Western rationalist 'common sense' 'idea theory of the meaning of words', and 'thoughts' or 'beliefs' as the common-sense mental counterparts of sentences. This latter component of Western folk theory anchors the 'belief-desire' theory of human *free, rational* behavior and its role in the Western puzzle about human free will.

The ancient Chinese masters instead operate with a primary focus on social *practice* and its contrary, *natural* guidance, the guidance implicit in the Chinese *path* (*dào*) metaphor. The implicit goal of 'knowledge' was not of picturing a material reality, but of competence, mastery, and know-how in behaving in real contexts. They didn't believe in the importance of correct belief/thought. They

Chad Hansen

neither focused on sentence-sized units of language, of mind (beliefs, thoughts), of natural (causal) process (events), nor of human behavior (actions). The first sentence of the first complete book of learning, the *Confucian Analects* (ca. 5th c. BC), begins 'to study and regularly practice, that is the life!' Confucius' conception of the good life operates within a seemingly mereological conception of nature and language. There are larger, more inclusive, and smaller parts of nature. There are also parts of language, longer and shorter compositional strings of strokes, characters, phrases, slogans, descriptions *etc*. They are two separate compositional structures.

Chinese thought focused on the individual word or character. The character could be a part of these strings (whether on scrolls or spoken) and it in turn had parts, pictographic, indicative, or rhyming components that made up the individual characters each designed to fit in its square 'box' in the vertical bamboo strips of Classical texts. Characters can be compounded in many ways to represent sums or intersections of things (物 *wù* natural kinds and 器 *qì* artifacts, implements, tools) as well as interactions in social behaviors (事 *shì* affairs, business).

3. Idea Theory of Meaning

One way to query whether traditional 'idea theory' is an intuitive, common-sense account of human experience or an optional cultural inheritance is to look at the earliest arguments for it. It turns out common sense is not all that common and usually has an evolutionary history behind it. It emerges most recognizably in Aristotle (via Plato). While the origins of idea theory may lie in a long and obscure pre-history of the languages of the ancient civilizations stretching from India to Egypt that eventually adopted the Phoenician invention of a segmentally phonetic alphabet, alphabetic writing motivated the Classical Greek theory of the intellectual, rational realm of being. It has been around long enough that we routinely take it for granted in our way of teaching each other about language. With the typical Greek genius for elaborating a concept by giving it an argument, Aristotle spelled his theory out this way:

> Now spoken sounds are symbols of affections in the soul, and written marks symbols of the spoken sounds. And just as written marks are not the same for all men, neither are spoken sounds. But what these are in the first place signs of—affections

A New Look at the Classical Chinese *Dào*

in the soul—are the same for all; and what these affections are likenesses of—actual things—are also the same. (Aristotle, *De Interpretatione*, 16:3, Ackrill (trans.), 1963, p. 42)

Chinese theory of language is as old as that of the Greek rationalists. Parmenides and Heraclitus to Plato and Aristotle overlap with Confucius to Mozi, Mencius, Zhuangzi, and Xunzi. The Chinese masters implicitly shared a theory of language-world relations that more closely resembled Kripke's (1972) modern alternative to idea theory – the causal, historical-conventional account of language reference. The role of characters in Chinese theory is widely misconstrued in academic orthodoxy by one side in a long-running debate about how to describe Chinese characters: whether to use the term 'ideograph' or to adopt some 'more accurate' neologism such as 'logograph.'

Peter Du Ponceau (1838) functions like a prophet of the 'logograph' side of the debate:

> Chinese characters represent the words of the language and are intended to awaken the remembrance of them in the mind, they are not therefore independent of sounds, for words are sounds. It makes no difference whether those sounds are simple and elementary, as those which our letters represent, or whether they are compounded from two or three of those elements into a syllable. There are syllabic alphabets, like that of the Sanskrit and other languages, and it has never been contended that they do not represent sounds. And it makes no difference that the Chinese syllables are also words, for that does not make them lose their character of sounds. But, on account of this difference, I would not call the Chinese characters a syllabic, but a logographic system of writing. This being the case, it seems necessarily to follow, that as the Chinese characters are in direct connexion with the Chinese spoken words, they can only be read and understood by those who are familiar with the oral language. (Du Ponceau, 1838, Appendix, p. 110)

Du Ponceau was channeling other Western theorists of language like Ferdinand de Saussure (1983) and Leonard Bloomfield's (1914) 'scientific' principle that empirically confirms Aristotle's view that language = speech, and that written language *necessarily* represents speech and things in the world indirectly through the medium first of speech, then of ideas. They take the word 'ideograph' to deny this fundamental principle of linguistics and claim writing directly (without mediation) *represents an idea or concept*.

185

Chad Hansen

Their remedy ignores a less familiar difference between Western and Chinese 'folk theories' of language. Chinese theory of their own language did *not* say it represented Aristotle's 'images in the mind.' They thought characters represented natural objects directly because of their history. They didn't have a *mental idea* or *picture* theory of the relation of words and world.

That fact seems to opponents of the word 'ideograph' to entail that they did not have a theory of *meaning* since Western folk theory turns *meaning* into an *object in mental space*, a mental construct, conception, or abstract object. This distorts traditional Chinese philosophy of language into a silly version of Aristotle's theory – one where pictures (pictograms or ideograms) *represent* the mental pictures (ideas, meanings, concepts) which in turn represent objects and, theoretically explain how speech itself has meaning, links to the world. This coloring of traditional Chinese language learning theory is thus saddled with the conclusion that speech represents writing rather than the obvious 'scientific' law that writing represents speech.

John DeFrancis (1984) turns the alleged empirical law into a tautology by stipulating a distinction between a full and partial writing system. A writing system is full only if it can represent every expression of *the* spoken language. This allows him to dismiss other obvious ideographs in Western writing such as 1, 2 and &, @, and $. The alternative for advocates of 'logograph' is to treat them as representing the English sound 'o-n-e' and 'd-o-l-l-a-r.'

This is, quite frankly, just the insistence that the *Western* theory of teaching their languages (idea-thought theory) is right (for all languages) and the Chinese theory of teaching theirs is wrong. Further, it is baldly wrong about Chinese languages. The error is continuous with our practice of calling Chinese a language, rather than a language family, a group of related languages. The real value of Bloomfield's 'spoken language priority' dictum is to recognize that Chinese is not a single language, but 40+ (depending on degree of mutual intelligibility) distinct spoken languages. It reminds us that China is roughly equivalent to Europe in the number of related but distinct languages. In Europe, we appeal to writing to help us distinguish between different spoken *languages* and different *dialects* of the same languages. In China, continuity with this European practice has led to calling Cantonese and Hokkien *dialects* rather than *languages* of Chinese.

There is no 'Chinese' language in that sense other than the Classical, literary writing – which copies the spoken form of none of the spoken vernaculars. What Chinese 'ideographs' wear on their face is that they are a language of a meta-linguistic community, a

A New Look at the Classical Chinese *Dào*

family of spoken languages, but neither a language 'spoken in China' nor a language of the mind. 'I have no books,' for example, 我沒有書 uses the negation form of Mandarin, 吾無書 uses the probably unspoken literary negation (and the literary first-person pronoun) and 我冇書 uses the Cantonese negation form. Other triggers might be the third person pronoun, 佢 vs. 他, linking verbs, aspect markers, and a plethora of common expressions as well as direct and indirect object order. Each *could* be read in the other's language (except, of course, for the unspoken literary form) as a stilted, awkward, or literary way to speak. It would almost always be unnatural speech – considerably more unnatural than how reading written English essays is unnatural in comparison to giving a lecture in English.

Similarly, logogram advocates note that the translation of, e.g., an English word takes two characters in Chinese and conclude that the individual characters are morphemes not words. Europeans use the conventions of writing spaces to individuate and count words and so we get the contrast of 'long words' of German because German compound words omit spaces. How can we criticize Chinese for similarly individuating their 'words' with the box-like space within which they write each character (especially when the various Chinese languages typically read the character as a single syllable word)?

If Chinese characters 'stand for' Chinese words they do so in the same way English written words *stand for* (represent) English words – to wit, usually not at all. If I want to refer to an English word, I put it in quotes or italics or otherwise signal that I am referring to the word, mentioning it, not using it in talking about us in a natural world environment. Normally, we use a word or phrase in either script to pick out or draw attention to some proper part of the world, not to a sound. I can, of course, refer to the sound, but the token of 'can' eleven words back in this sentence does not refer to a sound. It simply *is* a written word and if my wife says c-a-h-n and I say c-a-n, we say the same word as was written. If the speech-first argument shows Chinese is logographic, it equally shows that English is logographic. The written word 'can' is the English word 'can,' not its different spoken variations. The spoken variations are equally tokens of the English word 'can.'

So it is with Chinese 可 (Mandarin *kě* Cantonese *hǒ* can, may). The obvious difference is that European written languages are alphabetic with segmental phoneme structure, and Chinese is not. It's something else and the different neologisms proposed to replace ideographic cannot make it 'just like phonetically impoverished English.'

Further, the Mandarin and Cantonese pronunciations of the character are words in different but related spoken languages, not dialectal

Chad Hansen

variations in sound. The spoken pronunciations of Chinese characters by speakers of Hokkien, Cantonese, and Mandarin are also words but different spoken words of different languages.

This should make us wonder what sound reasoning would make us so vehemently reject calling Chinese characters ideograms. The parallel with '&' is apt. But DeFrancis (1989) is wrong to conclude it *represents* the English word 'and' any more than it does the German 'und.' Nor does the logical '·', the mathematical '+', or set theory's '∩' and '∪', or Chinese 同. We write two of the tokens using a segmental phoneme alphabet, and that is it! 'Ideogram' remains a perfectly viable candidate for these other examples of written units. We need not infer that they refer to objects in a mental space envisioned in idea-thought theory. They are words that *could be read* or re-written in other symbolic or linguistic form and pronounced in various spoken languages.

4. Socio-Linguistic Practices

The Chinese tradition's own account of the characters themselves is of a socio-historical process, not of the implicit psychological history of the child's gathering impressions into an abstract pictographic mental language (mentalese) to facilitate her learning of English from her parents. The typical Western 'folk psychology of language' presupposed in the argument for calling Chinese characters 'logograms' is one the Chinese example requires us to re-examine, not to enshrine it in an *a priori* principle.

A typical Chinese introduction to their writing system might start with *indicatives* (指事 *zhǐshì* pointing to a social interaction) – characters, like *above* (上 *shàng*), *below* (下 *xià*), and *center* (中 *zhōng*) and 一二三. The obvious parallel of the latter with '123' is a reasonable first start to understanding Chinese theory of language. There is a kind of obvious way to use them in sharing information about our situation in the world. *Indicatives* are typically the first in traditional lists of the several different structural principles of constructing Chinese characters.

The second traditional Chinese category of their characters are *pictograms* and the account of them recounts the Chinese myth of culture-heroes who invented language and both the social roles and the conventional practices using them. These culture founders started the chain transmitting (teaching) them to today. These *Sage Kings* are wise but not omniscient – mortal humans. The central tradition credits the Yellow Emperor's historian, Cangjie (now the name

A New Look at the Classical Chinese *Dào*

of a character-based computer input keyboard) as the inventor of *pictographic* characters. He was inspired by a hunter who recognized tracks of animals as marking the path to finding them. He scribbled ⊙ to record information about the sun. It 'evolves' as others use it into ⊡ then 日, the current graph for a day, or daily, and semantic component of characters related to the sun like 旦 (dawn, morning *etc.*). Similarly, 𝔻 is the causal-historical ancestor of *moon* (月 *yuè* month(ly)).

The Sages then used hundreds of indicatives and pictographs in compound metaphorical characters. The Chinese name for this category, *meeting of images/plans* (會意 *huìyì*), is the one we are most inclined to translated as 'ideograph'. The classic example is combining the two natural sources of light above to form 明 (*míng* bright, clear, understand, insight *etc.*).

The translation of *huìyì* as 'ideograph' is apt enough for this category, but we needn't infer that they 'directly invoke ideas.' It is because *huìyì* work structurally a bit the way Lakoff and Johnson's metaphorical gestalts explain meaning. The compound graph relates other concepts in an inferentially linked structure of pictograms and indicatives to simulate the gestalt of a familiar bodily encounter with the natural world. The *gestalt space* is structured around the concepts that play roles in that bodily situation – 'getting to first base', 'strike three', 'way out in left field'.

A core example of how this type of character evokes a situation gestalt is 德 (*dé* power, excellence, virtuosity), the famous companion character to dào. Its earlier forms 德 and 德 combine the crossroad-like paths formed between separated rice paddies (a pictogram that is completed in the early versions of 'walk' or 'behave' 北 北 and 辶) with pictograms of the eye and heart. The bodily gestalt of finding and following a path becomes the term for good, skilled, correctly learned behavior. This path metaphor, rather than the sentential metaphor of a threateningly powerful male's verbal command, becomes the Chinese conception of a norm of behavior.

This third type of character structure is the most engaging and emphasis on it provokes opponents of 'ideograph' to stress instead the fourth structural type where, rather than a visual or bodily metaphor, the structure combines a pictographic category (e.g., man, fish, tree, grass, water, ice *etc.*) with a phonetic or rhyming component – 'the kind of fish that sounds like 'sam' or rhymes with 'mammon' in some, many or most Chinese vernacular languages'.

Opponents of 'ideograph' like to focus on these semantic-phonetic compounds instead. They make Chinese a 'full' written language by providing a formula for constructing a character for every word of any Chinese spoken language. They object to focus on the other three

Chad Hansen

categories partly on grounds that a large Chinese dictionary will have far more phonetic compound characters than any of the others. This is an unsurprising observation since there are more species than genera, more types of fish and flowers than two.

Were we to focus on the correct characterization of Chinese written content, the traditionalist could count the ratio of *occurrences* of the other three on a 'typical' page of print. Then the proportion of semantic-phonetic compound type would shrink substantially, especially if we include the times a pictogram or indicative is used as a character component! Nor need we infer that since the component is relevant to its contribution to the information in the character that it could not also be semantically or metaphorically relevant as well. The meaning need not be irrelevant.

However, this is to assume that our concern here is with how to scientifically characterize the language. It isn't. We are interested in how their philosophy of language, which their language obviously influences, further shapes their wider philosophy – their metaphysics, ethics, *etc*. For this purpose, it is important not to distort Chinese *theory* of their own language into a pastiche formed by illicitly mixing it with Western idea-thought theory.

5. A Compromise Resolution

Armed with their traditional conventional-historical account, the temptation among Chinese theorists of language to invent another immaterial language of abstractions to explain the relation of sounds to natural objects almost completely disappears. 'Almost' because the ancient Chinese thinkers were clearly aware of imagination, memory, planning, and dreaming. These played roles in their accounts of humans choosing and following natural world dàos (paths), but not recruited to explain how language links to the natural world. With a real-life instance of Wittgenstein's reductio of idea theory, (Wittgenstein, 1964) an outward sign-object, they would not need an 'occult' sign to serve as the meaning of their sign. They would see easily that the norm of use of the written character is not another occult mental character but a social-historical practice – a dào of the word.

The traditional name of the third type of character, the metaphorical mix, uses the Chinese non-semantic conception of these internal goings-on (意 yí idea, intent). We can plan, imagine, remember and dream many kinds of behaviors including speaking, writing, advising etc. The conventions I practiced as a child gave me a start on navigating with the norms of use in my linguistic community. The relevant picture of meaning would be a map of correct behavior showing, e.g., where to take my turn speaking.

To picture normative guidance and natural information is to map possible paths of behavior. Words (characters or spoken words) act more as signposts that help communicate and share path-choice-relevant information. The signpost could indeed be pictures or picture-like, as road signs are in the modern world. However, it would have been obvious to Chinese theorists that the capacity to recognize the sign for horse (馬), a picture of a horse, and a horse are the same capacity. One does not explain the other. We become competent in using *mǎ* to call attention to the animal, to the picture and to the pictogram in basically the same way.

Classical Chinese thinkers described the information received from the senses as *biàn* (辯 distinction, discrimination) of, e.g., light from dark, red from blue, sweet from sour, hard from soft *etc*. Their psychology could otherwise be characterized by those committed to Western idea theory as 'naïve realism'. They do not assume the eyes convey *mental* pictures of *mental* objects consisting of *mental* substances painted in subjective inner qualia (properties, attributes) which may (or, for sense skeptics, may not) correspond to the color of natural objects. They say their eyes working normally accurately discriminate red from not-red objects in the world and red and not-red written characters. Their eyes discriminate the shape of a horse from the shape of an ox. When one's eyes are abnormal, e.g., one is color blind, then the eyes *fail to discriminate* X from non-X. This may be the result of distance or disease.

> Mozi said: a blind human can say 'Bright things are white; dark things are black' and the keen of sight will not correct them. But if we mix black and white things and invite the blind to pick one out, they would not know how to do it. This is why I say the blind do not know black from white, not because they cannot use the words correctly, but that they cannot pick one out from the other. (Mozi (ca. 4th c. BC), 12:8)

Inferences we routinely draw in English also would not strictly follow. Chinese thinkers needn't and probably wouldn't think of the characters either as 'meanings' or as having meanings. They have a history linking them via the experience of *some ancient coiners* and generations of transmissions and alterations to the *paths* of present use. Those paths are the norms outlining ways of using the words. The ancient Chinese masters neither felt nor had any need for a separate term with the conceptual role of 'meaning' in

Chad Hansen

Western idea theory. A conception of the norms (the *dào*s) of *kě* (可 permissible or possible) usage are functionally adequate.

Those norms are learned and practiced: 'learn and regularly practice; is that not fulfilling?' (Confucius, *Analects*, ca. 5th c. BC, 1:1). No one guesses merely from seeing the character 明, how to use it. We learn that from patterns we 'see' in adult usage and experiment within our own practice. The metaphor in the story used to help teach students the structure of the indicatives, pictographs, ideographs, and even the semantic-phonetic compounds assist learning, memory, and understanding.

One line of anti-ideograph attack is that the stories we tell in this way about the structure of the characters are sometimes inaccurate as accounts of the etymology and evolution of the character. With our focus on the ideology taught along with the language, the teaching slogans and assists that help learning, and the ways they impact the wider body of social-political naturalist thought, we needn't spend time worrying about that alleged problem. The teaching techniques that work can continue and those interested in actual evolutionary history can still submit their dissertations.

As Ancient Chinese thinkers appreciated, once a social practice is in place it continues to evolve. Conservative Confucians may want to 'rectify names' to bring them back into conformity with the 'original intent' of the ancient sages (Confucius, *Analects*, ca. 5th c. BC, 13:3), but Mohists can plausibly urge that any rectification should benefit people today given today's conditions. Elaborating the implicit metaphor in the character can facilitate mastery, but knowing the story is different from mastery. That comes with use in coordination with others in a real environment.

6. Types and Tokens

The key point here is that our concept of a word is vague in ways central to the dispute. A standard philosophical treatment distinguishes between word-type and word-token. In European languages, given that distinction, it is natural to treat spoken and written tokens as tokens of the *same* word-type. However, once we have that apparatus in hand, we can use it to help think about other linguistic categories, both broader and narrower in scope. We naturally treat differences in written tokens like 'harbor' and 'harbour' as tokens of the same word, but we could treat them as tokens of a spelling type and pronunciations as tokens of a dialect-pronunciation type.

A New Look at the Classical Chinese *Dào*

What Chinese orthography reminds us of is that concepts also have a history within what we can call a concept community. The character in the *Analects* passage translated above as study, 學, is pronounced *hôk* in Cantonese, *xué* in Mandarin, and *gaku* (Han reading) or *benkyoo* in Japanese. Each occurrence in its context is a token of one type in all these written languages. It is a token of the same written word type, the written morpheme type. Here we can begin to blend in the role of the semantic-phonetic compounds without jumping to DeFrancis's conclusion that Chinese is simply impoverished phonetic writing. Chinese characters token, in addition to word-types, cognate types (for recognizably borrowed words from other languages).

7. Cognates, Synonyms, and (Correct) Translations

We would treat English 'book' and German 'Buch' as cognates – words in different languages with the same meaning and derived from an earlier history of borrowing the spoken word-type. Clearly many of the tokens of Chinese characters would token cognate types for many of the different language communities of East Asia. This explains how a token of a written word/character would also token a cognate type. It thus acknowledges the relation of Cantonese *hôk* and Japanese *gaku*.

We similarly treat different spoken words within a language as synonyms when they have the same meaning. We could say tokens of the two synonyms token the same *concept*. *Xúe* and *benkyoo* are not cognates, but they play the same role, have a similar *dào* of use with other words in a concept cluster.

Throughout China's long and varied historical evolution of written and spoken forms of language, the writing system provided *an interpretation* of different spoken languages in the sense of linking both cognates and synonyms. This explains how Chinese written characters could underwrite a kind of translation among all the vernaculars of the Far East.

In this sense, the graphs do not represent ideas directly. However, functionally they do what ideas do in Western idea-thought theory. They underwrite translation among culturally linked languages that historically had shared words and inferentially linked concept structures like the *dào*, *dé*, eye, heart, walking/behavior structure discussed above in the example of *meeting of images/concepts* (會意 *huìyì*). When two linguistic communities interact enough to learn one another's theories, they learn these gestalt conceptual schemes, these *dào*s or patterns of inference linking clusters of concepts.

Chad Hansen

The characters originally provide a link to translating, interpreting, and understanding other Chinese languages. Japanese, Korean, and Vietnamese borrowed Chinese theories, hence concept clusters and inference patterns among them. If they developed a local approximation of the borrowed Chinese pronunciation, the character could token a cross-language cognate type. If they began to read the character using one of their already existing word types with a similar pattern of inference relations, a similar *dào* of use, they would be like inter-language synonyms. Correct translations of the same spoken theory in different languages could be (and were historically) written with the Chinese characters.

The spoken word is part of *a language* characterized as whole, not a *naturally representing,* phonetically structured atom (that is to say, sound does no magic bonding of word & object). Neither does the Chinese character. Chinese students learn its norms of use as she does other linguistic items, as parts of larger units of language. A word-token (in Europe) is typically also a concept-token and sometimes a cognate token. In the former case, we may token other word-types in that context while conforming to the *dào* of the language. The other terms share a mapped role in the concept space.

Correct translations would also token the concept while conforming to the *dào* of the translating language. This does not imply that between more widely separated mega-linguistic communities translation is either impossible or substantially more difficult. What it requires is that easier or more simple-minded translation works better between historically related and co-evolving language families. It is also better for examples like 'sun' and 'moon' and natural kind terms like 'fish' and 'water'. We can expect other terms, like 'mother' and 'father', to occur in all languages.

This doesn't follow, however, for historically entrenched theories of distinct cultures, no matter how intuitive and obvious they come to seem to speakers in that linguistic community. Monotheistic creator-God theories, however widespread south-west of the Himalayas, is not a natural kind theory nor such that the structure of natural human societies underwrites expecting it in all languages. The missionaries who came to China searching for the Chinese term for the God in their religion with the inference relations to 'rational', 'good', *etc.* should be prepared not to find it.

The missionaries could, still, teach their religion by coining a new compound using existing concept-characters like *Landlord of the Sky* (天主 *tiānzhǔ* Catholic translation for 'God'). Protestant missionaries alternately chose to pick a term from existing Chinese theories with a partially similar inference pattern. The *Emperor Above* (上帝 *shàngdì*)

A New Look at the Classical Chinese *Dào*

was the first ancestor of ancient and traditional Chinese Ancestor Worship who tops the afterlife hierarchy of normative authority whose bottom link is following one's father's *dào*. They could proceed to teach whoever would listen their theory of this unseen object using other terms (created light and dark, humans in male and female *etc.*) and expect their followers to start to draw inferences to the other existing terms of Chinese in ways that followed the *dào* of talking about God in their religion.

They would be disappointed to discover that they could not convince (and convert) any of the literate class (starting with Confucius) who had skeptically abandoned the talk of ghosts that survive in an afterlife social hierarchy and with it the normative authority of any imagined *emperor above* even earlier. The Zhou Dynasty (10th to 3rd c. BC) doctrine of the *mandate of heaven* claimed justification over the Shang Dynasty (16th to 10th c. BC) by appealing to the authority of *sky-nature* (天 *tiān* sky, the heavens, constant *dào*s) and dismissing the authority of any humanlike affiliation or endorsement. The natural forces leading to rule are not a promise or agreement, but the way nature unfolds. The paradigm of how nature unfolds are the constant *dào*s of the heavenly bodies.

The very learned 17th c. Jesuit missionaries in China tried to teach their Chinese intellectual counterparts logic so they could deploy one of their several powerful versions of the rationalist, logical proof of God – the ontological argument. It was taken in the West to show on purely rational, logical grounds that God's existence was *necessary* – logically necessary. The argument assumes immaterial, abstract ideas are the meanings of words. These ideas compose thoughts, some of which are necessarily true. The conclusion of the argument is 'God exists' is true. So, their Mission Impossible was to convince Chinese Confucian philosophers that 'there is a landlord of the sky' (有天主 $\exists x$ (Sky-Lord$_x$)).

Suppose you, the Confucian, were to accept the first premise:

P$_1$ *Sky-Lord* is the epitome of normative value (God is perfectly good)
(e.g., on grounds that sky-nature was the ultimate source of normative authority so if there were an owner of sky-nature he would embody good.)

The Jesuit then wants you to accept the inference (translation) of P$_1$ to its synonym P$_2$:
P$_2$ *Sky-Lord* has all good predicates to the highest conceivable degree.

Chad Hansen

Now the Jesuit must teach not only logic, but the Aristotelian theory of subject-predicate structure of sentences and thought. Further, it must include the Aristotelian subject-predicate (substance-property) conception of a thing. Chinese grammar does not require a subject so can't require that there be an underlying substance with properties for something to exist. If we don't have a name for it or words to describe it, so much the worse for our language. What naturally exists, exists. It's our job to fit it into our language.

The Jesuits are not trying to prove what Chinese naturalists already accept — that we may not fully understand or be able to fully describe nature (natural *dào*) in language. They are trying to prove there is an author-creator of nature — including sky-nature. The Chinese philosopher has no trouble *understanding* the conclusion, but there is no pattern of inference from P_2 to that conclusion following the norms of Chinese written or spoken languages.

Of course, Chinese can be converted to Christianity just as some were historically to Buddhism and Islam. Depending on how many of the related clusters of concepts are given character, character compound or character phrase translations they could come to draw inferences in shared ways. Chinese has had extensive co-evolution with Mahayana Buddhism since the 2nd c. and 真 (*zhēn*) *authentic-natural* (as opposed to socially constructed) had already acquired the reality vs. illusion-based sense of 'true' before more extensive contact with the European West.

8. Aftermath: Natural Objects and Science

The Jesuits might have concluded that Chinese culture was inherently resistant to logic. Still, it quite readily absorbed logic in the 19th and 20th c. when it came as part of the package with natural science. It was resistant to Western self-conceptions of reason and thought when packaged in the supernatural imaginary of idea and thought theory. Buddhism, for all the intellectual excitement it brought, did not take hold partly because it too was too committed to an image vs. reality conception of philosophy.

While it is true that the science that impressed China also came with gunships and armies, what impressed the earliest Chinese advocates of Western learning and logic was evolution, the scientific account of the *dào* of life, of our place in a natural, physical world. Traditional Chinese Daoism stressed the unity and continuity of nature, the unity of life with natural process. It was naturally more impressed with evolution and science than the more conservative Confucians.

A New Look at the Classical Chinese *Dào*

Its concept of reality was one of a whole with parts that were *natural* (自然 *zìrán* self-so) or 'so of themselves'. Things, natural kinds, are parts of the whole that is nature. Different things unfold in different natural causally possible processes – follow their part of the natural *dào*. Humans and other living organisms are equipped by nature to be able to distinguish the boundaries and shape of their changing possibilities in the natural world. The theory of evolution helped fill out the account of how this came about without attributing an intention, idea, or plan to the universe or its creator.

Each thing has its *dào* which is part of the *dào* of the larger thing of which it is a part. This non-dualist picture of reality was implicit in its traditional picture of human language – different Chinese communities with diverse ways of speaking, spoken languages in the larger Chinese linguistic world which used the literary tools that evolved through the centuries to write and communicate with others in that larger community. The common characters and plethora of different pronunciations were parts of that larger linguistic whole.

If we understand that naturalist picture of language correctly instead of distorting it into an unworkable version of semantic idea theory, it need not matter whether we characterize the package as ideographic or logographic. What we should not do is impose our mind-body, idea and thought metaphysics of language in defining those terms. Chinese language theory did not hold that characters represent *ideas* directly or indirectly. Their theory played a role in Chinese teaching of their language that is broadly like the role ideas and thoughts play in Western teaching (Aristotle's) of their language. It could work because of the relation of writing to the languages of China that make the ways of reading those characters either cognates and/or synonyms.

'Logograph' would also not be objectionable if it were not accompanied by a definition that implies the Western teaching theory of spelling and writing – that characters 'refer to a word-sound in a spoken language'. If we attend to the full role of 'logos' in classical Western rationalist theory, so it embraces *discourse, law, logic* and *-ologies* in general, then it would preserve its link to natural science and make it a vehicle of sharing information about natural *dào* – as multiple translators of Daoist texts have suspected (Carus, 1898; Hansen, 1992, 2009; Zhang, 1992).

References

Aristotle, *Categoriae* and *De Interpretatione*, J.L. Ackrill. (trans.), (Oxford: Clarendon Press, 1963).

Chad Hansen

L. Bloomfield, *An Introduction to the Study of Language* (New York: Holt/London: Bell, 1914).

Paul Carus, *Lao-Tzu's Tao-Te-King* (Chicago: Open Court, 1898).

Confucius, *Analects*, ca. 5th c. BC, in D.C. Lau *et al.* (ed.), *A Concordance to the Lunyu* (論語逐字索引) (Hong Kong: Commercial Press, 1995).

John DeFrancis, *The Chinese Language: Fact and Fantasy* (Honolulu: The University of Hawaii Press, 1984).

John DeFrancis, *Visible Speech: The Diverse Oneness of Writing Systems* (Honolulu: The University of Hawaii Press, 1989).

Peter Stephen Du Ponceau, *A Dissertation on the Nature and Character of the Chinese System of Writing* (Philadelphia: American Philosophical Society, 1838).

Chad Hansen, *A Daoist Theory of Chinese Thought* (Oxford: Oxford University Press, 1992).

Chad Hansen, *Laozi: Tao Te Ching on The Art of Harmony* (London: Duncan Baird, 2009).

Saul Kripke, 'Naming and Necessity', in Gilbert Harman and Donald Davidson (eds), *Semantics of Natural Language* (Dordrecht: D. Reidel, 1972).

Mozi, (ca. 4th c. BC), in *Harvard-Yenching Institute Sinological Index Series* (Taipei: Chinese Materials and Service Center Inc., 1973).

Ferdinand de Saussure, *Course in General Linguistics*, Roy Harris (trans.), (London: Duckworth, 1983).

Ludwig Wittgenstein, *The Blue and Brown Books* (Oxford: Basil Blackwell, 1964).

Zhang Longxi, *The Tao and the Logos: Literary Hermeneutics, East and West* (Durham: Duke University Press, 1992).

Index of Names

Aristotle 159–60, 181, 184–6
Ashcroft, B. 17–8, 24
Austin, J.L. 5, 76, 117n4
Baldwin, J. 15–6, 20, 27
Blackburn, S. 1
Bloomfield, L. 185–6
Bruner, J. 10, 158–62, 166, 168
Buckley, W.F. Jr. 15–16, 20
Burke, K. 158
Carroll, L. 116, 146, 150
Confucius 182–5, 192, 195
Davidson, D. 21
DeFrancis, J. 186, 188, 193
Delgado, R. 99
Dennett, D. 161, 164, 172
Du Bois, W.E.B. 17
Du Ponceau, P. 185
Fine, K. 145
Fish, S. 89, 92

Fodor, J. 52, 55, 145, 154
Forster, E.M. 143–4, 155
Frege, G. 9, 146–55
Gadamer, H.-G. 33, 36–9
Glissant, É. 2, 28–9
Grice, P. 7–8, 108–11, 139n3, 154
Habermas, J. 39, 41–4
Haslanger, S. 3, 4, 48–50, 59
Heidegger, M. 37, 38, 42
Kierkegaard, S. 166
Kripke, S. 146, 150–5, 185
Kuhn, T. 19–21
Lewis, D. 5, 73–4, 77
Locke, J. 36
MacIntyre, A. 163–4, 168
Mill, J.S. 92, 94, 102, 149, 152–3
Mink, L. 10, 158–60, 168, 176

Mozi, 185, 191
Murdoch, I. 175–6
Nguyen, C. Thi 24–5, 169, 172
Nietzsche, F. 40, 175–6
Plato, 143, 181, 184, 185
Rorty, R. 1, 147
Saussure, F. de 185
Scanlon, T. 102
Schiffer, S. 145
Schleiermacher, F. 36–7
Strawson, G. 163
Thiong'o, N.W. 22–4
Tirrell, L. 74, 90–1, 95–6
Velleman, D. 161, 164, 172
Whorf, B.L. 54
Williamson, T. 65, 108
Wiredu, K. 39–41, 44
Wittgenstein, L. 1, 33, 36–9, 143, 145, 181, 190